DAILY LIFE IN

Immigrant America, 1820–1870

Recent Titles in
The Greenwood Press "Daily Life Through History" Series

Civilians in Wartime Early America: From the Colonial Era to the Civil War
David S. Heidler and Jeanne T. Heidler, editors

Civilians in Wartime Modern America: From the Indian Wars to the Vietnam War
David S. Heidler and Jeanne T. Heidler, editors

Civilians in Wartime Asia: From the Taiping Rebellion to the Vietnam War
Stewart Lone, editor

The French Revolution
James M. Anderson

Stuart England
Jeffrey Forgeng

The Revolutionary War
Charles P. Neimeyer

The American Army in Transition, 1865–1898
Michael L. Tate

Civilians in Wartime Europe, 1618–1900
Linda S. Frey and Marsha L. Frey, editors

The Vietnam War
James E. Westheider

World War II
G. Kurt Piehler

Immigrant America, 1870–1920
June Granatir Alexander

Along the Mississippi
George S. Pabis

DAILY LIFE IN

Immigrant America, 1820–1870

JAMES M. BERGQUIST

The Greenwood Press "Daily Life Through History" Series

Daily Life in the United States
Randall M. Miller, Series Editor

GREENWOOD PRESS
Westport, Connecticut • London

Library of Congress Cataloging-in-Publication Data

Bergquist, James M.
    Daily life in immigrant America, 1820–1870 / by James M. Bergquist.
        p. cm. — (The Greenwood Press daily life through history series. Daily
life in the United States, ISSN 1080–4749)
    Includes bibliographical references and index.
    ISBN 978–0–313–33698–0 (alk. paper)
    1. United States—Emigration and immigration—History—19th
century.   2. Immigrants—United States—Social life and customs—19th
century.   I. Title.
    JV6453.B47   2008
    305.9'06912097309034—dc22   2007035360

British Library Cataloguing in Publication Data is available.

Library of Congress Catalog Card Number: 2007035360
ISBN: 978–0-313–33698–0
ISSN: 1080–4749

First published in 2008

Greenwood Press, 88 Post Road West, Westport, CT 06881
An imprint of Greenwood Publishing Group, Inc.
www.greenwood.com

Printed in the United States of America

The paper used in this book complies with the
Permanent Paper Standard issued by the National
Information Standards Organization (Z39.48–1984).

10 9 8 7 6 5 4 3 2 1

Contents

Series Foreword

The books in the *Daily Life in the United States* series form a subset of Greenwood Press's acclaimed, ongoing *Daily Life Through History* series. They fit its basic framework and follow its format. This series focuses on the United States from the colonial period through the present day, with each book in the series devoted to a particular time period, place, or people. Collectively, the books promise the fullest description and analysis of "American" daily life in print. They do so, and will do so, by tracking closely the contours, character, and content of people's daily life, always with an eye to the sources of people's interests, identities, and institutions. The books in the series assume the perspective and use the approaches of the "new social history" by looking at people "from the bottom up" as well as the top-down. Indian peoples and European colonists, blacks and whites, immigrants and the native-born, farmers and shopkeepers, factory owners and factory hands, movers and shakers and those moved and shaken—all get their due. The books emphasize the habits, rhythms, and dynamics of daily life, from work, to family matters, to religious practices, to socializing, to civic engagement, and more. The books show that the seemingly mundane—such as the ways any people hunt, gather, or grow food and then prepare and eat it—as much as the more profound reflections on life reveal how and why people ordered their world and gave meaning to their lives. The books treat the external factors shaping people's lives—war, migration, disease, drought, flood, pest infestations, fires, earthquakes, hurricanes and tornados, and other natural and man-made disasters that disrupted and even shattered daily lives— but they understand that the everyday concerns and routines of life also powerfully defined any people. The books therefore go inside homes, workplaces, schools, churches, meeting halls, stores, and other gathering places to find people on their own terms.

Capturing the daily life of Americans poses unique problems. Americans have been, and are, a people in motion, constantly changing as they move across the land, build new communities, invent new products and processes, and experiment with everything from making new recipes to making new governments. A people always in the process of becoming does not stand still for examination of their most private lives. Then, too, discovering the daily life of the diverse American peoples requires expertise in many disciplines, for few people have left full-bodied written accounts of their prosaic but necessary daily activities and habits and many people have left no written record at all. Thus, the scholars writing the books in the series necessarily borrow from such fields and resources as archaeology, anthropology, art, folklore, language, music, and material culture. Getting hold of the daily life in the United States demands no less.

Each book at once provides a narrative history and analysis of daily life, set in the context of broad historical patterns. Each book includes illustrations, documents, a chronology, and a bibliography. Thereby, each book invites many uses as a resource, a touchstone for discussion, a reference, and an encouragement to further reading and research. The titles in the series also promise a long shelf life because the authors draw on the latest and best scholarship and because the books are included in Greenwood's Daily Life Online, which allows for enhanced searching, updated content, more illustrative material, teacher lesson plans, and other Web features. In sum, the *Daily Life in the United States* series seeks to bring the American people to life.

Randall M. Miller

Preface

During the last century, the study of the American immigrant has gone through several transformations. Earlier, there were spokespersons and advocates for the immigrants who responded to the accusations of nativists with testimonies about the useful record of American immigrants as citizens, and about the significant contributions they had made to American life and culture. Then many Americans who recognized that their own background lay within the stories of the millions of immigrants began to search the genealogical records, seeking to find their individual ancestors' stories amid the "huddled masses." By the 1960s, other themes came to prominence. There was something of an "ethnic revival," in which descendants of immigrants sought to recover some of the cultural heritage of their ancestors. More significantly, academic historians began to examine the immigrants' world with some of the concerns of the social scientist—probing the inner workings of ethnic groups, analyzing immigrant societies, and dealing with the dynamics of emigration, dispersal, and integration. Many of their studies approached these questions on a grassroots level, through closer examination of a particular locality or groups of a particular ethnicity.

This book makes use of much of this previous work, especially the localized studies, but it has a somewhat different purpose. It seeks to recreate the world of the immigrant, as much as any such thing can be done, in order to understand the daily life of the immigrant as he or she lived it. By seeing the environments through which these immigrants passed on their very mobile and diverse careers, we can better understand what they did and how they reacted to the considerable challenges they faced. Readers who reflect on this complicated world may form their own theories of how individuals made their own way through it.

The accounts given here may be disillusioning to some who are used to an optimistic and uplifting view of the immigrants' progress. America in the early nineteenth century was not always a welcoming place; it was rapidly expanding and changing, often consumed with internal conflicts, and developing a very disorderly political culture. The stream of new immigrants included many honorable and hard-working people, but also had its share of rogues, criminals, and fakers. Fortune did not always reward these newcomers with fairness; there were successes, but also failures. Yet from these troubled times a different America would eventually emerge, and the millions of immigrants who came would have their own role in forming it.

Many people and institutions have been helpful in my exploration of immigrant life. I have a long indebtedness to the resources of the Balch Institute for Ethnic Studies, especially its collections of ethnic newspapers; these are now incorporated in the holdings of the Historical Society of Pennsylvania. At my own university, Villanova, I had access to the McGarrity Collection of Irish and Irish-American materials. The special collections of Bryn Mawr and Swarthmore Colleges also provided some useful rare materials. I also have benefited from the libraries of the University of Pennsylvania and the German Society of Pennsylvania. The Library of Congress provided some great visual materials from its resources.

At Villanova, I received valuable help from librarians Bente Polites, Michael Foight, and Sarah Hidding. Eric Pumroy and Barbara Grubb at Bryn Mawr and Amy McColl at Swarthmore facilitated greatly my search for useful illustrations. June Alexander and John Alexander also gave me some very useful advice.

I am indebted to Paul Bartels and to Craig Bailey for reading various parts of the manuscript and giving useful suggestions. I also thank my wife, Joan Solon Bergquist, a professional editor in her own right, for reading the drafts, but also for many other helps and favors rendered, for which my thanks are woefully inadequate.

Randall Miller, the series editor for these Daily Life works, originally suggested that I undertake this project. I thank him for his careful editorial work and suggestions, which have improved my efforts greatly. I also thank Greenwood editors Michael Hermann and Mariah Gumpert, who have been understanding and encouraging despite my sometimes tardy progress.

Inevitably, a work of this comprehensive nature will omit some important details, and some readers will feel that I have shortchanged their particular interests. I can only apologize, and take full responsibility for my errors and omissions.

Chronology

1815   January 8: Andrew Jackson defeats British in Battle of New Orleans, final battle of War of 1812.

June: Congress of Vienna concludes, ending the Napoleonic Wars.

June: Napoleon banished to the island of St. Helena in the South Pacific.

Major wave of migration to the western United States begins.

1817   New York legislature authorizes Erie Canal; construction begins.

1818   Steamboats begin to operate on the Mississippi and Ohio rivers.

Regular scheduled packet service established between Liverpool and New York.

The federally financed National Road completed from Cumberland, Maryland to the Ohio River at Wheeling, Virginia.

1819   The "Panic of 1819" begins, starting a period of economic depression; slows western development.

The ship *Savannah* makes a successful (but unprofitable) voyage across the Atlantic, the first steam-powered ship to do so.

March 2: U.S. Congress passes "An act regulating passenger-ships and vessels," requiring ship captains to file passenger lists with the authorities upon arrival in U.S. ports.

1820 8,385 immigrants arrive in the United States.

March: Missouri Compromise divides western territories into free and slave regions.

1821 9,127 immigrants arrive in the United States.

1822 6,911 immigrants arrive in the United States.

1823 6,364 immigrants arrive in the United States.

1824 7,391 immigrants arrive in the United States.

1825 10,199 immigrants arrive in the United States.

October: Erie Canal completed, opening water link between New York and the Great Lakes.

1826 10,337 immigrants arrive in the United States.

1827 18,875 immigrants arrive in the United States.

Mercantile interests in Bremen establish the port of Bremer-haven to facilitate transatlantic trade.

1828 27,382 immigrants arrive in the United States.

1829 22,520 immigrants arrive in the United States.

March 4: Andrew Jackson inaugurated president of the United States.

April: Catholic Emancipation Act passed in British Parliament, granting civil rights to Irish Catholics.

May: States in the German Confederation form a customs union, or *Zollverein*.

Influential guidebook to the western United States published by Gottfried Duden in Germany.

1830 23,322 immigrants arrive in the United States.

1831 22,633 immigrants arrive in the United States.

1832 60,482 immigrants arrive in the United States.

Cholera epidemic spreads through Ireland, then to the United States.

1833 58,640 immigrants arrive in the United States.

Western land boom underway in United States.

1834   64,365 immigrants arrive in the United States.

Another epidemic of cholera strikes on both sides of the Atlantic.

A mob destroys an Ursuline convent near Boston; tensions strengthen over nativism.

1835   45,374 immigrants arrive in the United States.

1836   76,242 immigrants arrive in the United States.

March 1: Texas declares its independence from Mexico; becomes independent republic.

1837   79,340 immigrants arrive in the United States.

March 4: President Andrew Jackson leaves office, succeeded by Martin Van Buren.

"Panic of 1837" introduces another period of depression, slowing western expansion and immigration.

1838   38,914 immigrants arrive in the United States.

1839   68,069 immigrants arrive in the United States.

1840   84,066 immigrants arrive in the United States.

1841   80,289 immigrants arrive in the United States.

1842   104,565 immigrants arrive in the United States.

1843   52,496 immigrants arrive in the United States.

June: The American Republican party, a nativist party, formed in New York.

1844   78,615 immigrants arrive in the United States.

March 1: Texas is annexed by a joint resolution of Congress.

March 28: Mexico breaks off diplomatic relations with the United States.

May–July: a series of nativist riots in Philadelphia.

1845   114,371 immigrants arrive in the United States.

July 5–7: Native American party organized in Philadelphia.

October: A blight begins to appear on the potato plants of Ireland; western Germany also affected by crop failures.

1846   154,416 immigrants arrive in the United States.

Potato crop in Ireland is a total failure.

April 25: Clash between U.S. and Mexican troops along the Rio Grande.

May 12: Declaration of war against Mexico by the United States.

June 26: Britain repeals its Corn Laws, which had imposed tariffs on agricultural imports.

July 15: ratification of the Oregon treaty with Great Britain, giving the United States territory south of the 49th parallel.

1847   234,968 immigrants arrive in the United States.

A serious epidemic of typhus spreads from Europe to the United States and Canada.

Typhus and increasing famine in Ireland mark the year as "Black '47"; pressures for emigration increase.

Hamburg-America shipping line begins service between Hamburg and New York.

An investigation by the New York legislature leads to the establishment of the New York State Commissioners of Immigration.

1848   226,527 immigrants arrive in the United States.

Another major potato crop failure in Ireland.

January 24: Gold discovered at Sutter's mill in California.

February 2: Treaty of Guadalupe Hidalgo signed, ending Mexican War; transferred California and much of the southwest to the United States.

February: Riots in Paris, causing abdication of King Louis Philippe; beginning of revolutions of 1848.

May 18: Frankfurt Parliament convenes, seeks to achieve a unified German republic.

June: Attempted rebellion in Ireland soon fails.

1849   297,024 immigrants arrive in the United States.

Gold rush to California from all parts of the world.

About 325 Chinese begin migration of Asians to California.

March–April: King Frederick William of Prussia rejects constitution written by the Frankfurt Parliament; revolutionary and nationalist movements in central Europe collapse.

1850   369,980 immigrants arrive in the United States.

The census counted 2,244,602 foreign-born living in the United States.

April: California territorial legislature passes the Foreign Miners' Tax, imposing heavy taxes on the foreign-born miners.

January–September: Congress adopts Compromise of 1850, making California a free state, leaving rest of Southwest up to "popular sovereignty" to decide the question of slavery.

1851   379,466 immigrants arrive in the United States.

June: The "Maine law," a liquor prohibition law, adopted in the state of Maine; leads to efforts to adopt similar laws elsewhere.

1852   371,603 immigrants arrive in the United States.

1853   368,645 immigrants arrive in the United States.

1854   427,833 immigrants arrive in the United States; the peak immigration year before the Civil War.

May 30: Kansas-Nebraska Act allows slavery in new territories under "popular sovereignty," arouses controversy about future of slavery in the West.

New nativist party, the American or "Know-Nothing" party, gains strength.

1855   200,877 immigrants arrive in the United States.

New York establishes principal immigration station at Castle Garden, in lower Manhattan.

Bremen surpasses Le Havre in numbers of emigrants passing through the ports, reflecting greater emigration from eastern Germany.

1856   200,436 immigrants arrive in the United States.

May–September: A localized civil war breaks out in Kansas between abolitionist and proslavery forces.

November: James Buchanan, Democrat, defeats John C. Fremont, Republican, for the presidency; Republicans carry 11 northern states, showing remarkable strength.

1857   251,806 immigrants arrive in the United States.

North German Lloyd shipping line establishes regular service between Bremen and New York.

August 24: Financial panic, the "Panic of 1857," slows economy and reduces flow of new immigrants.

1858   123,126 immigrants arrive in the United States.

1859   121,282 immigrants arrive in the United States.

1860   153,640 immigrants arrive in the United States.

The census counted 4,138,697 foreign-born living in the United States.

November: Abraham Lincoln, a Republican, elected president.

December: South Carolina secedes from Union.

1861   91,918 immigrants arrive in the United States.

January–February: 10 more southern states secede from Union.

April 12: Southern artillery in Charleston harbor fires on Fort Sumter, beginning Civil War.

April 15: Lincoln calls for volunteers to suppress the insurrection; response includes many ethnic militia units.

1862   91,985 immigrants arrive in the United States.

May 20: Homestead Act passed; immigrants qualify for land grants.

July 1: Pacific Railway Act authorizes building of transcontinental railroad.

September: Otto von Bismarck becomes minister-president of Prussia.

1863   176,282 immigrants arrive in the United States.

January 1: Lincoln issues Emancipation Proclamation, freeing slaves behind Confederate lines.

March 1: Conscription Act establishes draft; males 20–45 liable for military service.

July 1–4: Southern incursion into Pennsylvania turned back at battle of Gettysburg.

July 13–16: Serious riots against draft in New York City.

1864   193,418 immigrants arrive in the United States.

May–September: General Sherman's army marches through Georgia; takes Atlanta September 1.

July 4: Congress passes the Emigrant Aid Act, allowing emigrants to sign employment contracts of not more than one year's duration before embarking for the United States.

November: Abraham Lincoln reelected to the presidency.

1865 248,120 immigrants arrive in the United States.

April 9: General Robert E. Lee surrenders to General Ulysses Grant at Appomattox, Virginia.

April 14: President Lincoln assassinated.

1866 318,568 immigrants arrive in the United States.

May 31: "Fenians"—Irish nationalists—fail in an invasion of Canada near Niagara Falls.

1867 315,722 immigrants arrive in the United States.

1868 138,840 immigrants arrive in the United States.

Fourteenth Amendment to the Constitution ratified; defines citizenship as belonging to persons born or naturalized in the United States.

1869 352,763 immigrants arrive in the United States.

May 10: Transcontinental railroad completed.

1870 387,203 immigrants arrive in the United States.

The census counted 5,507,229 foreign-born living in the United States.

July 19: France declares war on Prussia.

September 1–2: France defeated at the battle of Sedan, leading to capitulation and end of the Franco-Prussian war.

1871 January 18: William I, King of Prussia, becomes Emperor William I of Germany.

April 14: Constitution of the German Empire adopted, achieving national union of the former German states.

1

Overview: Immigration by the Numbers, 1820–1870

In 1820 both Europe and America were passing from an era of upheaval and instability to one of vast transformation. The wars and internal conflicts that had tormented both continents for decades had come to an end. Europe had spent a quarter of a century embroiled in the wars that followed the French Revolution and then continued into the reign of Napoleon Bonaparte. In June 1815, the defeated Napoleon was banished to the remote island of St. Helena (where he would die six years later). In that same month the Congress of Vienna redrew the map of Europe and restored power to most of the old monarchies and principalities of the eighteenth century. Conservative political settlements, however, could not restrain the powerful social and economic forces that were about to be unleashed, including the relentless advance of industrialization, the unprecedented growth in the continent's population, and the complex migrations that would follow.

In America, the stage was also set for vast changes. The War of 1812 between Great Britain and the United States ended in 1815 with a treaty that simply returned affairs to the pre-war status quo. Nevertheless, Americans still could claim victory after the decisive triumph of Andrew Jackson over the British at New Orleans that same year. Americans' exuberance over having freed themselves from British intrusions led them into a new era of nationalism and expansion. The entire Mississippi Valley was now open to settlers, free of British and Indian obstruction. In New England and elsewhere in the Northeast, new factories, some established during the war years when European goods were difficult to obtain, began to signal the birth of the Industrial Revolution in the United States. The developing transportation network, spurred on by projects such as the National Road and the Erie Canal, opened up new land for settlement and new markets for both industry and agriculture. The cotton kingdom of the South would soon extend its domain across the Gulf states.

The American story of a republic created by overthrowing a European monarchy would inspire young intellectuals in Europe and elsewhere. It was already inspiring the colonies of Latin America to take advantage of the distractions of their Spanish and Portuguese overlords during the wars of Napoleon. Between 1811 and 1821 many of those colonies would declare their independence from European powers and become republics.

IMMIGRATION AND SOCIAL SCIENCE

The raising of the republican ideal was part of the heritage of the Enlightenment, which had grown in European intellectual circles in the last part of the eighteenth century. The Age of Reason also caused inquiring men to try to discover the order behind natural phenomena. By the first decades of the nineteenth century they were beginning to subject human affairs to scientific inspection, and thus what would be known as "social science" began to emerge. One of the leaders of the establishment of a social science was Adolphe Quetelet (1796–1874), a Belgian astronomer who was elected in 1820 to the Royal Academy of Sciences in Brussels. Charged with taking the Belgian population census, he began to subject the results to mathematical analysis, devising such measurements as birthrate and mortality tables. Quetelet asserted that the causes of human affairs could be discerned from studying the probabilities of human behavior. He can justifiably be considered the father of the science of demography.[1] Countries had taken censuses before this time, but largely for the purpose of raising taxes or raising armies. Now they began to use statistics to gauge the ongoing course of human affairs such as population growth, economic changes, and migration.

In 1820, the United States began to collect statistics (imperfect as they were) on people who entered the country on ships, although it was not until 1850 that the U.S. census began to include questions about the birthplaces of the population. European countries also began to take more careful censuses and to record the numbers of people leaving their domains. By the end of the nineteenth century, enough statistics had been collected to reveal some underlying causes of one of the greatest phenomena of the century, the vast migration of peoples from their ancestral homes to new places, both within and outside of their native countries.

COMPLEX CAUSES, MULTIPLE MOTIVATIONS

The complexities of these movements of peoples should not be oversimplified. Intertwined were several factors: the increasing pressure of growing population in the rural lands of Europe, the rise of industry in areas of western Europe, the decline of village life and economy, the technological development of various forms of transportation, and the lure of areas across the oceans with their promise of freedom and prosperity. Caught in the midst of these forces, a specific individual might respond in many different ways, be confronted with many different choices, and make many different decisions. Some might initially move within their country or region. In fact, many who eventually made their way to America first migrated to another part of their native country, tried a different way of life, and began the process of adapting to a new environment—all of this before deciding to cross the Atlantic to make a new beginning.

The Pressures of Population

Europe's growing population during the nineteenth century was one obvious factor in the movement of peoples, but analyzing all the reasons for that growth is difficult and controversial. An estimated 184 million people inhabited Europe in 1800; by 1850 there were 266 million and by 1900 over 390 million.[2] However, these figures do not include the millions who had left the continent for America and other places around the world. One reason for the increase was certainly improved health conditions, which led to less infant mortality and a general lengthening of the average lifespan. As more children survived into adulthood and more adults lived longer into old age, the total number of persons at any given time increased. At the same time there was an increase in agricultural production, partially in overseas places that now supplied Europe, and a decrease in the occurrences of famine and pestilence, which led to generally better nutrition. There would still be agricultural crises (such as the Irish famine in the 1840s), but for many, these local shortages could be made up for by food imported from other countries.

The pressure of population was particularly felt in rural areas where the land was limited and the growing population left many without opportunities to till the land. Landowners could split up their land holdings to distribute among several sons, but there eventually were limitations to doing so when the plots of land simply became too small to support a family. Requirements to divide land equally among all male heirs would eventually fall into disuse. Often the eldest son could continue to farm the land, but others had to seek a living elsewhere. Although the Netherlands drained some land to provide new farms, generally new farmland was available only in eastern Europe, in North and South America, or in Australia. Others who could not or would not farm would have to look to other opportunities such as working as artisans in a village, seeking a career in the church or the professions, or migrating toward the developing urban and industrial areas. All these options required a willingness to change dramatically one's established ways of life.

Industrialization and the Transformation of Society

During the post-Napoleonic era, the Industrial Revolution—a dynamic factor in British society since the mid-eighteenth century—was now underway in continental Europe. The growing number of industrial jobs was an outlet for the many young men who were forced off the farms, but those jobs often provided only unskilled and low-wage labor. The Industrial Revolution also served to undermine the small village economies in the rural areas of Europe. Local artisans who provided consumer goods found their market threatened by factory-made goods from industrial areas. The choice many of them had was either to accept the less-skilled work that industry offered or to migrate elsewhere—often to America.

The Attractions of America

As an expanding country in the early 1800s, the United States offered much to attract the prospective immigrant. When peace came after 1815, new lands, from which the native Americans had been driven, now became available in the regions north of the Ohio River and across the Gulf states. Later, areas to the west beyond the Mississippi were opened. Migrating Americans reached Texas in the 1820s, even while it was still governed by Mexico. U.S. government lands were sold at low prices, beginning at $1.25 per acre. Even developed lands in the regions previously settled were much less expensive than comparable lands in Europe. It was now possible for many farmers migrating from western Europe, where most feudal restrictions on land had been abolished, to sell their lands and buy much larger tracts in the United States with the proceeds from their sale. Many new agricultural areas in the United States were located close to transportation—first the river system, later canals and railroads—so that farmers were able to sell their surplus to either domestic or overseas markets.

Even though land was cheaper in America, wages were generally higher than for comparable work in Europe. Those migrants who lacked the means or the abilities to turn to farming could easily find wage-labor jobs. Many newcomers were recruited off the docks for the burgeoning work of extending the transportation system. This included the building of canals in the boom of 1820–1837; the building of railroads, which escalated in the 1840s and 1850s; and eventually the building of the transcontinental railroad just after the Civil War. Those who followed the new transportation lines to the West often remained among the populace of the new towns and cities that were established along those routes. These offered construction work and common-labor jobs for newcomers. The same newly developing towns and cities also offered opportunities for those immigrants who were skilled workers or professionals.

Migrants who did not go west might find jobs in the mines, mills, and mechanical trades being created by the Industrial Revolution. For example, by the early 1840s, in the textile mills of New England, Irish workers were rapidly replacing the locally recruited "factory girls." In periods of economic depression in the United States, both rural and industrial life would be affected because agricultural crops fell in value and industries would lay off workers. These unfavorable conditions were quickly reported to friends and relatives in Europe, and during these periods of depression (e.g., the early 1820s, the late 1830s, and the late 1850s) America seemed less attractive, and immigration would decline.

THE EBB AND FLOW OF THE IMMIGRANT TIDE

The fluctuation of conditions in both Europe and in America—the "pushes" and "pulls" that drove the process of migration—accounted for the rise and decline in the flow of migrants during the period from 1820 to 1870. The official immigration numbers for this period were derived mostly from ship lists—reports on passengers as recorded by ship captains and submitted to customs officers when the ship arrived in an American port. These numbers do not account for persons who stayed only temporarily and then returned to Europe, or for those who re-migrated to other places such as Latin America. They also do not account for persons who entered the United States over land. Since the federal government was only minimally involved in immigration matters until the late nineteenth century, the numbers must therefore be considered as approximate calculations. Nonetheless, they do reveal the general trends of the flow of migration throughout the years.

Immigration in the early 1820s was inhibited by an American depression beginning with a crisis in the financial markets (the Panic of 1819) that was followed by plunging agricultural prices, largely due to the decline of trade with Britain, and then by the resulting urban unemployment. In 1820 about 8,000 immigrants arrived in American ports; in 1823 the annual rate declined to about 6,000 and then began to rise. By 1828, the year Andrew Jackson was elected president, about 27,000 immigrants arrived. The American economy was on the rise during most of Jackson's presidency, and the expansion of the West provided the new arrivals with job opportunities such as constructing the new canals and building new towns and cities. At the same time, new land was opened up for sale in one of the biggest land-sale booms in American history. The expansion affected not only the states of the Old Northwest, such as Ohio, Indiana, and Illinois, but also the Cotton Belt now being developed across the states of Georgia, Alabama, and Mississippi. In 1837, the year Jackson left office, 79,000 immigrants arrived. But that year also marked the beginning of another major depression—the Panic of 1837. News of hard times reached Europe as quickly as sailing ships could bring it, and by 1838 the number of immigrants had been cut in half to about 39,000. Land sales dropped drastically, canal-building nearly came to a halt, and unemployment was widespread. The immigration flow (like the economy) revived only gradually, with 114,000 newcomers arriving in 1845.

Then there began one of the greatest waves of immigration in American history, driven by a strong combination of both "pushes" from Europe and "pulls" from the United States. The best-known of the pushes was the terrible potato famine in Ireland, which broke out in 1845. The famine sent 1.8 million people fleeing to North America to avoid the starvation that took the lives of perhaps another million people who did not leave.[3] In the states of western Germany, there were also crop failures with attendant food shortages and high prices, as well as widespread political unrest during the Revolutions of 1848. All of these factors led to a wave of emigration from those regions.

At the same time, America offered a variety of pulls to attract the distressed and disillusioned of Europe. Transportation expansion revived with the building of a vast network of railroads, especially across the upper Midwest. This construction provided many jobs for immigrants and also provided access to new lands for the land-hungry. The conclusion of the Mexican War (1846–1848) led to the annexation of most of the American Southwest, with its additional possibilities for development and settlement. A fortuitous but fateful development during those years was the discovery of gold in California. Immigrants, both new arrivals and those who had arrived previously, joined the gold rush. Among them was a small but significant group of Chinese, the first sizable Asian additions to the American population. The flow of gold into the American economy helped to fuel a general economic boom that lasted into the early 1850s, and the supply of jobs was abundant.

The total number of immigrants in 1846 was 154,000; the number rose rapidly to an annual average of about 375,000 in the early 1850s. In 1854, immigration peaked at 427,000 people—a level that would not be exceeded until 1880. The immigrants of this period were disproportionately male. In the 1820s, the number of males approached 75 percent of the total and hovered around 67 percent in the early 1830s. As time went on, the figures settled to around 60 percent male each year through 1870, although among the Irish the proportion of females was greater. The immigrants were also generally a young group. During this time, around 90 percent of immigrants were 40 years of age or younger. Just after the Civil War, the 40-and-under group fell slightly to about 87 percent.[4]

Irish Immigration by the Numbers

The flow of immigration varied among the diverse groups originating in western Europe. The emigration from Ireland was the largest overall during the period from 1820 to 1870. In the early 1820s, those leaving Ireland numbered only a few thousand per year. The majority were still Protestant Irish from northern Ireland; they had also been the predominant Irish immigrants in the eighteenth century. However, the proportion of emigrants who were Catholics grew steadily as time went on, and by the mid-1830s Catholic emigrants were in the majority. By 1837 Irish emigration across the Atlantic had reached 48,000, but the depression years that followed showed a marked drop in the numbers of emigrants. By 1842 the numbers had risen again to 93,000, despite warnings from America that there still were insufficient jobs.

When the famine of the mid-1840s struck, however, desperation opened the flood-gates. In 1845 about 75,000 left Ireland for the United States and Canada. The annual numbers increased dramatically, from 106,000 in 1846 to 214,000 in 1847, and reached a peak of 245,000 in 1851. By 1855 emigration from Ireland had receded to 63,000, a figure more consistent with pre-famine totals. In that single decade (1845–1855), over a million and a half Irish had fled to the United States, with another 300,000 or more fleeing to Canada, whence many found their way to the United States. And in that same decade, the population of Ireland had shrunk from about 8.5 million to about 6 million. In the years before the Civil War (1856–1860), over a quarter of a million Irishmen would emigrate to North America. In the next decade, during and after the war, another 730,000 would leave Ireland. The U.S. census of 1870 counted 1.8 million Irish-born, making the Irish the largest immigrant group in the country.[5]

German Immigration by the Numbers

German-born immigrants, who accounted for about 1.7 million by the time of the 1870 census, were only slightly behind the Irish in their numbers. Germany was not one unified nation in the early nineteenth century. The region was still a patchwork of separate principalities, duchies, and kingdoms, each of them with their separate bureaucracies and differing laws concerning migration. Procedures for regulating and keeping track of emigration varied widely among them. The region would not be unified until 1871, under Prussian authority. Before that, many immigrants thought of themselves as having come from Bavaria, Württemberg, Hanover, or one of the many other states. The emigration in the years just after 1820 stemmed mostly from the southwestern German states, but more emigrants began to come from eastern and northern Germany as the decades passed. In the early 1820s, the Irish sent many more emigrants to America than did the Germans, but the German arrivals gradually rose in number until they were approximately equal to the Irish in 1837. Thereafter the Irish outran the Germans, particularly during the famine years, when two or three times as many Irish as Germans entered the country. By the late 1850s, the Germans prevailed slightly, but Irish newcomers outnumbered Germans during the Civil War. In the years following the war, the Germans' numbers again considerably exceeded those of the Irish.

In the 1820s, over half of the German emigrants leaving their homelands went to overseas locations other than the United States, particularly to Latin America. By the 1830s, with improved transatlantic transportation and the attraction of the developing American West, emigration to America was consistently over 90 percent of the total German emigration.[6] Before 1830, the number of recorded arrivals of Germans did not exceed 2,000 annually. In the early 1830s the numbers rose to a high of about 29,000 before the Panic of 1837 discouraged the emigrants. By 1845 the numbers were back at a new high of 36,000, rising again to 58,000 in 1846, to 79,000 in 1850, and reaching a pre-Civil War high of about 215,000 in 1854.

This flood of German immigrants, which came at the same time as the Irish famine migration, shared some of the same causes. There were similar famines and crop failures in Germany, which exposed again the long-standing problems of too many people occupying too little land. The Industrial Revolution, just in its beginning stages in Germany, would leave many artisans without a living. Added to such socioeconomic disruptions was the political unrest that culminated in the Revolutions of 1848. The political upheavals brought a small but significant number of professional and intellectual refugees from the revolutions to America, along with many others who simply tired of the political turmoil. After the high point of 1854, the number of Germans arriving fell to 72,000 the next year, and remained below 100,000 annually until the end of the Civil War. Wars in both Europe and the United States probably served to discourage Germans from emigrating during those years. The numbers in the late 1860s rose modestly to 131,000 in 1869 and 118,000 in 1870. The next big wave of German emigration was yet to come, in the 1880s.[7]

British Immigration by the Numbers

The migration from Great Britain (including Scotland and Wales), the third largest migration stream of the period from 1820 to 1870, provides a somewhat different story. British immigrants arrived speaking English and sharing a culture that had been implanted in America since colonial times. There were generally not serious problems of assimilation, and the British newcomers could often disappear quietly and without resistance into the general American social fabric. They represented a wide variety of professions, including farmers, industrial workers, professional men, preachers, financiers, artisans, shopkeepers, and many others. The variety of motives, pressures, and pulls operating upon these individual emigrants was probably greater than for any of the emigrants from other countries. Their opportunities for upward social mobility were also greater than those open to other immigrant groups.

While British emigration at earlier times had been carefully controlled and sometimes restricted, policies changed in the early 1820s. Concerned about building the population of Canada for defense purposes after the War of 1812, Britain experimented with some assisted emigration in the early 1820s. In 1827 the British Parliament removed all restrictions on emigration. Also in the 1820s and 1830s, trade between the United States and Great Britain grew rapidly, and Britain soon became America's foremost trading partner. The consequence was a great increase in transatlantic shipping, offering cheap and frequent transportation between the two countries. From an annual average of two or three thousand British immigrants in the 1820s, the volume rose to a yearly total of 39,000 in 1840, with only a slight downturn during the depression of 1837. During the 1830s and 1840s canal and railroad development in the United States (much of which was financed with British money) opened up new opportunities for British immigrants. Migration fell to 14,000 in 1844, due mostly to slow economic conditions in America, then began to rise, to 35,000 in 1848, 55,000 in 1849, and to a high of 58,000 in 1854. The booming gold-rush economy of the United States in the early 1850s also had its effect. Immigration from Britain slowed during the late 1850s due to a languishing American economy, remained low in the early years of the Civil War, then began to rise again; 67,000 British immigrants came in 1863, and 82,000 came in 1865, the year the war ended. Immigration from Britain remained strong through 1870, when 107,000 arrived in U.S. ports. The U.S. census of 1870 found 771,000 British-born: 555,000 from England, 141,000 from Scotland, and 75,000 from Wales.[8]

Other Immigrant Groups by the Numbers

Many other groups were planting their roots in American soil in the mid-nineteenth century, and, while their numbers were small compared to the numbers of Irish, Germans, and English, their set-tlements would become beacons for those who would follow. The Scandinavians provided only handfuls of immigrants in the 1820s and 1830s. Their numbers increased in the great wave of migration of the decade after 1845; their largest annual total was 4,222 in 1854. Immigration from the Scandinavian countries then declined until near the end of the Civil War, and reached a new peak of around 44,000 in 1869. Swedish migrants between 1820 and 1870 were mostly farmers, and a significant minority of them came as dissent-ers from the state Lutheran church. They settled predominantly in the upper Midwest, a region just being opened up to settlement in the period before the Civil War. In the same period, groups of Norwegians formed communities in states such as Illinois, Wis-consin, and Minnesota. Of the Danes arriving in America before 1870, many went to the valley of the Great Salt Lake, attracted there by Mormon missionaries who had made Denmark one of the first of their missionary fields in Europe. The federal census of 1870 counted (by country of birth) 97,000 Swedes, 114,000 Norwegians and 30,000 Danes.

In the same year census takers counted 116,000 persons born in France and 66,000 born in the Low Countries (Belgium, Nether-lands, Luxembourg). These people were widely distributed geo-graphically. The Italian-born numbered about 17,000 in 1870, but they had established coherent communities in New York, San Fran-cisco, New Orleans, and Philadelphia. Italians were usually found in urban places, were mostly from the northern parts of Italy, and contained in their numbers many skilled craftsmen, artists, musi-cians, merchants, and intellectuals.

Chinese, the first major Asian migrants into American society, came primarily as a result of the annexation of California and the gold rush. Approximately 100,000 of them were recorded as arriv-ing between 1849 and 1870. But many of these were sojourners, who intended to return after a period of hopefully profitable work. The census of 1870 found 63,000 Chinese, most of them on the West Coast. Their increasing involvement in common-labor jobs was already beginning to arouse the enmities of Westerners in general and laborers in particular.

THE TRAIL OF THE IMMIGRANT

The transportation revolution that occurred both in America and internationally also had its influence on the flow of migration.

Improvements in transportation after 1820 stimulated an increased flow of migrants—but also channeled it in new directions. In Europe, the main rivers had provided the traditional route to the sea for emigrants: down the Rhine to Rotterdam, down the Weser to Bremen and Bremerhaven, down the Elbe to Hamburg, down the Seine to le Havre. As the era of canals was followed by the era of railroads, transportation networks developed outward from these original routes, and emigration from the interior of Europe was greatly facilitated. German emigration from the eastern provinces increased during the 1830s and 1840s as the railroads reached further to the east. Scandinavians took ships to ports in Germany, France, and England, whence they emigrated to America.

Ports of Emigration and Immigration

Ireland in the early nineteenth century still had the traditional ports from which emigrants had gone to North America since the early eighteenth century. Among them were Belfast, Dublin, Cork, Limerick, and Galway. For Irish emigrants, land journeys to one of these ports were usually fairly short. As time went on, these ports became for most Irish mere way-stations in their route to America, as they increasingly traveled first across the Irish Sea to Liverpool, which became the prime port of embarkation for those going to America. The reasons for the rise of Liverpool were several. Liverpool was emerging as the great center of trade between England and America, and the numbers of ships arriving there (and often returning to the United States with much less cargo) tended to lower the cost of the trip for immigrants willing to occupy the steerage. In 1818 packet service (meaning ships operating on a regular schedule) was established between Liverpool and New York. The packet ships carried both cabin and steerage passengers. At about the same time, the Erie Canal opened up a water route from the Hudson Valley into the Great Lakes region, enhancing the desirability of New York as a transatlantic destination for trade of all sorts. During the 1830s, the price of transportation from Liverpool to New York dropped to a point equal to or less than the price of transatlantic voyages from ports in the west of Ireland. As steamboat service was introduced in the 1820s to carry passengers from Irish ports across the Irish Sea to English ports, the cost of deck passage on those ships was minimal and the voyage relatively short. By 1826 about a third of Irish people emigrating to New York went by way of Liverpool. The numbers increased in the following decades, and the great majority of Irish emigrating during the famine went to America by way of Liverpool.

The Liverpool-New York connection became by mid-century the main stem of migration to America from Europe. By 1851 Liverpool was far ahead of other continental ports both in terms of trade and in terms of number of immigrants. That year there were recorded 455 ships carrying 159,000 passengers leaving Liverpool for New York. Le Havre meanwhile sent 124 ships with 32,000 people, and Bremen sent 19,000 people in 132 ships to New York.[9] Emigrants from Germany or elsewhere in Europe increasingly took ship from North Sea ports to Hull, on England's east coast, then traveled by train to Liverpool on the west coast. Although New York far surpassed other American cities as a port of immigration, there were regular migration routes to Boston, Philadelphia, Baltimore, and Charleston. As land opened up in the Mississippi Valley, the port of New Orleans became a prime port of entry for immigrants headed toward the Midwest. Immigrants to the United States also came by way of Canada, using ports such as Quebec City and St. John, New Brunswick.

The Transatlantic Voyage

The transatlantic voyage in the 1820s and 1830s was a daunting one. While sailing ships still dominated the trade, the westward journey across the Atlantic took at least 25 days, more commonly 60 days, and as much as 100 days during stormy weather and adverse winds. Immigrants generally took passage in cargo ships and found accommodations in bunks in the steerage. The ships often carried produce from the New World to Europe—heavy materials such as timber, tobacco, wool, flax, and cotton; many would have to return empty were it not for taking on immigrants as passengers. While the passengers in steerage were charged very low fares for their passage in these rudimentary accommodations (around $20–25 per person in the 1830s), they were often obliged to bring their own provisions. Poor sanitation on the ships encouraged the spread of many illnesses, including typhus and cholera, and deaths on the high seas were not uncommon. Before arriving in port, passengers had to be examined at a quarantine station, and those with diseases were detained. Shipwrecks were always a possibility, and storms might drive the ships far off course and toward an unexpected destination. In the 1820s more packet ships specifically designed for passengers were put into service, offering cabin accommodations and many amenities for those who could afford them. But most such ships still offered steerage passage, and the poor immigrants who traveled in steerage saw only modest improvement in their circumstances.

Conditions improved somewhat with the development of steam power for ships. While Robert Fulton inaugurated steamboat service on the Hudson River in 1807, and steamboat transportation on inland waters developed rapidly over the next two decades, it took longer for steam to be introduced into transatlantic service. Sailing ships assisted by steam began to appear in the 1830s, but it was not until the 1850s that fully steam-powered ships came into their own. When they did, the trip across the Atlantic could be shortened to as little as 10 days. With the formation in the 1840s and 1850s of large shipping concerns such as Cunard, Hamburg-America, and the North German Lloyd, the process of migration became somewhat more standardized and safe, although steerage passengers would still complain of their sufferings compared to the cabin passengers.

The Continuing Chain of Migration

Thus there were established in the second quarter of the nineteenth century paths of migration leading to America and continuing onward to immigrants' new homes within the country. Back across the same routes there developed a flow of information telling those in the homeland of America's possibilities. The attractions offered by emigration to America were made known in many different ways. By correspondence from those immigrants already arrived in America, relatives and friends in the old country could be advised of American conditions and warned of the pitfalls that might occur along the way if they were to follow. Groups of newcomers who concentrated in a particular town or region would encourage others from their hometowns to follow, setting up a process called chain migration. The promise from familiar acquaintances to assist the newcomers in getting settled in the New World served as a strong inducement in determining a destination. Others, particularly in Germany, might be influenced by organized emigration ventures. These were undertakings set up by specific emigration societies, by church congregations and missionary societies, and sometimes by groups organized by German states motivated to encourage emigration. But most migration was a much more individual undertaking. Those who had no family or friends to greet them relied instead upon guidebooks produced specifically for emigrants. People who had no guidance at all might fall prey to those who met them at the docks—"runners" who tried to induce them to a certain rooming house, agents who marketed steamboat or railroad tickets, and recruiters who were paid to find laborers for employers. Emigrant-aid societies and state agencies tried to prevent the exploitation of newly arrived immigrants, but what they could do was limited in the face of the overwhelming numbers of arrivals.

Spreading across America

In all these various ways—sometimes planned, sometimes random—newcomers were distributed across the expanding breadth of nineteenth-century America. Those without any means to travel further might find themselves taking lodgings and laboring in the port where they had arrived—often in menial tasks such as working on the docks, paving the streets, digging the sewers, serving the wealthy as housemaids, and driving the teams hauling wagons. Others with some skills might find work in the shops of craftsmen, as leather workers, iron workers, wagon makers, carpenters, and other common tradesmen. Those who did not speak English might seek work within their ethnic community and its businesses. As industries developed, some might go to factory towns nearby for work. Others might be recruited to join the numbers being employed as laborers on transportation projects—first the canals, later the railroads. In the early 1820s the great project of the Erie Canal was underway, and immigrants from all lands were being transported from New York up the Hudson to work on the canal. Many of them would stay behind when the canal was completed to provide the labor needed for developing new cities along the canal. The success of the Erie Canal inspired other efforts to expand the waterways along the East Coast and also in the Mississippi and Ohio watersheds. By the late 1830s, the canals were giving way to railroads, and Irish immigrants in particular worked on the railroads that opened up new areas to settlement. The multiplication of new towns and cities in the West offered new opportunities which attracted other immigrants. Thus inland cities that were transportation centers began to emerge as centers of immigration. St. Louis, Cincinnati, Louisville, Pittsburgh, Buffalo, Memphis, and New Orleans developed ethnic communities along the river and canal systems. Later, the railroads would stimulate immigrant settlement in Chicago, Milwaukee, Cleveland, Columbus, and Indianapolis, to name a few.

While many who left farms in Europe abandoned agricultural life forever, others found their way to rural areas in America. The Irish in America tended to become urban people, partly because many could not afford land, partly because they could not adapt to the drastically different conditions of rural life in America. The Germans and Scandinavians, however, contributed greatly to the opening up of new agricultural areas in the United States. In the decades before the Civil War, Germans established farms in the rapidly growing states of Ohio, Indiana, Illinois, Wisconsin, and Missouri. Their landholdings were usually in areas close to the new transportation routes, which made commercial farming possible. While Germans were less common in the South, they established some concentrated areas of settlement in Texas. After the Civil War, immigrants began to follow the western railroads out onto the Great Plains, where railroads encouraged settlement in and near towns established completely by groups from Germany. The Scandinavians opened up farms on the northern plains, and towns that were exclusively Swedish, Norwegian, or Danish sprang up in Wisconsin, Minnesota, Iowa, and eventually the Dakotas. Many immigrants of these ethnicities were able to buy farms with capital brought from the sale of previous land in Europe, and could use the proceeds for a much larger or more fertile tract in America. While new unimproved land could be bought cheaply from the federal government, the preference of many was to buy farms near the railroads' rights-of-way, or farms already developed by others. Those who lacked capital to buy farms could become tenants or hired hands, hoping to one day acquire land of their own. Immigrant farmers commonly practiced very intensive farming, similar to what they had known in the old country; but changes in their traditional crops and methods were often brought about both by climate and by market conditions.

UPWARD MOBILITY, DOWNWARD MOBILITY, OR STABILITY?

There is an infinite variety of stories about the success or achievement of the nineteenth-century immigrants. It is certain, however, that rags-to-riches stories in the pattern of the Scots immigrant Andrew Carnegie, who made his way from poverty to wealth in the iron and steel industry, are the rare exceptions to the general pattern. Far more common were the stories of those who found success merely in a stable existence with continued employment, enabling them to raise a family and own their own home. Social mobility—movement from one social class to another—was often seen only in the advance of the second generation, when children of the working class found white-collar or mercantile occupations. In an era when the economic cycles of depression and prosperity could make and unmake the wage-earner, a workingman felt lucky to maintain his position on one rung of the social ladder. And on the farm, the immigrant who acquired land and was able to retain it and maintain a stable existence in spite of the economic cycles was generally considered a success.

One can only speculate on the numbers of immigrants who found no employment, were overcome by disease, fell victim to a disabling accident, or succumbed to homelessness and despair. There are many recorded instances of immigrants who abandoned wife and family and disappeared into the vastness of the expanding country. There were also those who gave up and eventually decided to return to the mother country from which they came. The exact numbers of such cases are in dispute, but at the time nearly everyone in an immigrant community knew of them. Return migration was less common among the Irish, who, despite their nostalgia for the old country, knew that there was little there to welcome them back, and little promise of a steady living.

CONFLICTS AND CHALLENGES FACING THE IMMIGRANTS

The middle years of the nineteenth century saw increasing examples of a confrontation between cultures, particularly in the major urban areas of the United States. Conflicts emerged more frequently with the rise of nativism, or anti-foreign hostility, especially during the 1840s and 1850s. Opposition was aimed particularly at Catholic immigrants, who included most of the Irish and some of the Germans. Catholics were being seen for the first time in many areas of a heretofore overwhelmingly Protestant nation. To the anti-Catholic prejudices that traced back to the Protestant Reformation in England was added the American conviction that Catholic traditions could never be harmonized with the ideals of a democratic republic. Outgrowths of this nativism were seen in clashes in New York and elsewhere over the issue of religion in the schools, and in the working-class riots that broke out in Philadelphia in 1844. By the early 1850s nativism took political form in the American or

Know-Nothing party, which made political gains in many areas of the North. This party's platform included the denying and delaying of citizenship to immigrants. Another form of cultural tension was found in the growing anti-liquor crusade. Although there was doubtless a serious alcoholism problem in American society at the time, immigrants who saw the consumption of alcohol as a regular part of their social and cultural life interpreted the "temperance" or "prohibition" reform movement as simply another form of hostility to foreigners.

THE PACE OF ASSIMILATION

Despite the tensions between native and immigrant cultures, a process of interchange and adaptation went on between them. This assimilation should not be seen as a sudden crossing of the lines between cultures; it occurred in gradual steps, in minor compromises, in differences between generations, and in disappearances of old habits that were now no longer viable. This occurred much more readily in the cities and towns than in the countryside, where immigrants in isolated ethnic settlements could preserve their traditions more easily. Immigrants in urban workplaces that were part of the general economy had to adapt to the practices that prevailed there. Urban America was already becoming ruled by the clock, and rural Americans and rural foreigners alike had to abandon the more leisurely ways of their old culture and adhere to the more rigorous schedules of the new. The sons and daughters of immigrants—the second generation—might find less reason to preserve old customs and stick to the language of a country they did not remember. In the long run, one of the most effective instruments of assimilation was the American political system. When their right to voting citizenship was challenged, immigrants generally found their own defense by becoming part of the democratic system— something generally outside their previous experience. The Irish, whose only previous political experience was that of protest and resistance, were especially quick to take hold of the machinery of politics by the force of their numbers, and came to dominate many large cities by the time of the Civil War.

IMMIGRANT INFLUENCES UPON AMERICA

Also underway was the other side of the process of assimilation: the influence that the presence of many new immigrants had upon the host culture to which they came. It could be seen in the gradual if grudging acceptance of the immigrants into the structure of the main society—as, for instance, when native-born Americans found themselves shopping at the German butcher's store, or native-born politicians found themselves speaking to an Irish rally in the midst of a political campaign. By the time of the Civil War, German lager beer had come to dominate the American market, generally eliminating the English ale that formerly prevailed. And public celebrations and festivals (even on Sundays) in the European style had begun to replace the more staid observances of the Anglo-American culture. America was gradually easing into the diversity that would become a hallmark of American cities by the end of the century.

Behind the statistics that measure the flow of immigrants into the United States, behind the mass movements through the transportation network, behind the enumerations of census-takers, behind the recordings of births and deaths and marriages, lie the individual stories of millions of people. And none of them were the same. In the chapters which follow, these stories will be examined from the point of view of the individuals themselves. We can never recover the entire immigrant experience, but we can have some sense of what their lives were like.

NOTES

1. Victoria Coven, "A History of Statistics in the Social Sciences," *Gateway: An Academic History Journal on the Web* (spring 2003), available from http://www.grad.usask.ca/gateway, accessed 14 May 2005.

2. Herbert Moller, "Introduction," in *Population Movements in Modern European History*, ed. Herbert Moller (New York: Macmillan, 1964), 5.

3. Kerby A. Miller, *Emigrants and Exiles: Ireland and the Irish Exodus to North America* (New York: Oxford University Press, 1985), 280.

4. *Historical Statistics of the United States, Colonial Times to 1970* (Washington, DC: Government Printing Office, 1975), 106, 112.

5. Miller, *Emigrants and Exiles*, 193–201, 280, 291–93, 346–53, 569.

6. Wolfgang Köllmann and Peter Marschalk, "German Emigration to the United States," in *Perspectives in American History* 7 (1973): 518–19.

7. *Historical Statistics of the United States*, 106.

8. Ibid.

9. Gordon Read, "Liverpool—The Floodgate of the Old World: A Study in Ethnic Attitudes," *Journal of American Ethnic History* 13 (1993): 31.

2

Leaving Home, 1820–1845

Across western Europe after the fall of Napoleon, one thing was becoming clearer: the circumstances of everyday life were changing rapidly, and in such a way as to lead many to question whether they could pursue the traditional ways and customs of their ancestors. From that realization came decisions that would lead more Europeans to join the growing stream of migrants to America.

THE DECISION TO EMIGRATE, AND ITS CONSEQUENCES

Behind the statistics of the ebb and flow of migration lie the stories of millions of individual immigrants. There were no typical immigrant experiences, and the beginning of each story of migration is one individual's decision to abandon the familiar surroundings of a homeland and begin a journey to America. For some it was a decision to break ties with an ancestral community of many centuries; for others it was a decision that came after previous wanderings within the European homeland. The decision might be made with hope and optimism or with fear and regret. It might reflect confidence in the future, or it might reflect sheer desperation. Regardless of the emotions involved, those who decided to go to America would recognize this decision as the most crucial one of a whole lifetime, one which, given the difficulties of the sea voyage, they did not expect to be easily reversed.

Understanding why people chose to emigrate involves much more than simply categorizing their motives as economic, political, or religious. Those contemplating departing their homeland were confronted with numerous alternatives and responded to a variety of circumstances as they came to a decision. And while there were common themes underlying emigrants' decisions in different lands, the particular circumstances that elicited the decision to emigrate varied considerably from one country to another, and, indeed, within any single country.

A Norwegian Idealist

On April 7, 1837, Ole Rynning, then 28 years of age, left Bergen, Norway, on the sailing ship *Aegir*. He was one of 84 passengers bound for America. The son of a minister of the established Lutheran Church of Norway in the parish of Snaasen, he had originally planned to enter the church himself, and for that purpose had spent four years at the University of Christiania, where he completed his studies in 1833. By that time he had decided against entering the ministry and had returned to Snaasen, where he conducted a school for advanced students. By 1836 he had begun to feel disillusion with his hometown environment, and also some differences with his father. Some accounts suggest that his father had disapproved of his plans for marriage. He also seems to have come to differ from his aristocratic father ideologically, and was known to have expressed sentiment for democracy and sympathy for the plight of the ordinary peasant. He had himself undertaken to purchase a tract of land in Snaasen for four hundred Norwegian dollars, but then was unable to raise the necessary amount.

A variety of influences, then, seem to have influenced Ole Rynning's decision to go to the New World. He linked up with a group that was planning to go to the Fox River Valley of northern Illinois, where other Norwegians who had been among the pioneering emigrants of 1825 in Fulton County, New York, had resettled in 1833. The group included many who were religious dissenters from the Lutheran state church of Norway. The emigrants arrived in New York after a two months' journey, and immediately embarked for their Illinois destination. They followed the established route by steamboat up the Hudson River, then by an Erie Canal boat to Buffalo, then via Lake Erie to Detroit, and finally by another boat trip across the Great Lakes to Chicago.

When they arrived in Chicago, then little more than a frontier village, they were encouraged by promoters to avoid the Fox River Valley and go instead to the new community of Beaver Creek, located in Iroquois County on the prairies of eastern Illinois, about seventy miles south of Chicago. Leaving the rest of the group in Chicago, Ole and three others traveled to Beaver Creek, approved of the site, and recommended it to the others. About fifty of the emigrant group decided to go; the remainder headed instead to the Fox River settlements.

It would become clear by the next spring that the choice of Beaver Creek had been a mistake. Land that had seemed dry and promising in the fall proved to be swampy and untillable when the spring rains fell. The scourge of the early frontier—malaria—appeared and began to claim its victims. Ole Rynning, close to destitution, worked for a while digging the just-begun Illinois and Michigan Canal, and was probably weakened by the hard work and the unhealthy, malaria-ridden environment. Construction was suspended on the canal in the wake of the financial panic of 1837. During the winter of 1837–1838, Ole traveled on foot across the Illinois prairie, returning to Beaver Creek with feet severely injured and frostbitten. While he seemed to have recovered by the spring, he fell victim to a new wave of disease during the summer. After a lingering illness, Ole died of malaria and typhoid fever in the fall of 1838 at the age of 29.

In the winter before his last illness, Ole Rynning had undertaken to write a book of advice for prospective Norwegian immigrants. Titled *True Account of America for the Information and Help of Peasant and Commoner*, it was published in Norwegian late in 1838. As its title implied, it took into consideration the aspirations of the common people. In addition to the usual practical advice about ocean voyages and land acquisition, Ole Rynning emphasized those aspects of America that would appeal to the peasant and artisan, namely, the availability of land, better wages than existed in Norway, freedom of religion, the democratic society, and the possibility of forming a communal society with fellow countrymen. The book would have a considerable influence on Norwegians contemplating emigration in the ensuing decade.

A fellow settler at Beaver Creek remembered Ole for his selflessness. "He hoped to be able to provide the poor, oppressed Norwegian a happier home on this side of the sea. . . . Nothing could shake his belief that America would become a place of refuge for the masses of people in Europe who toiled under the burdens of poverty."[1] Following Ole Rynning's death, the Beaver Creek community disintegrated, most of the survivors going to the Fox River Valley, to Missouri, or to Wisconsin.

A Faithful German Wife

Henriette Geisberg, known to her family as "Jette," was brought up in comfortable middle-class circumstances. Born in 1813 in Oelde, Westphalia, where her father was a tax collector and later the mayor, she went to live in the city of Münster with her uncles after the death of her mother in 1827. There she received the education common to well-bred young women of the time: languages, music, and homemaking. In 1831 she returned to Oelde to care for her dying father. There she met a physician, Dr. Bernhard Bruns, fifteen years older than she, and agreed to marry him, despite some opposition from within her family. The wedding occurred in May 1832, after the death of her father.

After their wedding, Dr. Bruns, feeling various dissatisfactions with life in Oelde, broached the idea of removing to the New World. He was particularly interested in the young state of Missouri. The principal influence acting upon him was the famous guidebook written by Gottfried Duden, *Report on a Journey to the Western States of North America and a Stay of Several Years along the Missouri (during the Years 1824, '25, '26, and 1827)*.[2] Duden painted a romantic picture of the possibilities of emigrant farm life in Missouri: ample and productive land, a beautiful landscape, a political and social environment of freedom, and prospects of a prosperous income.

Jette recalled in her autobiography that, while her husband was a highly regarded physician with an extensive and remunerative medical practice in Oelde, he was unhappy that so many of his patients were poor people who had difficulty paying for his services. "That his income had to come from poor people was the beginning of his dissatisfaction. . . . At that time there was an emigration fever in the air and it was furthered by reports of Duden, von Martels, Löwe, and others. Bruns kept himself well-informed, and we discussed it often."[3] The discussion went on for nearly two years.

"For me it was a hard struggle between inclination and duty— anyway I thought it was. When the latter won, a big fuss broke out, but I had given my husband my promise to follow him to the New World."[4] The "big fuss" came particularly from Jette's own relatives. They appealed to her responsibility to help care for her seven younger brothers and sisters. She herself (still just 18 when she was married) felt an obligation to her siblings, but her concern was partially relieved when her two oldest brothers said they wanted to go to America with her. Dr. Bruns was unwavering in his desire to emigrate, but agreed to make the trip to America first and assure his family of a definite and secure place for their home.

Bernhard Bruns left for America on June 12, 1835, traveling cabin class in the ship *Elise,* and arrived in Baltimore on August 6. Over the next seven months he traveled to Missouri, appraised the surrounding region, and chose a site in Gasconade County (later Osage County), where he bought property. He described the site to Jette in terms that were designed to be attractive to her: a landscape with a beautiful river valley (the Maries, a tributary of the Osage), fertile land, much wildlife. And, he reported, a number of friendly Germans were already there—in fact, the settlement was named Westphalia because many of the inhabitants came from there. When he returned to his wife in Oelde in January 1836, Bruns elaborated on the beauties of the place: a colony of Germans, with a village already supplied with a teacher and a shoemaker, a Catholic church to continue their religious traditions, and a house already under construction for her to occupy. "I am agreeable to everything," said Jette in a letter to her brothers. "I believe that I can be quite content with everything."[5] Nevertheless, Jette showed some ambivalence as she turned over the care of her younger brothers and sisters to her uncle Caspar: "To be sure, I believe that I am fulfilling my primary duty as a wife, and I hope to God that bitter remorse will not torture me in the future, but I fear that the heart's pure and serene peace will be forever denied me!"[6]

On July 6, 1836, Dr. Bruns, his wife Jette, their young son Hermann, just under two years old, and Jette's two brothers Franz and Heinrich Geisberg, accompanied by a maid and her young daughter, sailed from Bremerhaven, arriving in Baltimore on September 16. Dr. Bruns's brother David was also in the party. Others from Westphalia were in the steerage, but Jette, pregnant at the time, traveled in the cabin. Six weeks after landing in Baltimore, having traveled by the railroads and canals of the Pennsylvania Main Line, by rail over the Allegheny Portage in Pennsylvania, by steamboat down the Ohio River and up the Mississippi to St. Louis, they arrived at the small village of Westphalia, Missouri. Very soon the realities of frontier life began to dissolve the romantic images that had inspired them to come. The family's first home was a one-room log cabin with one window. There were delays in finishing the larger house on higher ground which Bruns had promised. The next spring brought floods, and the crops for the year were meager. "We could plant only very few vegetables because the little fellow [her new son Maximilian, born in February 1837] took too much of my time. . . . Now we have many people and little to eat."[7] Jette and her husband would have a total of eleven children, ten of them born in America; of those, five would die in childhood. Three of these died of dysentery in 1841. Jette resigned herself to the hard work of a farm housewife, but complained of loneliness and boredom. Dr. Bruns's practice was time-consuming, spread across a large area, and not always as financially rewarding as he had hoped. In 1851, after 15 years at Westphalia, the family moved to a larger farm on the Osage River. The loss of her children, frequent family illness, and an apparent depression took its toll on Jette. She admitted in 1853 that, while still only 39, she appeared very elderly. The family moved to Jefferson City, Missouri's capital, in hopes of a better life, but Dr. Bruns suffered for a while a state of severe depression and then contracted pneumonia. Jette later recalled that time as the worst period of her life. By 1856, Dr. Bruns had recovered sufficiently to visit Germany with his wife. Jette confessed that she felt somewhat disoriented there after twenty years' absence. And by now, enmeshed in the ties of family and community in America, there was no thought of a permanent return to Germany.

After their return to Jefferson City, Dr. Bruns became more involved in both politics and land development, which increasingly occupied more of his time than did his medical practice. As the country drew nearer to civil war, Bruns, like many other Germans in the area, adhered to the new free-soil Republican party in the hotly contended politics of central Missouri. When the war came, the family was among the many Germans who resisted the secession; the division within Missouri between secessionists and Unionists would generate a guerilla war that would continue over the next four years. Jette's son Heinrich died in 1863 while fighting for the Union. Dr. Bruns served as a major and surgeon in the Union Army, then returned to Jefferson City and served as the city's mayor. He died of a rheumatic fever in 1864. Jette spent many years after her husband's death dealing with the complex financial matters he left behind. Otherwise, she spent time with her children, now widely dispersed, and lived at various times in Toledo, Ohio; in Seattle; in St. Louis (where she took in boarders for a while); and in Jefferson City. In 1882 she went to Germany for the summer, and remarked in a letter to her son in America that "All in all, everything has become quite foreign to me here."[8]

Jette Bruns died at her daughter Ottilie's home in St. Louis in November 1899.

An Outmoded English Artisan

Abel Stephenson, who left his native Yorkshire for the United States in 1837, was described by the historian Charlotte Erickson as "an honest but singular man" who was "irascible and violently inclined."[9] His irascibility no doubt grew out of the general unrest of workingmen that disturbed England during the 1830s. Some even labeled Stephenson a Chartist, a member of a workingmen's reform movement that had sprung up during that decade. Certainly like the Chartists he deplored the conditions of the poor, the lack of democratic government, and the general conditions brought on by the Industrial Revolution. Most particularly, the advance of the power-driven looms in the textile industry was making obsolete his own skill at hand-weaving. His family and his native community of Thurstonland in Yorkshire had long been involved in hand-weaving, but increasingly the inhabitants were becoming factory workers in the woolen and cotton mills. Those who remained in the home hand-weaving trade, like some of Abel's relatives, were increasingly impoverished as a result of competition from factory-made cloth.

Abel arrived in the United States in early 1838, just as the effects of the severe depression following the Panic of 1837 were beginning to be felt. He found that power looms were also taking over the American textile industry, and jobs of any kind were difficult to find. In a bitter letter written April 1838 to his relatives in Thurstonland, he had found the villains of hard times to be the same as those that had beset him in England. "I can give no good accounts of the times in this country in the manufacturing business. The rotten corrupt banking, it is a curs [sic] to this country. . . . I shall give [emigrants] no encouragement to come to this country except they turn into the land. . . . Machinery is increasing fast in this country, so that in a little time it will be as bad as it is in England."[10]

Abel searched for two years for a chance to make his living as a hand-weaver. He was employed in a factory in Pittsburgh, but left, denouncing his employer as a tyrant and a cheat. He remained optimistic, however, as he moved down the Ohio River to a job near Wheeling. "I begin to like the country better than ever."[11] In 1840 he turned up in Northampton, Massachusetts, after having apparently spent some time in New Orleans. He complained of the climate, of the lack of work, and of the "ague," the common term for malaria. In Northampton he found that the power looms had also taken over the textile business, and he was reduced to spinning woolen yarn for a living. About 1842 Abel moved to the new territory of Iowa and was able to purchase government land near Fairfield, in the southeastern part of the territory. Apparently acting upon his own previous assertions that the only way to advancement and independence in America was to take up farming, he encouraged his brother Richard, another hand-weaver just arrived in New York, to come to Iowa and settle on his land. Subsequently, Abel Stephenson seems to have disappeared, after announcing that he was going to Canada. His family did not hear from him again. They continued to farm in Iowa, but also were still striving to make money from hand-weaving—now a dying craft that could be plied only in the more remote sections of the frontier.

Land Hunger and the Luck of the Irish

A strong farmer from County Wexford on the southeast coast of Ireland, Martin Murphy, Sr., made a decision in 1820 to take his family to Canada. He was then 35 years of age. Long afterward, his grandson Bernard D. Murphy gave an account of the circumstances to a local historian in California: "As his family increased, Mr. Murphy, who was an intelligent, industrious and pious man, became more and more discontented with the disadvantages under which the Irish people were placed by the government of Great Britain, and with the meagre political liberty accorded them."[12] These feelings were not surprising in Wexford, which had been the center of the bloodiest battles of the failed Irish Revolution of 1798, and where emotions were frequently tense between Protestants and Catholics, especially between Protestant landlords and their Catholic tenants. Murphy was a pious and faithful Catholic, and he remained so all his life.

In Ireland in 1820 the Penal Laws, dating from the early eighteenth century, were still in effect. They put restrictions upon landholding by Catholics, forbade participation by Catholics in civic affairs, and prohibited the public celebration of Mass. In 1820 discontent was running high. Ireland's farmers were still suffering from the plunge in agricultural prices that had followed the Napoleonic Wars. Falling incomes and the tendency of landlords to consolidate their holdings and push tenant farmers off the land were motivating many to emigrate to America. For Murphy there may have been an additional problem: his family now consisted of his wife and six children, three of them sons. Although his land holdings would seem to have been fairly extensive (perhaps fifty or sixty acres), the prospects were slim that his children would have a healthy income after their parents were gone. If the then-traditional practice of primogeniture were followed, the eldest son, Martin Jr., would inherit tenants' rights to the land and Murphy's other sons would probably become agricultural laborers—at a time when work was scarce and wages were falling. Thus Murphy appears to have been one of many who decided to take the family's resources to America in order to buy more land there.

When the Murphys departed Ireland in 1820, they left two children behind: Martin Jr., age 13, and his sister Margaret, age 9. There is some speculation about the reasons for this, but the most likely answer is that Martin, Jr. stayed to retain tenant's rights to the land. Leases could not be sold without the consent of the oldest son, and then only when he reached the age of twenty-one. Who cared for the children and the land in the meantime is a mystery, but, in any event, on April 9, 1828, when Martin Jr. was 21, he and Margaret sailed from the city of Wexford, arriving in Quebec a remarkable 28 days later.

Martin Murphy Sr. had gone to Quebec, perhaps encouraged by British policies promoting emigration to that area. He had purchased land in the village of Frampton, a growing Irish settlement 35 miles southeast of Quebec City. His wife Mary had borne him three more children after their arrival. Martin Jr. remained for two years in Quebec City as a retail salesman. There, in 1831, he met and married Mary Bolger, who came from a family the Murphys had known in Wexford. In 1832 Martin Jr. purchased two hundred acres near his father's farm in Frampton. In the ensuing years, however, the Murphys began to consider the comparative advantages of looking for land in the United States, where economic conditions were better and the soil and climate seemed more attractive. In 1840 the elder Murphy and his family moved across the U.S. border and traveled to the western fringe of the expanding agricultural frontier—an area recently opened up to settlement in what would become Holt County in the Platte Purchase of northwestern Missouri, near the Missouri River. Martin Murphy Jr. and family would follow two years later and purchase 320 acres in the same settlement, now named Irish Grove. While the land was productive, it was not entirely healthy; in 1843 both Martin Sr.'s wife Mary and Martin Jr.'s infant daughter died of malaria. Over the next year the family seemed to have succumbed to the Oregon Fever that was affecting many areas of the West, an area not yet recovered from the hard times following the Panic of 1837. For the Murphys, however, the Oregon Fever changed to the more adventuresome spirit of the California Fever. A Jesuit missionary visiting the Irish Grove settlement persuaded the Murphy family that there were greater opportunities in California, still a part of Mexico. There extensive land grants were available, the country was receptive to Catholics, and the climate was nearly perfect. In 1844 the Murphy family and various associates, numbering 22 people, traveled up the Missouri to Council Bluffs, then known as the principal jumping-off point for the Oregon Trail. With the leadership of a mountain man, Elisha Stevens, they joined others and set out for California in a party of about fifty people. About half of the travelers, including the Murphys, made it to California; the other half branched off at Fort Hall in Idaho and headed to Oregon. The Stevens-Murphy party would go down in the history books as the first travelers to make it all the way from the Missouri River to the Sacramento Valley with a wagon train. The group was also the first to use the Truckee River route through the Sierra Mountains, through what would later be known as Donner Pass. The first of the party reached Sutter's Fort on the Sacramento River in early December. Others were forced to make winter camp near the headwaters of the Yuba River, and were rescued the following March.

With their arrival began one of the great success stories of early California. Both Martin Murphy Sr. and Martin Jr. became Mexican citizens. The elder Murphy quickly acquired about 9,000 acres of land in the region south of San Jose, near the seacoast. The younger Murphy originally purchased over 11,000 acres of land near Sacramento. There he would play a role in the events of the Mexican War. The Bear Flag Revolt arguably began on his ranch, where Americans stole 125 horses from a Mexican army company in June 1846, arming themselves for the insurrection that would follow. The Gold Rush of 1849, which came immediately after the war and the U.S. acquisition of California, led to changes in Martin Jr.'s life and in the lives of most others in California. Not wanting to risk his resources in prospecting and mining, Martin Jr. sold his ranch and 3,000 head of cattle in 1850 and took up residence in the Santa Clara Valley, near his father. The senior Murphy began to acquire large grants of land, and by wheat-raising and cattle-ranching made a fortune selling foodstuffs in the mining camps. His impressive residence and ranch was on the site of what would become

Sunnyvale, California. He became an American citizen and also played a role in the development of the young town of San Jose. Although illiterate, like many Irish immigrants of that time, he was among the benefactors who founded Santa Clara University in 1851 and was a benefactor of many other Catholic institutions in the region.

Martin Murphy Sr. died in 1865 at the age of 80. Martin Murphy Jr. died at the age of 77 in 1884, leaving an estate valued at between $3 and $5 million, including 92,000 acres of land stretching from San Jose south to Santa Barbara. The Murphys' sons and grandsons continued to prosper in California land development and civic affairs. The family that left a farm of fifty to sixty acres in Wexford found more land in America than they would have imagined in their wildest dreams.

MIXED MOTIVES AND CONFLICTING PRESSURES

A few examples, mostly drawn from literate and educated emigrants, do not answer all the riddles of why people from many countries and backgrounds chose to emigrate. But the complexities behind these decisions can be seen in the long list of possibilities. The desire for more or better land, the inability to acquire any land at all, the search for work to support a family, the weakening social fabric of a country town, the lack of a market for particular skills, the miserable working and living conditions in factory towns, the romantic appeal disseminated by guidebooks and advocates of emigration, the inviting letters from friends and relatives, the promise of a new "freedom" (however ill-defined), escape from a religion thought oppressive, the desire to continue a traditional way of life—all these considerations in varying proportions might find their way into Europeans' thoughts as they contemplated their futures. Beyond these were the much more personal motives: fidelity to one's spouse or family, estrangement from one's family, the hope to find a suitable spouse, a flight from the law or the authorities, a dispute with family or friends, the desire for the lack of restraint of a frontier society, the avoidance of military service, the need to escape from parental control—any of these might help propel emigrants on their way to a port of embarkation. To understand the background from whence these many motives came, one must consider more particularly some of the main sources of migration in the second quarter of the nineteenth century, and the daily living conditions of those who would decide to migrate.

Ireland and Its Dwindling Hopes

Ireland in the 1820s and 1830s was an island still mostly rural, and the majority of people made their living, however humbly, on farms. Over half the farmers were small landholders, cultivating tracts of no more than 10 acres. About three-quarters of the small farmers were tenants of landlords. The others held lands under some form of communal system, wherein specific tracts were parceled out to each small farmer under a traditional system called "rundale." These communal arrangements were on the road to disappearance in the early 1800s. Farm families occupied small houses of one or two rooms, most with traditional thatched roofs. The farmers were compelled to make the most of their meager portions of land. Every acre was cultivated intensively, using only hand-tools, since most small farmers could not afford horses or mules. The few livestock that the small farmer owned might have to be kept in the house at night with the family, for few farmers could afford to take up space with barns or other outbuildings. Since some marketable commodities had to be produced in order to pay the rent and to rise above the level of mere subsistence, a number of acres might be devoted to flax, wheat, other grain, and livestock-grazing. The poorer farmers seldom raised these commodities for their own consumption. Extra income was also sought by selling milk, eggs, and young livestock, by laboring on the larger farms of others, or by home industry such as spinning or weaving linen. For their own diet the families of small farms had come to rely almost entirely on the potato; a potato patch of one to two acres could provide much of the nutrition a family might need for the year. Clothing was usually made from homespun wool or linen.

In the early nineteenth century the Irish population was growing, increasing from about seven to eight million between 1821 and 1841. Of those eight million, just over three million still spoke Gaelic, the Irish language, although the numbers of Gaelic-speakers had been dropping steadily since 1800.[13] The pressure of increasing population upon the available land profoundly affected the conditions of small farmers. Over the previous century, when population had also been rising, farming families had survived by dividing their land among their sons. But "partible inheritance," as the practice was called, was increasingly impossible, for tracts of land less than

The harbor of Cork in the 1830s. In the days of the sailing ships, Cork was one of the leading ports from which emigrants left for both America and England. Drawing by W. H. Bartlett, from G. N. Wright et al., *Ireland Illustrated, from Original Drawings* (London: H. Fisher, Son and Jackson, 1834). Courtesy McGarrity Collection, Villanova University Library.

eight acres were generally insufficient to support a family. Thus one son, usually the eldest, might carry on the farm, but others could expect no inheritance and had to look elsewhere for a livelihood. The usual choices were to work as a laborer on a larger farm, to seek industrial work, to learn a trade, or to emigrate. For a young woman, the choice was to marry if she could, to enter a convent, to become a spinster spinning yarn at home as her contribution to family income, or to emigrate.

There were farmers who were somewhat better off; those who held between ten and thirty acres, so-called middling farmers, constituted about one-third of all the farmers in Ireland. While they might enjoy a somewhat higher standard of living than the small farmers, they still were often on the margin of insecurity. They might hire some laborers for their farms, raise somewhat more surplus crops for the market, own a draft animal, and be able at times to add a little fish, pork, milk, or chicken to the routine diet of potatoes. Yet, they too were often tenants who had to deal with rising rents and had to accept the risk of the crop failures which were part of the life of all farmers. Their houses, though humble, were somewhat more comfortable than those of the small farmers, and their

Ireland in the nineteenth century. From Kerby A. Miller, *Emigrants and Exiles: Ireland and the Irish Exodus to North America* (New York: Oxford University Press, 1985). By permission of Oxford University Press, Inc.

clothes might be the products of a tailor or dressmaker, but often were worn and ragged.

The highest level of farmers in the social scale were the strong farmers, who held lands ranging from thirty acres up to tracts of grazing land that were well over a hundred acres. Although they numbered only about one-sixth of all Irish farmers, the strong farmers held a majority of the land in Ireland. Most held their land in tenancy, and sometimes sublet lands to others. They were somewhat more secure in that their leases were often longer-term, sometimes lasting for a lifetime.[14] In good times, strong farmers could earn enough from their surplus crops to improve their farms, buy implements, and build houses more comfortable than most—two-story houses, sometimes built of stone and including slate roofs. Many had draft animals and could afford a more ample diet, including some meat. Often they were able to employ seasonal labor to help with the farm work.

Nearly all the farmers were beholden, either directly or indirectly, to the landlords who formed the top level of Ireland's agrarian society. "Fewer than 10,000 families literally owned Ireland, and several hundred of the wealthiest magnates monopolized the bulk of the land."[15] The landlord class was a genuine gentry, sometimes recognizing their obligations to their tenants, but sometimes tempted to evade those obligations when times changed for the worse. During the eighteenth century a generally rising British economy had led to profits for all agriculture and had encouraged many landlords to raise their rents. The Napoleonic Wars had also provided rising markets for grain, and Irish exports were booming. But the years after 1815 produced shrinking markets, and there were seasons of crop failures. These were the times in which landlords pressed their tenants for new leases with higher rents, or even turned tenants out in an effort to combine holdings for more efficient farming When cultivated land was turned into grazing land, fewer tenants were required.

The wealthiest of the gentry were often absentee landlords, preferring the social climate of Dublin or London, where they owned townhouses. They were often accused of spending their profits on luxurious living, neglecting the upkeep or improvement of their lands, and leaving the management of their estates to agents or middlemen. The middlemen, holding fairly large long-term leases, could subdivide their holdings at considerably increased and burdensome rents. Landlord-tenant frictions, long an irritating element in Irish society, became even more disruptive when economic conditions deteriorated.

At the bottom of Irish society were those who held little or no land and were primarily dependent on their own labor for survival. Suffering greatest hardship was a particular class of laborers called cottiers. These people would normally labor on the farms of larger landowners, receiving from them a small plot of land, perhaps an acre or two, with a small primitive cabin. They would pay rent to the owner, and could be hired (at will) by the owner for a small daily wage. Otherwise they might piece together a small living by pursuing weaving or other crafts, or by selling their labor to other farmers. Historian Kerby Miller described their living conditions:

Before the Great Famine, cottiers, landless laborers, and the poorest small-holders—those who can properly be called the peasantry—constituted about three-quarters of the rural population, and their wretched condition gave Ireland its deserved reputation for dire poverty. . . . The poorest cottiers and laborers dressed in cast-off rags, through which naked arms and legs protruded, and lived in one-room, mud-floored cabins without chimneys or windows. In 1841 nearly half a million such hovels dotted the Irish countryside, particularly in the South and the West. . . . [Their] furniture consisted generally of a few broken stools; beds were considered luxuries, and many poor families slept huddled together on straw laid on the bare floor.[16]

The cottiers were most vulnerable to the cycles of the economy. Their number had grown in the late eighteenth century as land-owners terminated many leases. They would continue to grow as efforts toward agricultural "rationalization" continued in the 1820s and 1830s, driving more tenants from their farms.

In contrast to other countries of western Europe at the time, Ireland offered few choices for those who could find neither land nor employment. Industry was not developing in Ireland, and the older Irish industries such as linen weaving were attempting to meet the British competition by increasing their mechanized production. That meant smaller earnings for the home spinners and weavers, and fewer wage-earners in the factories. Demand for labor could generally be found in England, and emigration across the Irish Sea toward England was already common in the 1820s. This movement had begun with the seasonal hiring of Irish labor in agricultural areas in Britain. Then the growth of British industries had further encouraged the surplus manpower of Ireland to search for perma-nent work in the cities of England. The cost of passage from Dub-lin to Liverpool was small compared to the cost of a transatlantic voyage. Emigration to America was generally not an option for the poorest of Ireland; the cost was simply too great without some form of financial assistance.

The social and class structure of pre-famine Ireland and its agri-cultural economy were profoundly influenced by religious divisions.

In 1834 a religious census classified about 80 percent of the population as Catholic, about 10 percent as Anglican Protestant and a slightly smaller percentage as Presbyterian. However, the distribution of adherents of these religions by region and within the social structure heightened the potential for conflict among them. The majority of the farmers were Catholic, except in Ulster and other relatively prosperous regions in the north, which were the strongholds of Protestants. The farming classes there were primarily Presbyterians. Landlords, government officials, and large mercantile traders were most often members of the Anglican Church of Ireland, the established church which all taxpayers were obliged to support with tithes.

The origins of these divisions were deep-seated, and went back as far as the Protestant Reformation of the sixteenth century and the English Civil Wars of the seventeenth century. England had for centuries attempted to gain control over Catholic Ireland, and when an established English Protestant church emerged during the English Reformation, greater bitterness and strife resulted. In the English Civil Wars of the 1640s, the forces of Oliver Cromwell invaded Ireland and effectively crushed all Catholic resistance. The result was that perhaps one-third of the island's Catholics perished, others fled to France, and others were taken prisoner and deported. Those Catholics who would not convert to the established church had their lands confiscated, leaving Protestants with ownership of about 80 percent of the land in all Ireland. Although during the Stuart Restoration after 1660, Catholics found some relief, the Glorious Revolution of 1688 led to the downfall of the Catholic King James II, and to the final suppression of Catholic resistance at the Battle of the Boyne in Ireland in 1690. After the additional confiscations that followed, Catholics owned about 14 percent of the land in 1700, an amount that further decreased to about 5 percent by 1750. A series of Penal Laws in the early eighteenth century placed further restrictions on Catholics. Catholics could neither purchase land nor lease it for longer than 31 years, and land bequeathed by a Catholic had to be divided among heirs by partible inheritance, unless the eldest son converted to Anglicanism. Catholics were likewise denied the franchise and were forbidden to enter the army and most professions. While the Penal Laws were sometimes evaded or ignored as the eighteenth century went on, any efforts of Catholics to rise in the social or economic scale were effectively foreclosed.

Conflicts with both Anglicans and other Protestants served to strengthen the Irish Catholics in their religion, although this did not necessarily mean they conformed to all the rules disseminated from Rome. Only 30 to 40 percent of Irish Catholics in the early nineteenth century attended Mass weekly, although most were in attendance at least several times a year. While the public celebration of Mass was formally forbidden by the Penal Laws, Catholics worshiped in secluded open-air locations, in private houses, or in discreet Mass houses. Many pursued private devotions at so-called holy wells, a practice that had gone on for centuries, in which worshipers observed a ritual of making rounds and reciting set prayers around wells devoted to particular patron saints.[17] Popular devotions like this would gradually diminish as the century went on and the Irish church underwent considerable reform, during which its religious observances would gradually conform more closely to those promulgated by Rome.

In the late eighteenth century, the Irish had increasingly agitated for emancipation from the Penal Laws. The movement culminated in a failed revolution in 1798, which had aimed to bring about an independent Irish Republic. In the wake of this failure, more conservative Catholic elements agreed to the Act of Union (1801), which abolished the separate Irish Parliament and merged England and Ireland under one parliament and one government. Catholics hoped for the abolition of the Penal Laws, but this did not follow immediately, and another thirty years of agitation, led by middle-class Catholic elements, followed. The final result was the Catholic Emancipation Act of 1829, wherein Parliament repealed the Penal Laws and granted Catholics the rights to vote and hold office. However, given the entrenched position of all parties in the land system, the relative economic statuses of Protestants and Catholics did not change greatly in the years before the Great Famine.

The Protestant Irish were divided into two main groups: Anglicans, who followed the established Church of Ireland; and Presbyterians, most of whom who were descended from migrants who had come from Scotland during the seventeenth century. In 1608 King James I of England, having confiscated the lands of various Irish chieftains in northern Ireland, began a policy of granting lands as tenants to many who were induced to migrate from the lowlands of Scotland. The purpose was to reinforce English dominance by pushing the Catholic Irish into less desirable areas. There were continued migrations throughout the seventeenth century, especially after the Battle of the Boyne in 1690 put an end to the Catholic resistance in Ireland. By 1700 the Presbyterians from Scotland dominated northern Ireland's population. Although the Scots were united with the Anglicans in the effort to subdue and control the Catholic Irish, there were also frictions between the two Protestant groups. England in 1699 passed restrictions upon the export of cloth from Ireland; the heaviest concentration of weavers in Ireland was among the Ulster Scots. The Presbyterians also were subjected in 1704 to a Test Act that disfranchised them and forbade them to hold office unless they were to swear allegiance to the established Anglican Church. In the early decades of the 1700s landholders in Ulster were confronted with greatly increased rents as their long-term leases expired.

The consequence was that the Scots from Ulster began a second migration, this time across the Atlantic, beginning after the end of Queen Anne's War in 1713 and continuing in stages until just before the American Revolution. The migrants included both farmers and those fleeing from the declining linen trades in northern Ireland. These migrants were identified by the English colonists in the American colonies as Irish, although they subsequently became known in America as Scotch-Irish. The predominantly Protestant migration from Ireland in the eighteenth century established a precedent for migration that would follow in the nineteenth century. The Scotch-Irish entered in largest numbers through Philadelphia, moved to the backcountry of Pennsylvania, then migrated southward through the mountain valleys of the Appalachians into western Virginia and the Carolinas. They would eventually become the vanguard of pioneers crossing the mountains into Tennessee and Kentucky. Catholics made up a rather small proportion of the migrants from Ireland before the American Revolution. When migration began to pick up again after 1815, Protestant Irish were still in the preponderance. Only in the 1830s did the Catholic Irish begin to outnumber the Protestants in the yearly flow of emigration.

The Anglican adherents in Ireland, perhaps about 10 percent in the early 1800s, were an outgrowth of the dominance of the English government, and so were often disliked intensely by both the Catholics and the Presbyterians. Many of them were of English birth or descent, and had acquired over the centuries control as landlords of much of Ireland's land, most of it confiscated from the Catholics. Others held major offices in the British government, or were able to monopolize many local offices. The business leaders in the centers of trade also were largely Anglicans. The ruling class, in short, was made up primarily of Anglicans. Anglicans could dominate the social and cultural life of the larger cities. Some of the other Protestants might join the established Church of Ireland, perhaps intermarry with the English, and thus gain entry into the upper class. But few Catholics would do the same.

Although Ireland had in general been enjoying a rising economy since the middle of the eighteenth century, the growth benefited large landowners and commercial interests, and not the small farmers who were the bulk of the growing Irish population. Irish exports (which went primarily to England) supplied the increasingly urbanized English population with food and textiles. The markets were good during the industrialization of England, and also while the long wars of the Napoleonic era increased demand for military supplies. A depression in the years following the end of the wars proved the vulnerability of the economy. Of all the Irish, the most vulnerable were the small tenant farmers. They might see their lands taken over by landlords intent on increasing productivity, their farms might be subdivided to satisfy multiple heirs, or their rents might be increased as a result of rising market prices. Economic downturns would also devastate the cottiers and laborers, whose income was always unpredictable. The inequities in the economy would be revealed by potato famines, such as occurred in 1822 and again in 1830–1831, both limited primarily to the poorer areas of western Ireland. These famines set off movements to emigrate. In 1832 the desire to emigrate was further stimulated by a cholera epidemic, against which there seemed to be no defense. Ironically, some of the migrants of those years simply took the disease with them and started an epidemic in North America.

The poorest of Ireland, however, did not provide the principal stream of migrants to America in these years. They were too poor to pay the cost of transporting a family to America, so they more commonly paid the small price of deck-passage on the steamer to Liverpool, and became part of a growing Irish population within England. More commonly, those who boarded a sailing-ship for Philadelphia or New York were of the moderate middle class. They might include strong or middling farmers who could no longer see their land broken up, or artisans who saw their livelihoods disappearing in the face of manufactured goods, or laborers who sought a steadier and more profitable wage in America. The economy and society were showing the weaknesses that would become more obvious in the future, and the emigrants were establishing the precedents and pathways for many others to follow.

Germany: Changing Economies, Changing Ways of Life

Germany in the early 1800s was far from being a unified nation, however much that ideal might have glowed in the minds of nationalist intellectuals. At the Congress of Vienna (1815), following the end of the Napoleonic wars, the centuries-old patchwork quilt of petty states in Germany was reorganized into a still-complex German Confederation, comprised of 35 principalities and 4 free cities. The largest of these was Prussia, whose dominion spread across northern and eastern Germany, but which also ruled provinces in the west along the Rhine. The only thing these various states had in common was the German language, and even that was represented by widely varying dialects, so that people from the southern states might have difficulty understanding those from the north.

Germans who migrated to America continued to acknowledge identities derived from their provincial origins, and even from their villages and towns. They remained acutely aware of the differences among them, calling themselves Westphalians or Badenese or Bavarians even as Americans characterized them all under one label as Germans. Most significant of the divisions among them were those of religion, for the Germans had greater religious diversity than any other immigrant peoples. They were divided into Catholics, Lutherans, and Calvinists; besides these there were adherents of other Protestant pietistic sects, such as the Mennonites and Moravians, who had formed an important element of the previous colonial migrations. There was also a significant minority of German Jews, who in many ways identified culturally with the other Germans. In addition, a growing element of freethinkers aroused the animus of all the other groups. Many of the German states at that time continued to support an established church, and thereby created an element of dissenters from the state religion. In Silesia, a province of Prussia, there was resistance to the 1835 policy of combining Lutherans and Calvinists in one state church, giving rise to the emigration of self-styled Old Lutherans. Other emigrant groups of Old Lutherans, many of them espousing what they called the Unaltered Augsburg Confession of Martin Luther, followed in the late 1830s from Saxony, Brandenburg, Pomerania, and elsewhere.

The division of Germany into many small and separate states with varying trade and economic policies had long inhibited the development of a more modern economy. There were efforts in the 1820s to coordinate trade policies and eliminate barriers among states in a customs union or *Zollverein*. Under increasing influence by the Kingdom of Prussia, separate customs systems finally were integrated by 1834 into one *Zollverein*, which included most of the German states. The removal of tariff barriers among the participating states helped to create a larger economic structure through which trade, goods, and people might flow. At the same time, other developments, especially in the southwestern states of Germany, were helping to modernize the economy. The transportation network in that region relied primarily on the river systems for the movement of goods. Western Germany particularly benefited from the Rhine River and its tributaries, which flowed northward through the Netherlands to outlets in the North Sea. Steamboats, introduced in larger numbers by the 1830s, revolutionized the river trade and made it less expensive. Germany got its first railway in 1835, and thereafter the growing network of railroads provided competition for the river traffic, which still had to deal with numerous tolls and fees imposed by states and localities along the riverbanks. The general effect of these developments was to transform the economy in such a way as to open new markets to producers of goods, and also to afford the population more mobility, in response to economic pressures and changes in the labor market.

The basis of the German economy during the first half of the nineteenth century was agriculture. Modern mechanized industry was still in its infancy before 1845, and most individuals' livelihoods were made from the land or from trade in agricultural products. For those who farmed the land, land tenure systems were of critical importance. In the regions of southwestern and western Germany— regions from which the majority of emigrants were coming in the early nineteenth century—feudal systems requiring service from the peasants had largely been abolished by the end of the Napoleonic period. Tenant obligations were now reduced to paying rents to landlords. Land in these regions could be passed to one's heirs by right, but there were generally laws requiring partible inheritance. Dividing one's land among several sons led to smaller and smaller parcels, making it increasingly more difficult to maintain a family. The problem was compounded by the general increase of population throughout Germany, with numbers increasing from around 25 million in 1815 to 34.5 million by 1845. Thus in southwestern Germany, which in some respects had the most advanced economy, the agricultural system was stubbornly pre-modern. The economist Friedrich List characterized the system as a *Zwergwirtschaft*—a dwarf economy. Seen in human terms, the farmers within this economy became more and more vulnerable to economic depressions and crop failures as their diminished landholdings were increasingly hard put to produce enough to support a family.

Also increasing in number were the artisans and shopkeepers in the small towns and cities of Germany. They felt disadvantages of their own, as the generally expanding and modernizing economy made them increasingly marginal and vulnerable. The widening markets meant more competition from goods made elsewhere, some of them in British factories or other places abroad. Since their customers were drawn primarily from the agricultural elements, crop failures could severely affect the business of craftsmen and shopkeepers as well. Many weavers of southwestern Germany were unable to compete with the rise of factory weaving, which in Germany as in England was the beginning stage of the Industrial Revolution. It would not be until the second half of the century that heavy industry such as iron-making would begin to drive forward Germany's Industrial Revolution.

The emigration in the 1820s was drawn mostly from the states of southwestern Germany, such as the Grand Duchy of Baden and the Kingdom of Württemberg. This movement continued patterns of emigration that had prevailed in the eighteenth century. By the 1830s regions further north along the Rhine became subject to the same forces. The states further east in northern Germany did not have laws requiring partible inheritance, meaning that agriculture remained in larger holdings; however, those unable to inherit land were consigned to the labor market. The same general pattern seen in southwestern Germany—increasing pressure of population on the limited supply of land—held true in those eastern regions. A study of the migrants from mid-nineteenth century Hesse-Cassel found that those more likely to emigrate included substantial farmers with the means to emigrate, young men left out by the practice of inheritance by primogeniture, and skilled laborers who envisioned greater opportunity in America.[18] In those parts of Prussia east of the Elbe, agricultural land was primarily held in large estates by nobles and worked by peasants with no claim on the land. In the early nineteenth century, emigration from these eastern regions in times of hardship was mostly toward regions further east, in Poland or Russia. Czarist Russia had been encouraging the settlement of Germans since the mid-eighteenth century. Thus the general center of emigration flow moved from the southwest to the north, then to the east, until, in the late nineteenth century, the easternmost parts of Germany would provide the largest flow of migrants. Mack Walker, historian of the German emigration, gave this characterization of the migration of 1830–1845:

The Auswanderung of 1830–45 was, with the exception of certain northern areas, decidedly a movement of what may be called the lower middle class: neither great landowners nor harvest hands, but small farmers who cultivated their own land; not apprentices, nor unskilled laborers, nor great merchants, but independent village shopkeepers and artisans; next to no one from the larger towns and cities. They were people who relied upon their own skills and wished to do so in the future, who had property that could be turned to cash; they traveled on their own resources. They were people who had something to lose, and who were losing it, squeezed out by interacting social and economic forces: a growth of population without a corresponding growth of economic bases, and the increased cosmopolitization and liberalization of the economy.[19]

Walker also observed that the motivations of most German emigrants were not to change a society but to "gain and conserve something old . . . to keep the ways of life they were used to, which the new Europe seemed to destroy."[20] Their efforts to find new roots in an old culture transplanted from Europe, however, would more often than not be frustrated by the dynamically changing society of America, as well as by the many different cultures found within that group that would become known collectively as German America.

Britain and the Fruits of the Industrial Revolution

As in the countries of the continent, Great Britain (including England, Wales and Scotland) was undergoing a dramatic rise in population during the first half of the nineteenth century. Census statistics show a doubling of the population (from 10 1/2 million to 21 million) between 1801 and 1851. The fixed amount of agricultural land and the pressure of increasing population led to movement out of the rural areas. But this mobility occurred not only among farmers and farm laborers but also among townspeople and artisans. These migrants were on the move mostly toward urban and industrial areas within Britain, and, in smaller numbers, out of the country. In the case of Britain, emigration was not only to the United States, but also to other parts of the British Empire, especially Canada, Australia, and New Zealand.

The British economy was also on the rise, continuing a long-term expansion that had begun in the late 1700s. This was primarily due to the growth of the country's overseas trade. An increasing proportion of these exports was the product of Britain's Industrial Revolution. In the middle of the eighteenth century, the revolution had begun with the expansion of textile factories, in which handweavers were assembled for mass production of woolen and cotton cloth. Toward the end of the century, the textile factories were being relocated near water-mills so that they could take advantage of the

power machinery that was transforming the industry. The spinning jenny, for example, introduced in 1766, allowed one worker to
produce a number of threads at once, outmoding the old spinning
wheel. Crompton's Mule, a spinning device that produced stronger
and more consistent yarns, was another critical development. The
power-loom, invented by Edward Cartwright in 1785, proved eventually to be the device that transformed cloth-weaving and reduced
the number of hand-weavers. By the 1820s, after some technological improvements, the power loom was becoming more common
in factories. The machine required about one-fifth of the labor that
was required to produce the same amount of cloth by hand-weaving.
Another innovation beginning to be adopted by factories during
the 1820s was the steam engine, which could allow the factory to
drive its power machinery without being tied to a location beside
a stream.

Textile-making was at the heart of the British economy, and the
staple of its overseas trade. Textiles accounted for over 60 percent
of Britain's exports during the first half of the nineteenth century.
While the value of exported woolens had exceeded that of cotton
before 1800, cotton products were in the majority after that date.
The swing toward cotton production was caused by the increased
supply of cheap raw cotton coming from the United States after
the invention of the cotton gin. British shipping interests quickly
adapted themselves to this trade, and the ships bringing raw cotton from the United States returned carrying both finished textiles
and other manufactured goods, with enough room for emigrants
as well.

The massive changes in the economy that were taking place in
the early nineteenth century were felt through all elements of British society as well. The rural areas were being changed by various organized efforts of large landowners and public authorities to
rationalize agriculture and make it more efficient. These efforts had
been underway for a long time, but were intensified by the decline
in prices for agricultural crops that occurred after the Napoleonic
wars. Greater productivity was to be achieved by consolidating
holdings of individual farmers that had previously been distributed
through the open fields; by enclosing pastures and other common
lands and adding them to the farmers' holdings; and by encouraging more intensive methods of cultivation. England was not
affected as greatly by the micro-farms that had developed because
of systems of partible inheritance in Ireland and southwestern Germany. British farmers could generally designate which son would

inherit rights to the farm, and the remaining offspring were left to seek other occupations. Working as a laborer on someone else's farm was increasingly unattractive; the work was often seasonal, wages dropped consistently after 1820, and housing conditions for laborers on the farms were deteriorating.

More often than not, this surplus labor might find its way to the nearby towns, where artisans and shopkeepers still clung to their traditional positions, and apprenticeships and shop clerks' positions might be available. But eventually the growing oversupply of such occupations, and the increasing competition of manufactured goods from elsewhere, created surplus labor in the towns, and brought about a stream of migration outward to the cities and factory towns. London's population grew from 1.38 million in 1821 to 1.95 million in 1841; the population of the textile-making center of Manchester grew in the same period from 126,000 to 275,000. The rapid growth of urban areas inevitably led to depressed living conditions, as workers both employed and unemployed crowded into marginal housing—tenement dwellings and airless cellars, with sanitary conditions that were primitive and health-threatening. Food available to these urban classes was often adulterated and lacking in nutrients.

As happened in other countries, migration often took place first to locations within England, either other agricultural areas or the large cities and industrial towns, and then to other places abroad. In any event, the general picture of emigration from 1820 to 1845 shows a slight majority of emigrants of rural origin as opposed to those of urban and industrial origins. These rural emigrants were often farmers who were able to sell out and use the proceeds for a better farm in America, or shopkeepers from rural towns who had retained enough capital to start anew on the other side of the Atlantic. There were emigrants from the industrial sector as well, including some who would influence the development of industry in America. Those who were craftsmen made superfluous by industrial production—the hand-weaver Abel Stephenson, for example—were not the largest portion of industrial emigrants. Industrial workers tended to emigrate during periods of cyclical unemployment, as happened in 1826–1827, 1830–1831, and 1841–1842. Those among the unemployed who were unskilled laborers were less likely to emigrate; they had neither the means nor the marketable skills that would allow them to move. More commonly it was the more skilled factory laborers—the operators of the power looms, for instance—who would cross the ocean to seek new employment at higher wages in the budding textile mills of New England and the Middle Atlantic states. Another small but significant element in search of a better life was the highly skilled technicians and engineers who had designed and installed the new machinery that was driving the upward curve of English industry. Britain had attempted to prohibit the emigration of such high-skilled individuals, but the restrictions were removed in 1825. Thus occurred the transference of many techniques of the developed English Industrial Revolution to the still-developing American industries. The influence of such skilled Englishmen on the American economy was evident not only in the mechanization of textile mills but also in the opening of mines, the building of canals and, later, the construction of railroads.

In general, the emigration of English and Scots in the 1820s, 1830s, and early 1840s was not a movement of the poorest outcasts from the Industrial Revolution. The movement from the urban and industrial sector was primarily of those who still had the resources to emigrate, who expected a better reward for their labors in America, and who often had some capital and a spirit of entrepreneurship in envisioning their future in America. As for the agricultural migrants, the historian Maldwyn Jones noted that "in social composition and motivation English agricultural emigration in the 1830s was very similar to that taking place in southwestern Germany at the same time. In both countries it was not the pressure of existing want that induced people to emigrate, but uncertainty about the future. The emigrants consisted not of people who had already been engulfed by poverty but of those who feared a loss of status if they stayed where they were."[21]

Common Themes and Experiences

Among all the major immigrant groups, despite their seeming diversity, echoes of the same experiences were heard. Impoverished agricultural lives stirred people to leave their ancestral farms. Small-town craftsmen and shopkeepers saw futility in their futures there, and chose instead the adventure of another continent. Visions of an elusive, ill-defined freedom offered relief from the constraints of older societies. Religious divisions bred among dissidents the desire to practice their religion in their own way in a new land. The false promises of industrialization sent disillusioned workers in search of some way of retaining their traditional customs. People of moderate middle-class status feared the loss of their place in a rapidly changing society.

Other countries, too, were sending their people to America, and with many of the same emotions. In Norway, there was a highly stratified society, with over 90 percent of the people in rural areas in the fjords and mountain villages. The emigration was overwhelmingly comprised of rural people seeking the better lands of the American Midwest. By the 1830s the economy of Norway was growing stronger, but few in the rural areas shared in the increase. Instead, the rural population lived in a subsistence economy, bartering only a small surplus of crops for other essentials. The pressure of population was being felt: the number of inhabitants increased from 885,000 in 1801 to 1,195,000 in 1835. The famous Norwegian pioneer ship of 1825, the *Restauration,* carried dissenters, Quakers, and pietists; many were Haugeans, who claimed they sought to reform the Church from within, but apparently sought relief from it abroad. Other religious dissenters would follow.[22]

Sweden sent only about 15,000 emigrants to America before 1850, but the story of the Swedish emigrants was remarkably similar to that of the Norwegians. Between 1820 and 1850, the population grew from 2.3 million to about 3.5 million. The emigrants came from mostly mountainous rural districts with poor agricultural conditions. In rural areas, impartible inheritance was the existing land custom, and those who were not chosen to inherit the land provided many of the early emigrants to America.[23] Yet, in the words of the scholar Robert Ostergren, "few were forced from their former existence by impossible circumstances."[24] As in the case of other countries, the very poorest could not afford to emigrate. Dissent from the rationalist state Lutheran church was also rife among the rural people, and in a wave of religious revival many followed the pietist preacher Eric Jansson, who founded a pioneering colony of Swedes at Bishop Hill in Illinois in 1846.

In the Netherlands, the emigrants of the early nineteenth century were far removed from the seventeenth- and eighteenth-century Dutch settlers of New York and New Jersey. Religious dissent played a role among the nineteenth-century Dutch emigrants. A religious schism of 1834, in which certain Dutch ministers seceded from the official Dutch Reformed Church, led to a growing number of Calvinists who rejected the official church because of its attachment to the ideas of the Enlightenment. These dissenters contributed disproportionately to the emigration to America. Although there were some who came out of land hunger and began a movement to the Midwest, the lists of those arriving in America between 1820 and 1845 seem to show mostly people who were merchants, artisans, and tradesmen, at least one step removed from the land.[25] Pioneering immigrants from other countries also tended to show the same middle-class origin.

French immigrants during this period were of very diverse origins. They included such constituent elements as musicians, artists, restaurateurs, teachers, skilled craftsmen, missionary priests, and nuns (whose convent schools were valued by the native-born American elite). Motives either entrepreneurial or missionary characterized many of them. The predominantly middle-class French, many of them already removed from agriculture, gravitated mostly toward urban areas, but some rural emigrants found their way to farms in Louisiana. Concentrated urban neighborhoods of French were found only in New York and New Orleans.[26] Italians of the early 1800s likewise came mostly from northern Italy to urban areas in America, and their numbers included artists, merchants involved in the trade with Italy, musicians, music teachers, and skilled craftsmen.

CATCHING THE FEVER

Before making the life-changing decision to leave their homelands for America, immigrants generally went through a process of weighing the consequences, evaluating the possibilities of America, and overcoming their fears. By the 1830s, there were guidebooks in the major languages, agents representing ship captains eager to sell passage to America, and newspapers and magazines that published articles and letters from the New World. There were also government publications, particularly in Norway and some of the German states, that sought to discourage emigration. But probably most influential of all were the letters written by those who had already made the journey to America. When written by a close friend or relative, these letters could earn a trust that was not possible with other publications. By describing the writers' emigration experiences, their homes in America, their problems and successes, the letters were answering the question in the reader's mind: should I go to America also?

Sometimes letters were frank about the challenge. Andrew Morris, a weaver from Lancashire who had taken employment in Philadelphia preparatory to searching for a farm, wrote his family in 1831:

My Father wants to know whether this country would do for brother William and him or no, to which I answer Yes, it will do for every person that is willing to work for a living as there is plenty of work and good wages. I am very desirous for William to come as he is young and if Father and Mother & him was here and living together they would do very well, and if they do come we will do what we can for them. . . . I have no doubts that we could do very well in the western country but we are doing well here and I think we had better stay as we are a while, as weaving is very brisk in Philadelphia and likely to be so.[27]

"America letters," eagerly awaited by relatives in the homeland, generally avoided exaggerating the attractions of America, their writers being always aware that they might eventually be called to task for misleading information. Yet the facts they stated about wages, availability of land, and the living conditions in ethnic communities, could exert a powerful influence. Wilhelm Stille, a farmer's son who had emigrated from Westphalia in 1833, wrote from Ohio to his family in 1836, describing his new job working for a merchant:

I get 10 dollars a month . . . plus board and washing, and that's all grand, and I don't have to work much . . . [I] enjoy a contented life such as I never had in Germany. Dear parents, someone wanted to know if we have German churches here, there are enough here, and it's a great pleasure for us to hear the gospel preached as well as in Germany, but I wouldn't tell any family to come here just because of that, except young people, for it's hard to travel as a family and it costs quite a lot, and when you first come to this country you don't know the language and face an uphill climb, that's why many people take a long time to get over their trip. But when they've been here for a while and get a feel for freedom, and see the good crops growing here and all without manure, and that the land is so easy to work, then they think differently, then they feel sorry for their friends who are still in Germany.[28]

Letters like this, aimed at the hearts of the recipients, conveyed the kind of information that energized the process of chain migration, in which families and communities from one side of the ocean reconstituted themselves on the other side. Those who went first paved the way for friends and relatives who would then be inclined to follow the same path. As time went on, the accelerating process would build upon itself. In its fully developed form, chain migration might bring emigrants from a small European town to a specific destination in America, where similar churches might welcome the pastor from the homeland, and stores might have owners who had left similar businesses to come to America.

The greatest barrier to the decision to leave home was fear of the unknown, and those fears were greatly allayed by the stories of close friends and relatives who had gone before, and the reassurance that someone would be waiting. Those remaining behind in Ireland often looked forward to America letters that might contain remittances, offering perhaps the only source of support for their own emigration. Sometimes emigrants would be sent prepaid tickets to America, and needed only to claim them from the ship owners. Thus William Smyth, writing in 1837 after he had been settled for several years in Philadelphia, advised his nephew Robert in County Antrim:

You are not coming to strangers. . . . you will come to the best home you ever had and if you are coming I wish you to come in the first vessel that will sail from Londonderry belonging to James Corscadden as I have paid your passage and sent you two pounds for pocket money which James Corscadden will pay you on presenting this letter to him.[29]

Not only did the America letters deal with the problem of whether to go, but they solved the bewildering problem of where to go: the places where family and friends waited.

America letters were generally passed around in the old country, and there were few who did not have the opportunity to read them or have them read to them. The few who did not could have recourse to the innumerable guidebooks prepared for prospective emigrants, but these were probably more useful to those who already had made the decision to emigrate. In the earlier stages of migration, books by advocates for life in America and guidebooks explaining the details of travel and settlement were widely used as the principal source of information. The pamphlet that Ole Rynning wrote in 1838 served for a number of years as an inducement for Norwegians, despite Rynning's own death and the failure of the Beaver Creek colony.[30] Many Germans contemplating emigration in the 1830s used Gottfried Duden's 1829 book about Missouri,[31] which in fact brought many to that state and even encouraged emigration societies in Germany to attempt model colonies in the region. Duden envisioned Missouri as a sort of new Rhineland along the Missouri River, and an excellent place for wine-growing (which was in fact pursued by some German followers). These early works were just the beginning of a flood of advice-books to emigrants. It has been estimated that over a hundred guidebooks for emigrants were published in Germany alone from 1827 to 1856.[32]

General-circulation newspapers featured mostly government pronouncements on emigration or advertising from agents seeking passengers on behalf of ship captains. However, by the late 1830s, newspapers and magazines catering to prospective emigrants were being published in both Germany and England, and their numbers increased as emigration increased. The emigration publications carried reports from abroad and information about new settlements in America. The English emigration papers concentrated more on those going to the British colonies, but the German papers were almost entirely devoted to America.[33] The Norwegian emigrant magazine *Norge og Amerika* (Norway and America) published detailed information about wages and costs of living in America in this anonymous 1845 letter:

Let us assume that a young able-bodied man from the country, who has saved up a small sum of thirty or forty dollars, leaves Norway with the intention of emigrating to America. He then presents himself in the *Great West* with a few dollars in his pocket. His intentions and wish must consequently be to get work, the sooner the better, and this he will soon be able to do by consulting those of his countrymen who arrived before him. Depending on the time of year and other circumstances, his daily wage will be from 60 to 100 cents (one cent equals approximately one Norwegian skilling). In the winter he will get 60 cents, in the spring 80 cents without board, and during the summer and autumn, when the harvesting of grain and hay requires many workers, 100 cents ($1) plus free board. Thus his average pay will be 80 cents, out of which he must subtract 30 for good board and clothing, and in this way he has saved 50 cents a day.

If we figure the number of working days at 250, at the end of the year he will have saved up $120. If he gets permanent employment he will be paid by the current wages here, $10—often $12—a month plus good board, and will thus get $120 a year, from which he must subtract the price of the clothing he will need. It is easily seen that after two years, this young man will have saved up $200 and consequently for $50 he can buy one sixteenth of a section, or forty acres of land . . . For the rest of the money he will build houses, buy animals, farming tools, and so on. Thus at the end of two years he has become an independent man and is in a position to marry without having to worry for himself or his family, and in all probability he may look forward to a pleasant and carefree future. . . .

Now if this young man had stayed in Norway. I do not think it will be necessary to prove my contention that at the end of the two years, he would have been in about the same position as he was at the beginning.[34]

Anonymous letters in newspapers such as this were similar to personal America letters in their specificity and their encouraging quality, but lacked the reassurance from friends or relatives promising help to newly arrived emigrants. Even less effective in inspiring people to emigrate were the increasing numbers of emigration agents, whose principal business was to sell passage for both individuals and groups on ships to America. They may be considered facilitators, something like latter-day travel agents, but they were not the prime force in influencing decisions to go to America. Emigration agents were particularly active in Germany, where there was often a longer trip from the interior to ports of embarkation, and they could offer complete arrangements for the entire voyage. They advertised through posters in public places and handbills distributed in villages; their advertising sometimes played to the emigrants' fantasies and desires and minimized the difficulties of the voyage. The agents typically received about 2 percent of the costs of passage, although their profits could sometimes be enlarged by charging a set price and then searching for a lower fare from the competing ship captains. Agents had been active in southwestern Germany since the 1700s, and in the early 1800s they helped people to emigrate down the Rhine River to Dutch or French ports. By the 1840s their numbers were growing rapidly, partly because, after the introduction of railroads, they began to promote alternate routes through Hamburg or Bremen. In 1850 the emigrant newspaper *Allgemeine Auswanderer-Zeitung* (General Emigrant News) foresaw the time coming when "there would be more agents than emigrants in Germany."[35]

By the late 1840s the agents in Germany increasingly worked under major brokers in the principal port cities. Eventually, with the rise of the transatlantic shipping lines, they would become employed agents of those corporations. In pre-famine Ireland the agents developed more slowly; until the late 1820s, when emigration proceeded mostly from Irish ports which were easily accessible to the emigrants, and when agents were located mostly in the port cities. After that, as Liverpool began to take over the emigrant trade, agents began to circulate in Ireland, especially in the west, advertising the advantages of emigrating through Liverpool, where the cost of passage was lower and the schedules of departure more predictable.

FAREWELLS

Eventually, when the decisions were made, when possessions were gathered for the trip, when arrangements for passage were completed, when a ship awaited in the harbor, the time would come for an emotional and perhaps anguished parting. This might be a quiet and almost secret affair, particularly in some German states where the authorities continued to discourage emigration. In Norway and some German states, the departure might be the occasion for a religious service and a sermon, especially if the emigrants were a group from one village.

In Ireland, a parting custom that was developing as early as 1830 was the so-called American wake—an all-night gathering of friends and neighbors that included both celebration and sorrow, patterned after the Irish wake for the dead. In the years when transatlantic transportation was difficult and hazardous and an emigrant could not confidently predict his or her return, the separation from loved ones seemed as permanent and irreversible as death itself. So the departing emigrant would be both praised and mourned. Besides traditional Irish melodies, the music might also contain tearful laments for the loss of a friend or relative. The mournful "keening" that characterized a funeral might also be heard in the laments of a mother who was about to say farewell to her emigrant son. Those ready to depart their home village might then leave as daybreak appeared, often accompanied or "convoyed" for a ways before

Irish emigrants receive the blessing of the parish priest as they depart for the seaport. From *Illustrated London News*, May 10, 1851. Courtesy Swarthmore College Library, via Bryn Mawr College Library Special Collections.

saying their last goodbyes. The emigrant then left, perhaps with a sense of remorse or guilt as well as of hopeful anticipation.[36]

And so from towns and villages across Ireland, England, and the continent of Europe, emigrants would begin their initial journey to a port—down the rivers to the North Sea, toward the fjords of Norway, down the muddy springtime roads, and at last to the waiting ships. For better or worse, there awaited an ocean voyage to the New World and a new life.

NOTES

1. Quoted in Theodore C. Blegen, introduction to Ole Rynning, *True Account of America for the Information and Help of Peasant and Commoner,* ed. and trans. T. C. Blegen (St. Paul: Minnesota Historical Society, 1917), 228.

2. The title is a translation of the original German edition, *Bericht über eine Reise nach den westlichen Staaten Nordamerika's,* published at Elberfeld in 1829.

3. Henriette Bruns, *Hold Dear, As Always: Jette, a German Immigrant Life in Letters,* ed. Adolf Schroeder and Carla Schulz-Geisberg, trans. A. E. Schroeder (Columbia: University of Missouri Press, 1988), 46. Gustav Löwig (not Löwe) and Heinrich von Martels had published other reports on the desirable life of immigrants in the United States.

4. Bruns, *Hold Dear,* 46.

5. Ibid., 58.

6. Ibid., 59.

7. Letter of Bruns to her brother Heinrich Geisberg, August 1837, in ibid., 79.

8. Letter of Bruns to her son Wilhelm, April 21, 1882, in ibid., 245.

9. Charlotte Erickson, *Invisible Immigrants: The Adaptation of English and Scottish Immigrants in Nineteenth-Century America* (Coral Gables, Fla.: University of Miami Press, 1972), 301.

10. Ibid., 303.

11. Ibid., 305.

12. Hubert Howe Bancroft, *Chronicles of the Builders of the Commonwealth: Historical Character Study,* 7 vols. (San Francisco: History Co., 1891–1892), 3:16. For other accounts of the Murphys, see Sister Gabrielle Sullivan, *Martin Murphy Jr.: California Pioneer, 1844–1884* (Stockton, Calif.: Pacific Center for Historical Studies, University of the Pacific, 1974) and Joseph A. King, "The Murphys and Breens of the Overland Parties to California, 1844 and 1846," in *Patterns of Migration,* ed. Patrick O'Sullivan (Leicester, England: Leicester University Press, 1992), 84–95.

13. Cormac Ó Gráda, *Black '47 and Beyond: The Great Irish Famine in History, Economy and Memory* (Princeton, N.J.: Princeton University Press, 1999), 216.

14. The categories and statistics of the Irish social structure (as of about 1840) presented here are those found in Kerby A. Miller, *Emigrants and*

Exiles: Ireland and the Irish Exile to North America (New York: Oxford University Press, 1985), 45–54.

15. Ibid., 42.

16. Ibid., 53.

17. Michael P. Carroll, "Rethinking Popular Catholicism in Pre-Famine Ireland," *Journal for the Scientific Study of Religion* 34 (1995): 354–65; David W. Miller, "Landscape and Religious Practice: A Study of Mass Attendance in Pre-Famine Ireland," *Éire-Ireland* 40 (2005): 90–106; and Diarmuid Ó Giolláin, "Revisiting the Holy Well," *Éire-Ireland* 40 (2005): 11–41.

18. Simone Wegge, "Migration Decisions in Mid-Nineteenth Century Germany," *Journal of Economic History* 58 (1998): 532–35.

19. Mack Walker, *Germany and the Emigration, 1816–1885* (Cambridge, Mass.: Harvard University Press, 1964), 47.

20. Ibid., 69.

21. Maldwyn Jones, "The Background to Emigration from Great Britain in the Nineteenth Century," *Perspectives in American History* 7 (1973): 40.

22. Odd S. Lovoll, *The Promise of America: A History of the Norwegian-American People* (Minneapolis: University of Minnesota Press, 1984), 7–15.

23. Florence E. Janson, *The Background of Swedish Immigration, 1840–1930* (Chicago: University of Chicago Press, 1931), 40, 55.

24. Robert C. Ostergren, *A Community Transplanted: The Trans-Atlantic Experience of a Swedish Immigrant Settlement in the Upper Middle West, 1835–1915* (Madison: University of Wisconsin Press, 1988), 112.

25. Judged from samples gathered from Robert P. Swierenga, *Dutch Immigrants in U.S. Ship Passenger Manifests, 1820–1880*, 2 vols. (Wilmington, Del.: Scholarly Resources, 1983).

26. In a study of immigrant arrivals in New Orleans, J. Hanno Deiler found that more than 60 percent of French immigrants to the United States in the 1840s came to Louisiana. However, he cautioned that many of the recorded arrivals might have been Germans who happened to emigrate via the French port of le Havre. Deiler, *Geschichte der Deutschen Gesellschaft von New Orleans* (New Orleans: self-published, 1897), 41–50.

27. Andrew Morris to his brother-in-law, November 19, 1831, in Erickson, *Invisible Immigrants*, 152–53.

28. Letter of February 16, 1836, in Walter D. Kamphoefner, Wolfgang Helbich, and Ulrike Sommer, eds., *News from the Land of Freedom: German Immigrants Write Home*, trans. Susan Carter Vogel (Ithaca, N.Y.: Cornell University Press, 1991), 69.

29. Letter quoted in Trevor Parkhill, "With a Little Help from Their Friends: Assisted Emigration Schemes 1700–1845," in *To and From Ireland: Planned Migration Schemes c. 1600–2000*, ed. Patrick J. Duffy (Dublin: Geography Publications, 2004), 69–70.

30. Ole Rynning, *True Account of America for the Information and Help of Peasant and Commoner*, ed. and trans. T. C. Blegen (St. Paul: Minnesota Historical Society, 1917).

31. Gottfried Duden, *Bericht über eine Reise nach den westlichen Staaten Nordamerika's* (Elberfeld, 1829).

32. Philip Taylor, *The Distant Magnet: European Emigration to the U.S.A.* (New York: Harper and Row, 1971), 67.

33. Stephan Görisch, *Information zwischen Werbung und Warnung: Die Rolle der Amerikaliteratur in der Auswanderung des 18. und 19. Jahrhunderts* (Darmstadt: Hesse Historische Kommission, 1991), 43–49.

34. Anonymous letter in *Norge og Amerika* 1 (January 1846): 97–101 as translated in Theodore Blegen, *Land of Their Choice: The Immigrants Write Home* (Minneapolis: University of Minnesota Press, 1955), 195–96.

35. Agnes Bretting and Hartmut Bickelman, *Auswanderungsagenturen und Auswanderungsvereine im 19. und 20. Jahrhundert* (Stuttgart: F. Steiner, 1991), 50–77; quotation from *Allgemeine Auswanderer-Zeitung,* June 13, 1850, in Bretting and Bickelman, 51 (my translation).

36. Arnold Schrier, *Ireland and the American Emigration, 1850–1900* (Minneapolis: University of Minnesota Press, 1958), 84–88 and Miller, *Emigrants and Exiles,* 556–68.

3

Across the Atlantic and into America, 1820–1845

In December 1844, a correspondent of the *Illustrated London News* described a scene of English emigrants making their way through the muddy roads of southeastern England, on their way to a port of emigration, the Royal Dockyard at Deptford:

There were two covered or tilted farmer's hay-wagons—one from a parish in Buckinghamshire, and the other (we believe) from the neighbourhood of Northampton; they had joined company on the road. The women and children, with but few exceptions, occupied the conveyances, which were loaded with packages, bundles, and boxes; a few of the more elderly females walked on the pathway by the side of their husbands and sons; the younger men trudging it with seeming glee, and carrying various articles we conjecture for immediate use. . . . The leafless trees and hedges—the miry road, with long serpentine wheel tracks; the yellow wagons, with their inanimate and living freight, covered with light canvas; the women habited in blue or red cloaks; the men in their frocks blending in colour with the many hues of the bundles; and, above all, the object of their journey was well calculated to excite human sympathy. Yet no one appeared sad or sorrowful—on the contrary, all seemed to be cheerful; and their clean and decent appearance bore witness to the propriety of their general habits: the whole looked remarkably healthy, especially the children.[1]

Not all those who found their way to a port and an emigrant ship may have been so cheerful; these English, after all, had only a short way to travel to their port. Some of them may have already made arrangements for ship passage, and during this particular year some were taking advantage of a new program established by the British Parliament to assist emigration to other parts of the British Empire.

For others, uncertainty and some amount of fear may have prevailed. The Irish emigrants in the pre-famine years were increasingly making their way by road, rail, or coastwise ship to Dublin, and then by deck passage on a steamer to Liverpool. For many, the uncertainties of finding a ship and avoiding the pitfalls of the port may have reduced their cheerfulness considerably. German emigrants from the southern and western states made the trip to a port by road or by water, most commonly down the valley of the Rhine and its tributaries. They went to ports in the Netherlands or to Le Havre in France, where they would find ocean-going vessels. At this point the cost of transatlantic transport tended to be lowest for ships departing from Liverpool, so Germans and Scandinavians often traveled to that port by ship. Some had their arrangements made by the ever-proliferating emigration agents that flocked

English emigrants traveling in a group toward the port of emigration, 1844. *Illustrated London News*, December 21, 1844. Courtesy Swarthmore College Library, via Bryn Mawr College Special Collections.

across southern Germany; however, these travelers might have had justifiable worries about whether their arrangements would be honored when they arrived at a port.

One can imagine the variety of emotions that affected nearly every emigrant in these first steps of the journey: anticipation of a better life; fear of the unknown; regret at abandoning family and home for a dimly perceived future; concern for the dangers of the high seas on the voyage; perhaps a feeling of freedom from the restraints of an old society; and a vision of greater freedom in the new. The object of their hopes and dreams—a place in America that would offer a new beginning—still seemed very far away.

PORTS OF EMIGRATION

Many different ports in Europe offered passage to emigrants destined for America, but all of them might present problems and trials to those who had never before been far from their native village or town.

Liverpool

By the early 1840s, Liverpool, on England's west coast, had become the preeminent port of emigration, not only for English and Irish migrants but also for those from the continent of Europe. The eighteenth century port had been the center of the English worldwide trade in African slaves, but the British Empire's abolition of the slave trade had brought that commerce to an end in 1807. After the Napoleonic wars, the city found a new route of trade—across the Atlantic to North and South America. The reason for this change in Liverpool's fortunes lay in the increase of the regular trade in all commodities between England and America, but particularly in Liverpool's developing relationship with the port of New York. Liverpool thus became tied to the rise of the New York port in a trade relationship that offered merchants and shippers assurance of regular and predictable service.

In 1818 regular scheduled packet boat service, carrying both passengers and cargo, was opened between the two cities. This development was important primarily for business travel and the transport of high-quality merchandise, but it also helped to cement economic relationships between the two ports. Another incentive driving the consolidation of the transatlantic trade between Liverpool and New York was the 1825 opening of the Erie Canal in New

York State. This development offered an attractive water route into the American interior, allowing travel from the Hudson Valley via canal to Buffalo, and then through the length of the Great Lakes into the northern Midwest. New areas developing in the Midwest could export heavy commodities such as wheat, lumber, and lead through the Erie Canal to New York port. In the eighteenth century, Boston and Philadelphia had handled a greater volume of trade to Europe than had New York, but by the 1820s these two ports had yielded much of their commerce to New York, with its superior harbor and its Liverpool connection.

This thriving trade relationship created opportunities for emigrants. Ships arrived at Liverpool from New York and other American ports, loaded with basic commodities that Europe needed, including lumber, wheat, fruit, rice, flax and flaxseed, raw wool, tobacco, and, of course, cotton from the rapidly developing Cotton Belt of the American South. Liverpool offered easy access to the cotton-hungry textile mills of Lancashire and the growing manufacturing enterprises of the Midlands of England. The return ships along the transatlantic route, however, had items to carry that were less bulky, including manufactured goods, utensils and dishes, tools, and especially finished textiles. In short, ship captains had much extra room available, and the cargo space in steerage—the space beneath the top deck but above the cargo hold—could be used to house emigrants. Competition among shipowners for the emigrant trade thus led to lower rates for passage than could be found in other European ports. For the great mass of emigrants, steerage, not a comfortable cabin, was the standard means of transport.

In the second quarter of the nineteenth century, Liverpool was, then, already a prosperous city because of its thriving port, which included many impressive public buildings as well as stone docks and warehouses on the waterfront that were the envy of all other ports, whether in Europe or abroad. The thriving class of merchants and shipping interests supported an elegant society and culture. The trade and enterprise of the city attracted many laborers, both from the English countryside and from Ireland. The population of the city grew from 138,000 in 1821 to 286,000 in 1841, at a rate faster than that of any other British seaport.[2] In 1845 the number of ships trading through the port was recorded at 20,521.[3]

The arriving tide of emigrants came in greatest numbers from Ireland by deck passage on crowded steamers from Dublin or other Irish ports. Next in number came those from within England, arriving either by land or by water. Still others arrived by sea from

France, Germany and Scandinavia. In the 1820s and early 1830s, passengers from the continent came by ship directly to Liverpool. After the railroad-building boom of the late 1830s provided rail connections, emigrants from points on the continent sailed to Hull on the east coast of England, then went by train (or sometimes canal) to Liverpool.

The bustling port city appeared to most emigrants to be a place of confusion and possible danger. Few emigrants were able to go immediately to a waiting ship. Most often they had to find a place to stay, deal with emigration agents concerning their ship passage, and make choices about what ships they would use. This situation gave great opportunities to "runners"—predators who were paid to bring emigrants to a specific lodging house or a specific emigration broker's office. Emigrants had to watch their baggage, lest a runner pick it up and force them to follow him to his chosen lodging. Frequent complaints were lodged about the deception and cheating of both runners and boardinghouse operators, but the authorities were generally weak in controlling such matters. Landlords might demand more payment at the end of an individual's stay than they had quoted at the beginning. They might add fees for non-existent services. Many were the instances in which emigrants had to part with more of their savings than they had expected.

The emigrant lodgings, the emigration agents, the runners, and the export-import merchants were clustered both in the area of Goree Piazza, which had been in earlier times the center of Britain's African slave trade, and nearby along Waterloo Road, close to the waterfront. Most of the transactions the emigrants had to conduct took place in this run-down district. Dealing with the emigration agents or ship brokers was in itself a daunting experience. Those who had arrived with pre-arranged passage still had to work out with the agents what ships might be available, and, if possible, try to inspect them. Emigration agents were not employees of the shipowners, but worked for brokers who bought space in many different ships. Often they simply bought the unused space of a cargo ship after the cargo was loaded. That meant that sometimes they could not accommodate all those who had been promised passage, and some would then have to wait, possibly for weeks, for another ship. Or, the broker might simply send all the waiting passengers to the ship and pack them in beyond the legal limit, which at times was loosely enforced.

Emigrants who dealt with emigration agents had to be cautious and canny, and could not simply accept the first suggestion made in the agent's office. They were wise to inspect the various ships in the port in order to judge as best as they were able the seaworthiness, speed, and management of the ship. Emigrants were generally advised not simply to choose the cheapest passage, but to take into consideration that a higher price might bring better accommodations, more ample provisions, or faster transit across the Atlantic. It was, of course, sometimes possible to negotiate a more favorable price, especially if the ship was ready to leave with space still available.

The cost of passage might include provisioning by the shipowner, or the passengers might provide their own food while paying a lesser fare. Given the uncertain length of the journey in the age of sail, official advice was to prepare for at least a twelve-week journey; during the 1830s, that advice was reduced to 10 weeks. The commodities commonly taken aboard by emigrants included potatoes, cured meats (pork or beef), carrots, turnips, onions, dried peas, dried fish, biscuits or "hardtack," flour, rice, coffee, tea, cheese, sugar, and medications (including wine and brandy). Emigrants were also well-advised to bring tight-fitting containers or barrels to help preserve the provisions. The guidebook of A. C. Buchanan, published in 1828, suggested a very minimal list of provisions cost-

Emigrants boarding a sailing ship at Liverpool. Ships from Liverpool to North America generally carried a mixture of English, Irish, German, and Scandinavian emigrants. From *Illustrated London News*, July 6, 1850. Courtesy Swarthmore College Library, via Bryn Mawr College Library Special Collections.

ing about seven pounds for a family of five, but those seeking a more ample diet could easily spend two to three times as much.[4] Even those who had bought passage which included provisions often brought additional supplies of their own, for ship's stewards were sometimes known to be grudging with the day's rations.

Having bought the necessary provisions and paid for passage on a ship, emigrants could find themselves waiting days or even weeks for the ship to depart. Ship captains could be arbitrary and capricious about getting underway. The excuse might be to wait for more passengers, to try to find more cargo, or to wait for more favorable winds and tides. But sometimes it seemed only to be the whim of the captain that kept the ship in port. Delays in sailing were among the more frequent complaints of emigrants, and Liverpool authorities tried to impose some regulations, even demanding payment of a penalty to each passenger when the ship did not depart by the date contracted for. But the rules could not be imposed on ships of non-British registry, and as time went on, increasing numbers of the ships were American merchant ships. Meanwhile, emigrants languished in the miserable lodgings of the boardinghouses, to the delight of the avaricious keepers of those houses. When the captain finally relented and found conditions to his liking, the notice of sailing was sometimes sudden, allowing the emigrants little time to board.

A last barrier before boarding the ship was a required medical inspection, which was carried out by government doctors at a station near the docks. When Liverpool might be clearing thousands of emigrants in one day, these examinations were perfunctory, to say the least. Some witnesses claimed to have seen four hundred persons processed in one hour by the medical inspectors. Emigrants passed by a small window, were asked their name, told to show their tongue, and received a stamp of approval on their papers. This inspection probably did little to stop the spread of cholera and other diseases on board the ships. Complaints by reformers to the authorities did little to improve the situation.

Following the inspection, the emigrants could board their ship, either at the docks or by being taken to a ship waiting in the Mersey estuary. Despite the concerns about the voyage to come, most were only too glad to say farewell to Liverpool.

Irish Ports of Emigration

In the eighteenth century, virtually every Irish port had been a place of emigration, although emigration from Belfast and other ports in the North was more common while the Protestant Irish dominated the migration. By the early 1800s, emigration was becoming concentrated in fewer ports, including Belfast, Dublin, Cork, Limerick, and Londonderry. These ports had deeper waters to handle the larger ships arriving from America with cargoes of timber, tobacco, flaxseed, and other commodities. Many of the timber ships came from the maritime provinces of Canada and offered the cheapest passage to North America for the poorer Irish. This directed some of the Irish emigrant traffic to Canada, although many would subsequently find their way to the United States, and especially to New England. As the pioneer historian of immigration, Marcus Hansen, put it, "Celtic New England is the product of the New Brunswick timber trade."[5]

As emigration rose in the 1820s and 1830s, an increasing proportion of the Irish migrants went to the United States through Liverpool. The heightening trade between Liverpool and New York meant that many more ships were available there, leading to competition among ship captains for the emigrant business and lower prices for passage. Ships departed almost daily, offering greater assurance to Irish emigrants of a quicker passage. Additionally, the development of scheduled steamship service beginning in the 1820s from Irish ports to Liverpool greatly reduced the cost of travel across the Irish Sea. The steamships across the Irish Sea to Liverpool carried not only those Irish destined to go to America, but also those planning to settle in England, as well as seasonal migrants who worked on the harvest in English farms. Irish emigrants on the steamboats took deck passage, often sharing space with penned-up livestock. In calm weather, the voyage might take about ten hours, but in heavy seas and storms the passengers on deck were exposed to the elements for as long as a full day. The ease of transport to Liverpool transformed the whole picture of Irish emigration.

As the tide of emigration to America increased, the main Irish ports could continue to handle only a portion of the emigrants. They suffered from the fact that as the transatlantic trade in American exports was attracted more and more to Liverpool, the Irish ports had fewer arriving ships to take emigrants to America. By the 1830s the Irish ports saw only enough ships to handle about 35,000 emigrants annually going directly to America, and the increasing numbers of emigrants were exceeding that limit. In 1831 and 1832, over 65,000 emigrated each year.[6] Consequently, during the 1830s three basic changes in the flow of Irish emigration were taking place: the number of Catholic emigrants from the South was beginning to exceed the number of Protestant Irish from the North; the number going to the United States was beginning to exceed the number taking ship for Canada; and the proportion of Irish emigrants going to America by way of Liverpool was beginning to exceed those sailing directly from Irish ports.

The conditions of those using the Irish ports did not differ greatly from those at Liverpool. News of departing ships was generally advertised in the interior of Ireland by the newspapers in the north. In the south and west of Ireland, emigration agents increasingly spread the news by word of mouth and by handbills posted in Irish villages. The Irish in the interior, most of whom lived reasonably close to the seaports, learned not to go to the port until the ship was actually cleared for departure. The ports themselves harbored the same dangers of fraud and abuse as did Liverpool: agents whose ships did not exist, runners who practically took emigrants captives, and lodging-house keepers who charged high prices for miserable quarters. Those were wise who waited until the last minute before going to the port and boarding their ship.

Ports of Emigration in Northern Europe

In the 1820s and 1830s, when emigration from the continent came mainly from France and the western and southwestern parts of Germany, the most commonly used ports of emigration were Le Havre, near the mouth of the Seine, and ports in the Low Countries accessible from the Rhine River, such as Antwerp, Amsterdam, and Rotterdam. Travelers could come either by boat or by roadway down the valleys of those rivers, and there were emigration agents in the interior promoting all of those ports. Even in the 1820s, some of the emigrants used the ports on the continent as way stations en route to Liverpool. In the 1830s, when the railroad route across England was opened, traffic increased through Hull on England's east coast.

In the 1840s the American ship-broker Washington Finlay established his business at Mainz, near the Rhine, and actively promoted the ports of Antwerp and Le Havre to German emigrants. His principal selling point was the cheap passage to those ports from the interior. The trip by steamer to Antwerp from Mainz cost 15 francs for adults. Others were routed by rail through Paris to Le Havre, but that trip was more expensive. Finlay developed a remarkable network of agents across southern Germany. In 1849 he handled 12,743 German emigrants sailing to New York from Antwerp and Le Havre, and 2,682 Germans bound for New Orleans. The movement through those ports in the late 1840s was perhaps aided by the civil unrest and revolution in the German states. Those who had to escape the police or skip the country without permission knew that Antwerp and Le Havre, where personal controls were relatively lax, were the best emigration choices. Emigrants in those ports were seldom asked about the military obligations they might have left behind in Prussia or other states.[7]

Emigration from the north German ports developed more slowly. In the 1820s much of the overseas trade arriving in these cities was in sugar and coffee from Latin America, but new factors began to raise the importance of the emigrant trade to North America. Developments of the 1830s led to the rise of the free cities Bremen and Hamburg as ports of emigration, especially for German emigrants. First, the sources of migrants within Germany began to shift to the north and the east, and the river systems of the Weser and the Elbe offered easy transportation for those emigrants to Bremen and Hamburg, respectively. Then, the building of railroads beginning in the late 1830s began to offer alternative routes to migrants from the interior German states. The growing possibilities of the emigrant trade led to a competition between Hamburg and Bremen for that trade. A primary motivation was to provide cargoes of emigrants for ships arriving in the two ports with American commodities, so they would not have to return empty or seek cargo in other ports.

Bremen was already established by the 1820s as the center of tobacco trade between America—especially Baltimore—and Germany, and was increasing its business by gradually replacing the Dutch ports as the principal entrepôt for tobacco in all northern Europe.[8] New York, however, gained steadily on Baltimore, and by 1840 would replace it as the chief American port connecting to Bremen. But the trade of Bremen was beginning to suffer a disadvantage because of the silt accumulating in the Weser River, which impeded the movement of oceangoing vessels. The city responded by building in 1827 a new town, Bremerhaven, nearer the mouth of the Weser, which opened as a port in 1830. Traffic through the port grew slowly in the 1830s, but the merchants and city-fathers of Bremen, realizing that the trade in all goods from America depended on balancing the ships bringing cargo from the United States with ships returning full of emigrants, undertook active promotion of their port. They sent multitudes of emigration agents into the hinterland to stir up business, and undertook initiatives to deal with emigrants' complaints about exploitation by ship captains, agents, and lodging-house keepers. Beginning in 1832, the city passed a series of regulatory laws dealing with the emigration trade that were stronger than what existed in any other port. Lodging houses were inspected; ships were monitored for their seaworthiness; and captains were required to provide enough food for a trip of 90 days and to carry insurance for the passengers. Bremen's demonstrated concern for the welfare of the emigrants would serve to increase its share of the trade in German emigrants.[9]

As the movement of emigrants began to reach flood tide in the late 1840s, Bremen took further steps to protect the transatlantic travelers. In 1851 the city authorities established information bureaus for emigrants, with offices at the railroad station, at the river landing, and in the city's center. At these bureaus the travelers could bypass runners and get official information about places of lodging, stores, and ships—including their rates and schedules. In 1852 the city went further and erected its Emigrant House, which could provide lodgings for 2,000 people—along with eating facilities, a chapel, an information bureau, and an infirmary. Prices for room and board were an inexpensive 66 pfennigs per person per day. The Emigrant House proved to have great effect against the aggressive activities of the runners. In 1855 Bremen for the first time surpassed Le Havre in numbers of emigrants passing through the port, and continued to maintain its lead in the following decades.[10]

Before 1850 the free city of Hamburg ran far behind Bremen as a port of emigration. Its principal trade routes traditionally connected northern Germany with England and through England to Latin America. There were fewer ships bound directly for the United States. Hamburg handled much of the trade with England because of the political connections between England and Hamburg's neighboring kingdom of Hanover: the same royal family ruled in both Britain and Hanover. Hamburg employed many agents to promote itself as an emigration port, but it fared best by marketing as the cheapest way to America its route across the North Sea to England, then by land to Liverpool, and then to New York. There were numerous accusations of fraud and mistreatment of passengers against those brokers who handled the indirect traffic to America via England.[11] It was difficult to offset the favorable image of Bremen, which had consciously tried to reform the treatment of emigrants. Hamburg's efforts to regulate the emigrant trade met with stiff resistance from the shipping and mercantile interests of the city, and only in the late 1840s was Hamburg able to enforce regulations similar to those at Bremen. During the entire decade of the 1840s, Bremen handled 211,000 passengers from its port of Bremerhaven; Hamburg's port handled only 27,000.[12] The numbers handled by both ports would increase considerably in the 1850s and following decades. A great influence on the concentration of emigrants at the two Hanseatic ports was the two shipping corporations which would come to dominate the transatlantic traffic from the continent. These were the Hamburg-America line, which in 1847 began service from Hamburg to Southampton in England and to New York, and the North German Lloyd, which established regular service from Bremen to London and New York in 1857. Both established their own agents across central and eastern Europe, and would continue to flourish as steam replaced sail and, later, as iron ships replaced wooden ones.

THE EMIGRANT SHIPS

During the age of sail, the ships that most emigrants might board were of varied sizes, ranging from about ninety feet to over two hundred feet in length, and having displacements from about 250 tons to over 1,700 tons. Most were three-masted wooden ships with square rigging. Other smaller ships were sometimes used—the ship *Restauration*, which carried the pioneer group of Norwegians to America in 1825, was a sloop with one mast, and about fifty-four feet long with displacement of about thirty-nine tons. Such a small ship actually violated the American laws for passenger ships, which would have required a ship of at least 115 feet in length to accommodate the 52 people on board. As emigrant passenger traffic developed in the 1830s and 1840s, the economics of the trade encouraged the building of larger ships, capable in some instances of carrying over a thousand passengers. Emigrant ships became generally known as packets— originally a term meaning passenger ships which sailed on a regular schedule, usually between the same two ports. But eventually all sailing ships carrying passengers came to be called packets, even though they might be itinerant ships carrying freight to Europe and returning to America with emigrants. The more romantic and storied ships of the time, the clipper ships, were not so much involved in the transatlantic trade or in carrying emigrants. Their sharp-prowed narrow profile, designed for speed in calmer waters, did not do well in the turbulent waves of the north Atlantic. While the clippers dominated the Pacific trade, where speed was an economic benefit, the packet sailboats in the Atlantic could hold more cargo or passengers and brave the waves there as fast as most of the clippers.

As the emigrant trade grew during the 1830s and 1840s, the American-owned ships came to dominate the trade from Liverpool over the British ships, and they dominated the trade from Le

Havre as well. The American ships were larger—many were over a thousand tons—and they had a reputation for being better built and having more skilled and humane ship masters and crews—and much depended on how masters and crews treated their steerage passengers. The British vessels more often were built as cargo vessels, and took passengers mainly to fill up the space on the return trip to America. Particularly notorious were the timber ships which plied between England and Quebec. They often were far beyond their useful life, and their captains regarded the emigrants in the steerage as nothing more than ballast to avoid the ships' returning to Canada empty. The American ships were built more specifically for the emigrant trade, and their owners and masters were more conscious of their reputations.

In the rivers, harbors, and coastwise trade of both Europe and America, steamboats and steamships were taking over rapidly in the years after 1815. They offered speed and maneuverability in those waters that could not be achieved by flatboats, barges, or sailboats. But the use of steam power for transatlantic crossing was another matter. The possibility of steam passage across the Atlantic was demonstrated in 1819 by the first ship to make such a voyage— the *Savannah*, which sailed from its namesake port in Georgia to Liverpool in slightly over 29 days, about average for any ship at that time. The ship, about a hundred feet long, was a three-masted sailing ship with a steam engine and side paddle wheels that could be deployed or folded up as needed. Although the steam engine was used as an auxiliary to sails, providing an alternative when the winds were adverse or the seas becalmed, the ship proved an economic failure, as the engine and its necessary fuel took up so much space that there was little room for a payload. The ship toured European ports and was celebrated for its achievement, but after it returned to Savannah it never made another transatlantic voyage.

In the late 1830s and 1840s improvements were made in the technology of the steam-driven ships, equipping them with screw propellers instead of paddle wheels and improving their fuel efficiency. The steam engines were still used in combination with sails, but on the westward trips steam-driven ships were able to cut down the trip from Liverpool to New York to about sixteen days. This was an advantage to shippers, businessmen, and postal authorities, but the considerable cost of passage on the steamers made them unattractive to the mass of emigrants. The introduction of large wooden vessels powered exclusively by steam would come only in the late 1850s.

The general experience of most emigrants in the period before the late 1840s was in the steerage of sailing ships, the so-called packets. Those who had the money might travel cabin class, which was sometimes very elegant, but the cost of cabin passage from Liverpool to New York was five or six times as much as the $20–25 average per-person cost for travel in the steerage. The steerage was the space between the upper deck and a lower deck, technically called an orlop, above the cargo hold. The space was also called "tween-decks," or by the Germans *Zwischendeck.* The actual clearance in that space ranged from a head-banging five feet to eight feet. Beneath the orlop on some larger ships was another deck, even more cramped and crowded, that was sometimes used for additional sleeping space. On the eastbound passage the steerage might well have been used for additional cargo space. That meant that the nature of the cargo sometimes affected the conditions of the space used for passengers on the westbound voyage. Generally cotton ships were considered more desirable, since the steerage compartment usually remained clean and dry.

The steerage compartment was arranged into bunk areas on either side of a narrow aisle running the length of the compartment. On larger ships, eating tables might be placed in the central aisle. The bunks were mounted on stanchions, usually two bunks high. The bunks and stanchions were stowed away on the eastbound trip, and then put up for passengers leaving the European ports. The cooking facilities, separate from the galley that served the cabin class passengers, were usually sparse. The steerage galley might consist

The crowded steerage compartment or "between decks" on an emigrant ship. *Illustrated London News,* May 10, 1851. Courtesy Swarthmore College Library, via Bryn Mawr College Library Special Collections.

of a small room, about four by five feet, on the upper deck. The fire was made on a bed of stones or earth; above it was an iron grate occupying most of the space in the room. Pots or kettles could be hung on hooks over the grate. These meager facilities might have had to accommodate hundreds of steerage passengers, and there was often a desperate fight for access.

Life on Board the Emigrant Ships

The departure of the ship from the docks provided an emotional experience for most of the passengers as they contemplated what could have been the last view of the old country and of the friends and relatives that might be waving farewell on the docks. Nostalgia, fear, and uncertainty might all have risen to a peak. When the ship had scarcely left the mooring place, however, one last exercise of departure was performed: the roll call. All passengers were rounded up on deck at the stern of the ship, and made to wait while the crew searched the entire ship for stowaways. It was not unusual to find them, hiding under sacks of flour or inside a barrel in the steerage or even in a remote part of the hold. When the entire ship was cleared, the roll call began, and passengers who responded to their name were allowed to leave the confined area in the stern. Those unpaid passengers who were left after the names were called, along with the stowaways, were then put ashore by the pilot-boat or other small craft. Only then, given favorable winds, would the packet really set sail.

Favorable winds were not always available for the westbound emigrants, for the prevailing winds of the North Atlantic were westerlies. This meant that sailing vessels consumed a lot of time tacking against the wind, which added greatly to the time and distance of travel. The straight-line distance between Liverpool and New York, for instance, was about 3,000 miles, but the average mileage logged by the westbound ships was closer to 3,500. Eastbound ships could usually sail more quickly and directly with the prevailing winds. They could also take advantage of the Gulf Stream, which warmed them and carried them along in a more direct route. The westbound ships, however, had both to deal with the adverse winds and to steer away from the Gulf Stream current. This meant that the emigrant often experienced a trip of four to six weeks, and in a few cases as many as twelve. The eastbound ships, on the other hand, could often make the New York-Liverpool journey in about three weeks. Well-rigged ships and able crews thus were an important factor in the journey.

Life in the Steerage Compartment

Into the confined steerage space, the home of the emigrants for the long journey, might be packed hundreds of men, women, and children. Given the closeness of the quarters and the relative ignorance of basic hygiene shared by many of the travelers, the steerage could quickly become foul-smelling and disease-ridden. Toilet facilities were primitive, and there was virtually no provision for bathing. The small ration of water (perhaps two gallons a day per person) was mostly used for cooking and drinking, and even then it was not always palatable. Ventilation was inadequate; usually the open hatches to the upper deck provided the main source of air. The cabin passengers above who ventured near the open hatches frequently testified to the noxious odors emanating from the steerage. In storms and heavy seas the hatches and all other sources of ventilation were closed off, sometimes for days at a time. In such conditions steerage passengers were forbidden to go to the upper deck. The steerage passengers were prevented from going above even to cook food, and would have to make do with uncooked or raw provisions kept in the steerage. The most common memories of many emigrants were of seasickness, overwhelmingly foul odors, and nausea.

In more favorable conditions, the prevailing memory related by the immigrants afterwards was a sense of boredom. Initially, adults and children who had never before experienced ships or the sea could satisfy their curiosity by ranging about the ship, or at least the steerage and the upper deck. When their curiosity was satisfied and the ship no longer sailed within sight of land, they saw nothing for weeks but the sea, and the main source of excitement was minor changes in the weather. The sight of another ship might bring everyone out of the steerage and onto the deck. Sometimes, when the Grand Banks of Newfoundland were reached, it was possible to catch a fish or to purchase them from fishermen in their vessels. Quite commonly, passengers would devise word games or puzzles to pass the time. In well-run ships, the steerage passengers were usually required to perform housekeeping chores such as cleaning the steerage and cooking the food they had brought with them.

The Daily Regimen

Ships sailing to America from Bremen were known for their strict regulation and discipline (in contrast, the ships from Liverpool were often not as well-regulated). All steerage passengers were required to get up at 6:00 A.M., or 7:00 A.M. in fall and winter. After washing and dressing in the somewhat primitive facilities, the passengers, under supervision of the second mate, were responsible for cleaning the steerage compartment, making the bunks, and putting away equipment used during the night. After these chores were done, a few passengers would be selected to go to the upper deck, where cooking was done, and each would prepare breakfast for a particular group of eight to twelve persons. Ships from Bremen were required to provide provisions for the steerage passengers, although some passengers brought supplementary provisions of their own. The designated cook, who was usually the mother in the case of a large family, then prepared the meal. Other meals were handled in the same fashion. The three mealtimes were 8:00 A.M. (9:00 in the winter), 1:00 P.M., and 6:00 P.M. In fair weather all the passengers could go up on deck, and meals were generally taken there. When stormy weather made the deck conditions dangerous, passengers had to stay in the steerage, and were sometimes unable to have any cooked food.

The officers of the ship enforced rules zealously on the steerage passengers. Absolutely no open fire or flame was allowed. There could be no smoking of pipes between decks, no lighting of candles, and no handling of the fire equipment. Violators of the fire rules were locked up until arrival in port. Despite the terrible stench and contagion that might be present, passengers were particularly forbidden to fumigate their quarters by the time-honored method of plunging a red-hot iron into a bucket of tar, which provided the supposedly beneficial fumes. Ships had been known to catch fire and sink when using such methods.

Passengers were strenuously advised to keep the peace. There were stern rules against shouting, cursing, starting arguments, fighting, or raging against one another. Any disputes among passengers were to be settled by the first mate or the captain. Steerage passengers were strictly forbidden to enter the space reserved for cabin passengers.

When meals were to be cooked, access to the kitchen area was restricted to those persons chosen to do the cooking, and to some helpers who were assigned to peel potatoes, wash dishes, and do other chores. The cooks went to the storeroom to obtain the provisions for their groups. The fire was maintained in the kitchen from 6:00 A.M. to 7:00 P.M. A chief cook, a member of the ship's crew, presided.[13]

Hardships and Abuses

While the rules and procedures of the German ships present a picture of order and stability, emigrants on other ships were not always as lucky. Overcrowding of steerage passengers was a frequent complaint of emigrants leaving all of the ports. There were various attempts to regulate the problem, and it was one of the few areas where the United States attempted to control some aspect of immigration. In 1819 the U.S. Congress legislated that ships arriving in the United States could carry no more than two steerage passengers for every five tons of the vessel's displacement. A sizeable fine of $150 could be levied for each passenger carried over the limit. However, the law was difficult to enforce and was widely disregarded. In 1847, as larger waves of migrants began to fill the ships, a new U.S. law declared that each passenger in steerage must be allowed 14 square feet of space. This regulation too was seldom enforced, since customs officers were the only available enforcement officers, and they were largely concerned with the collection of customs duties.

Some captains found strong reasons for disregarding the rules. Ships sailing from the North Sea ports could at best make three round trips to America per year, and that only in the most favorable weather. Captains who saw that they could only make two trips to America in the year might try to make up the loss by crowding more people into the steerage. Some without assigned beds might have to sleep on mattresses in the aisles between bunks. The bunks themselves were customarily about six feet wide by six feet long, and were designed to be occupied by several people. Mother and daughter or a mother with two small children might be compelled to share a space only eighteen inches wide. Single emigrants might be assigned a bunk to be shared with strangers—although eventually regulations required single people to be separated from families and single men to be separated from women. Sometimes a kind of hut was built on the main deck to accommodate the excess passengers, and often these accommodations were not very tight against a stormy sea. The conditions were particularly unbearable when stormy weather forced all to go below and all the hatches were closed. The tight quarters, the oppressive stench, and the afflictions of nausea and seasickness left memories that few would forget.[14]

Distressful as the crowded conditions were, they were intensified by the actions of some captains and crews who mistreated and abused their steerage passengers. Reports of abuse were most common among the British ships sailing from Liverpool. These ships were often commanded by captains who were used to bringing timber from Quebec and regarded the emigrants traveling westward as a necessary nuisance. The captains were often abetted by crews who were themselves not happy at having to work for tyrannical officers. Over the years complaints accumulated concerning assaults by crew members on passengers, short-changing of rations, gouging and extortion for medical treatment or rations, neglect of hygienic conditions, and insensitivity toward the sick and dying. Many emigrants feared to air their complaints to the authorities after arriving in New York, often simply getting away from the ship as quickly as they could. The number of documented complaints is probably only a small proportion of the actual cases of abuse.

Two great fears, however, troubled nearly all passengers on the transatlantic voyages: life-threatening illnesses and shipwrecks on the stormy seas.

Disease and Death

The close quarters, crowded conditions, and unsanitary environment of the steerage were open invitations to disease. It was not unusual for ships landing in America to report to the port officers a number of deaths of passengers on the voyage. Among the causes frequently reported were smallpox, measles, dysentery, malaria, "ship fever" or typhus, and, most feared of all, cholera.

Cholera was one of the primary scourges that spread across Europe in the early nineteenth century. Originating in regions of India around Calcutta, it moved into the European continent in the 1820s. It struck quickly, with attacks of diarrhea leading to complete exhaustion and dehydration. The period from onset to death might be only a day or two. The cause of the disease was not well understood. It was attributed to "miasma," or foul air, and only later, in 1849, was the actual cause discovered: drinking water polluted by sewage. That meant it was a disease well-suited to travel along with passengers in a crowded ship.

In late 1831 the disease had reached England. In early 1832 it was afflicting the eastern part of Ireland, then spreading quickly westward across that entire island. The attempt to flee from cholera was perhaps one of the main reasons why there was an extraordinary exodus from Ireland to America during that year. Those emigrants gathering to take ship in Liverpool or in Irish ports spread the contagion and took it with them on board. The unsanitary conditions in the steerage compartment fostered close contact and little chance of escape from the disease. There was, for example, the unhappy trip of the *Brutus,* which departed from Liverpool with 330 passengers on May 18, 1832. Nine days into the voyage one 30-year-old male came down with cholera, and fortunately recovered. But then a woman 60 years of age contracted the disease and was dead within 10 hours. Then the cases of disease and the consequent deaths both rapidly increased. In one day, 24 deaths were recorded. The captain resisted appeals to return to Liverpool, but when the crew began to come down with the disease, he relented. On June 13, 1832, the ship arrived back in Liverpool. Out of the 330 passengers who had departed in the ship, 117 had contracted cholera and 81 had died.[15]

Immigrants arriving in America were quickly identified as the principal bearers of the disease. New York City immediately plunged into its own cholera epidemic in 1832, and the disaster was repeated in 1834. As immigrants moved to the interior, especially along the Erie Canal, the disease spread with them. Townspeople along the route organized militia to keep the immigrants on the canal boats from leaving their vessels. The epidemic of 1832 also struck Quebec and was rapidly transmitted to the populace of the city. Over 1,500 died within a few days.

Equally fearsome was typhus, a disease known as ship fever because it was believed to be produced by people living at close quarters—particularly those traveling in the steerage of ships. The real source of it, as would be found out much later, was lice, mainly those infesting rats or mice. The feces of lice found their way into dust, and were ingested or taken up in open sores. Typhus thus could spread rapidly in the steerage compartment. It came on suddenly, with chills and fever, muscular twitching, mental disorientation, and a dark rash on the skin. It spread quickly, and the few physicians on ships knew very little to do about it except to wait the disease out. The death toll could become heavy. The most serious outbreak was in 1847, among immigrants arriving in Quebec and New Brunswick. In August of that year, for example, the ship *Virginius* arrived in Quebec from Liverpool. Of the 634 who had left England in the ship, 158 had died during the voyage, including the captain, the first mate, and 10 crew members. Upon arrival another 106 were seriously ill with ship's fever. Other ships followed in similar distress, and the quarantine hospitals quickly filled up. At the end of the terrible plague season, authorities in London compiled some (probably incomplete) statistics: of 106,812 emigrants who crossed the Atlantic to British North America that year, 6,116 died on the voyage, 4,169 died while their ships were held in quarantine, and 7,180 died while in hospitals after arrival. That meant that one out of every six who left England for Canada died on the way.[16] This did not take into account the numerous residents of Quebec and New Brunswick who would also contract the disease from the immigrants. The fear of typhus was one of the main motivations for the port of New York, as well as others, to strengthen the regulations for quarantining ships and passengers upon arrival.

The fear of typhus could affect the motivation to emigrate to America; the number arriving in Quebec fell by half from 1847 to 1848 and was lower for several years thereafter. Yet many immigrants—particularly from Ireland, in those troubled years of high migration—felt they had no choice and took the risk anyway.

Shipwrecks

The other nightmare troubling prospective immigrants, especially those who had little acquaintance with the sea, was fear of the complete loss of the ship. Shipwrecks were unpredictable, and the stormy seas could take their toll at any time. While disease came and went in epidemics, there was no completely safe time to avoid shipwreck, although more dangers were present during the gale winds and high seas of winter. One could only look for a sturdy ship and a capable crew, and hope that the weather would be benign.

In the heyday of the transatlantic sailing ships (1824–1847), an estimated ninety seagoing vessels on the average were lost through shipwrecks each year. This figure included ships of all kinds, most of which were not in the emigrant trade. The emigrant packet ships probably had a better record than most. It was also estimated that there were only 22 wrecks of transatlantic packets out of some 6,000 ocean crossings during the period.[17] The average steerage passengers were probably not comforted by such statistics, if they even heard of them. There was one unsettling statistic on the other side: few of the emigrant ships carried more than four lifeboats, hardly enough for the hundreds in the steerage, and many ships carried only two. These boats would likely be used in an emergency by the cabin passengers and the crew. There was little hope for survival for the emigrants in case of shipwreck.

The story of the *William Brown,* an emigrant ship which crashed into an iceberg in 1842 while bound from Liverpool to Philadelphia, would naturally have given pause to all steerage passengers. One of the lifeboats that managed to get clear of the sinking ship contained

32 passengers. The first mate, Alexander Holmes, thought that was too many, and began to systematically throw overboard some of the emigrants, "just as freight might be jettisoned under similar circumstances."[18] Frank and Mary Carr, brother and sister, pleaded for their lives, but to no avail. Shortly after they were thrown overboard, the boat was rescued by a passing ship. Holmes would later be convicted of manslaughter in a federal court in Philadelphia.

Wrecks could occur from gale winds, high seas, and icebergs in the mid-Atlantic, and there were tales of several ships which went missing in the wintry mid-Atlantic and were never heard from again. Some of the more tragic incidents, however, occurred within sight of land—on the cliffs of the Irish coast, for example, or along the foggy shores of Long Island, or on the shoals off New Jersey beaches. Some of these tales involved spectators on the shore watching helplessly as the ship broke up under the pounding waves and the passengers threw themselves into the waters, only to drown.

AMERICA AT LAST

The fears that were part of every emigrant's story would then turn to relief when they sighted the American shores from a calm sea and headed into a harbor and, they hoped, a welcome.

Arrival in New York

On the morning of June 3, 1848, an English steerage passenger on his 38th day out of Bristol arose to have his first look at landfall in America, and then wrote in his diary:

Glorious morning! To the right is Long Island; to the left is Jersey State. What a fine country! Here at last is America. Yonder is Sandy Hook, with a lighthouse. What neat wooden cots [cottages] by the water's edge! Observe those forests of trees, with a house here and there peeping through the foliage. The sight now before us compensates for all our toil and trouble.

[The next day:] Up on deck by four in the morning. Arrive opposite Staten Island. . . . Eight o'clock—Two men came on board; these were custom-house officers. Then the doctor. Each passenger's name was called over, and every one had to pass in review before him. Then all below was examined; and the ship being pronounced healthy, was permitted to pass. . . . Almost all are on deck; the women and children much diverted with seeing the fishes play.[19]

The progress of the immigrant (for he or she was no longer an emigrant) to the landing place in New York City was slow, and sometimes delayed for weeks in case of illness. Sandy Hook, at the entrance to the lower harbor, was where incoming ships would take on a pilot to guide them around the shoals that lay across most of the passageway. Ships then proceeded six miles through the lower bay to the Narrows, a four-mile passage between Brooklyn and Staten Island. There they were required to stop at Seguine's Point for the quarantine station, located on the port side, on Staten Island. At this strategic entrance to the upper bay and its ports, the ship would be moored, and then boarded by the customs officers. These were federal officers who would receive the ship list with everyone's names and make (usually perfunctory) inquiries into the property being brought by the immigrants.

The inquiry by the health officer, a New York State official from the quarantine station, could pose greater problems. Ships and their passengers could be detained on a number of grounds, for example if there had been deaths on the seas, if passengers were found to have been exposed to a disease, or if the ship had come from a port where disease was known to be epidemic. Those found to be suffering from disease on arrival were placed in the hospital at the quarantine station. The hospital was supported by a head-tax on all entering emigrants; in 1845 this was set at 50 cents for steerage passengers. A ship known to carry disease might be required to wait a month, but the passengers might be able to leave sooner, to be taken with their baggage by a steamboat to the New York landing.

The trip across Upper New York Bay, which took about six miles, might be made by the steam ferry or on board the emigrant ship itself, which might require assistance from a steam tug if the winds were not favorable. There was no single arrival point for immigrants in the years before 1855. Instead, the ship was brought to any of the many wharves lining the lower Manhattan waterfront. In 1840 there were 113 wharves, of which 60 were along the East River, the location more favored by the transatlantic sailing ships. Each wharf might provide space for a number of ships; on one day in the spring of 1836, 921 ships were counted along the East River, another 320 along the Hudson.[20] Passengers on the arriving ships would see a vast forest of masts and rigging as they approached the landing place.

They would also see a crowd gathering to meet the arriving ship, whose approach was detected well in advance of its tying up at the dock. With luck, the immigrant might be greeted by relatives or friends who could immediately take the newcomer to shelter or to inland transportation. Others might find a representative of one of the emigrant aid societies, such as the Irish Emigrant Association (founded 1817), the Irish Emigrant Society (founded 1841), or the German Society of New York, which dated from 1784. There was also a Netherlands Emigrant Society and a British Protective Emigrant Society. These societies saw the protection of the newcomer as their mission, and the transatlantic travelers had usually been advised to seek them out. The societies could help find temporary lodgings, give guidance regarding the availability of employment, or help to make further transportation arrangements. They also served as a point of contact between previous immigrants already settled in the interior and the newcomers, who could find messages from their friends and relatives waiting for them.

In periods of high migration, however, the emigration aid agencies were often overwhelmed, and it became more likely that those coming off the ship would be at the mercy of the runners, transportation brokers, and employment agents who swarmed around the wharf. The scene on the wharf was often one of confusion, with family members calling to one another, and a scramble to find one's luggage in the helter-skelter pile in which it had been unloaded from the ship. Sometimes runners would find their way

Emigrants (who now become immigrants) arriving in New York. Some are met by friends and relatives; others are accosted by "runners" eager to take them to a favored lodging-place. *Harper's Weekly*, June 26, 1858. Courtesy Bryn Mawr College Special Collections.

onto the ferryboats which brought immigrants from their ships to the landing, or they might even manage to board the ships themselves, perhaps with the collusion of the ship's captain, at the Quarantine Station. The chances for fraud and abuse were great, despite all efforts to forewarn the arriving passengers. Some of the same practices that had assaulted emigrants in Liverpool were found again in New York: runners who snatched up the arriving immigrants' luggage and forced them to follow to a predatory lodging house; recruiters for employers who preyed upon the recent immigrants; and phony transportation brokers who sold tickets on non-existent steamboats or railroads, or tickets that would pay the fare only partway to a passenger's destination. The many abuses by runners were one of the chief reasons for an investigation by a New York legislative committee in 1847, which led to the establishment of the state's Commissioners of Immigration. The testimony of the police captain from the Third Ward to the investigating committee gave an account of the workings of the runners:

Many of the steamboats that land emigrants from Quarantine land at the docks in the Third Ward. There they are immediately visited by the runners from the emigrant boarding-houses, backed by bullies to assist in soliciting passengers to go to the different houses. As the emigrant attempts to take his luggage from on board the boat, the runner will endeavor to get it from him, and by force, unless there is a sufficient police to protect him, representing that they will keep them at sixpence sterling for each meal, and sixpence sterling for lodging, and no charge made for cartage or storage for luggage. When the emigrant comes to pay his bill, he is never able to get off at the contract price, but is compelled to pay from three shillings to fifty cents for each meal and lodging, one dollar and fifty cents for cartage, when if it was paid at the time, it could not, under the law, be but thirty-one cents and fifty cents per day for storage for an ordinary-sized chest, and other things in proportion.[21]

Another abuse of newly arrived immigrants was in the fraudulent sale of transportation from New York to the interior of the country. The most common route before the late 1840s was by steamboat up the Hudson River to Albany, then west by canal boat along the Erie Canal to Buffalo, then by steamer to various locations along the Great Lakes. Runners or agents would sell tickets which supposedly were valid for a trip all the way to a particular destination, but the travelers would find when they arrived at Albany that the rest of their trip was not covered. Or, exorbitant charges would be levied for carrying the luggage of the immigrants, not covered by the passenger's ticket. Even when valid tickets were sold, they could be at a price several times what was available normally at the carrier's ticket office. Some of the fraudulent sales of transportation had been made even before the emigrants left Europe. Agents in Liverpool or even in the interior of Ireland or Germany would try to sell tickets that would guarantee passage all the way to the final destination of the travelers. Tickets were sometimes offered on railroads not yet built or non-existent steamboat lines. Emigrant societies in the United States frequently tried to publicize this fraud, and to urge newcomers to buy only from the ticket offices of the established transportation companies, and not from any brokers or agents.

Many of the new immigrants stayed initially in New York, mostly because they could not afford to go any further, even if they wished to go to some place where friends or relatives awaited them. Employment agents waited on the docks and in nearby recruiting stations, offering new arrivals work at places both within the interior of the country and in the city itself. The offers of work along the canals or docks in the interior might provide transportation to a work site, but they also offered more opportunities for abuse, for the immigrants might have little knowledge of what they were getting into, and might find themselves on the frontier with few other alternatives to the hard and poorly compensated labor. In New York City itself, employers who did not pay a prevailing wage (even if at a low rate) might find their laborers deserting them for another job. If times were hard and unemployment was high, as in the years of depression following 1837, the new immigrant might be more vulnerable to oppression. But news of hard times spread quickly to Europe, and immigration dropped noticeably during periods of recession.

Irish newcomers, mostly from rural backgrounds, lacked many marketable skills and contributed to the unskilled workforce of the city. For the unskilled, the rapidly growing city offered many opportunities as dock-workers, water and sewer pipe-layers, street pavers, teamsters, construction workers, and factory hands. The Irish came to dominate the unskilled labor market by mid-century. The Germans, English, and Scandinavians, on the other hand, more often arrived with marketable skills, and found employment as tailors, jewelry workers, shoemakers, cabinetmakers, and stonemasons, among others. Women who were not with their families (as was often the case with the Irish) were often sought out as domestic servants, cooks, and chambermaids. Such work often provided shelter and security and avoided many dangers of exploitation. Irish women often had the edge in the general market because they knew English; German female servants, however, could still find work in German middle-class households.

For many, laboring in New York was only temporary, until the newcomers were able to move on to more attractive destinations. While the total numbers of foreign-born in New York City grew in the 1830s, 1840s, and 1850s, those who moved on into the interior of the country were constantly being replaced by new arrivals.

Arrival in New Orleans

By the 1840s, New Orleans had clearly become the second largest port of immigration, although it was a distant second to New York. There were two interrelated causes for the port's growth. Population movement into the Mississippi Valley region in the westward booms of the 1820s and early 1830s had opened up new areas there which were attractive to immigrants, and also had increased the production of agricultural exports which moved down the rivers to New Orleans. At the same time, cotton plantations spread across the Gulf states during the so-called flush times of the early 1830s. A large proportion of the product of the Cotton Belt was exported to Europe; thus, frequent cotton ships moved from New Orleans and other ports such as Biloxi to England and France, offering cheap passage to immigrants on their return. The Mississippi River, plied by frequent steamboats beginning in the 1820s, offered transportation for the newcomers all the way up to Iowa and Illinois, and to regions along the Missouri and Ohio Rivers as well. The steamboats, which greatly facilitated the export of the agricultural produce of the Upper Mississippi and Ohio Valleys, usually had less cargo returning upstream in those places, and so could offer cheap accommodations to the new immigrants.

New Orleans was itself a booming place in the 1830s. Its population doubled during the decade, from about 50,000 to 102,000. Furthermore, it was transformed from a largely black city to one in which the majority of the inhabitants were white. Arriving Germans, French, and Irish changed the character of the city. From 1820 to 1860 an estimated 550,000 immigrants passed through the port.[22] While this was far fewer than those coming through New York, it amounted to about one tenth of all immigrants arriving in the United States during the period. The city of New Orleans was already a cosmopolitan place because of its Creole population, descended from the early French settlers. This made it a desirable place for new French-speaking immigrants, both from France itself and from the West Indies, and Louisiana became the largest recipient of French-born immigrants in the early nineteenth century. From the 1830s to the early 1840s, the Germans were the most numerous European immigrants passing through New Orleans; the Irish would become more numerous in the great migration after 1846.

While New Orleans developed a sizable German and Irish population, the great majority of arriving immigrants made a quick transfer to steamboats which would carry them further north along the Mississippi and its tributaries. Many doubtless believed that the slave-owning plantation South offered little opportunity for immigrant farmers and laborers. Also, many feared the unhealthy reputation of the port, lying as it did in a swampy region well known for its epidemics of yellow fever. The cause of yellow fever, a virus carried by mosquitoes, was not yet known, but the swampy environment around New Orleans bred legions of mosquitoes which could carry the virus from one person to another. The native inhabitants of New Orleans tended to blame the yellow fever scourge upon the immigrants; epidemics seemed to coincide with the high tide of immigration (for example, in the peak year of 1853, there were more than 9,000 deaths from yellow fever in New Orleans). But yellow fever was in fact not a disease commonly carried into the country by immigrants; rather, arriving immigrants with no immunity to the disease might quickly contract it after arrival and then spread it among the local population.

Fears and uncertainties like these caused many arriving immigrants to take the earliest boat possible up the river, and ultimately would make most of them Midwesterners rather than Southerners. New Orleans became the principal port of entry for Germans headed toward St. Louis and the German settlements westward along the Missouri River, as well as those headed toward the river cities along the Ohio, the upper Mississippi, and their tributaries. Farming regions in southern Ohio, along the Wabash in Indiana, and in southwestern Illinois, gained German farmers. As for the Irish, they found common-labor employment in every one of those river cities, working on the river landings and building the urban infrastructures.

The heyday of New Orleans as a gateway for immigrants lasted until the late 1850s. As it turned out, this prosperity was directly linked to the peak years of the steamboat traffic on the river. By 1857 the railroads from the East were beginning to reach the Mississippi, immediately providing the new immigrants in eastern ports with a fast and cheap connection to the Midwest, and the steamboat trade rapidly showed a loss of business. The coming of the railroads also opened up newer areas for settlement in the northern Midwest, which became new goals for immigrants in the 1850s.

Arrival in Philadelphia

Immigrants who arrived in America via the port of Philadelphia had to travel about 200 miles further from European ports than those who went to New York. The trip required sailing to the southern end of New Jersey, around Cape May, then into the Delaware Bay and the Delaware River further north. The voyage became even more difficult in winter, for ice might freeze in the river, unlike in the New York harbor, which was ice-free all year. In the eighteenth century, Philadelphia had been the foremost port welcoming non-English immigrants, because the hinterland to the west of the city was the objective of both Germans and Scotch-Irish. That hinterland, by the time of the American Revolution, extended westward to the Allegheny Mountains, then southward into the backcountry of Maryland and Virginia.

After 1820, however, Philadelphia fell well behind New York as a port of immigration, since New York now had the Hudson River-Erie Canal gateway into the interior. The success of the Erie Canal as a route of trade and a route for immigrants inspired other seaboard cities to try to build their own routes leading to the West. Pennsylvania's answer was the Main Line of Internal Improvements of the State of Pennsylvania. Built in the late 1820s and early 1830s, it consisted of a railroad westward from Philadelphia to the Susquehanna River, then a canal leading up that river and up the Juniata River into the mountains. Once there, canal boats were lifted onto a steam-powered inclined plane and carried over the mountains to rivers on the west side, which brought them to Pittsburgh, at the head of the Ohio River Valley. New York's canal-building venture paid off well; the more complicated Pennsylvania system never completely erased its debt, which like New York's was based upon state-issued bonds. The trip through Pennsylvania was more expensive than traveling on the Erie Canal, but it was somewhat faster and did carry immigrants more directly to the growing region of the Ohio Valley. The Main Line route also helped Philadelphia and its growing industries and commercial interests to dominate the markets of the Ohio Valley before the Civil War, and the remarkable growth of manufacturing in Philadelphia provided an increasing number of jobs for immigrants.

In the 1820s, Philadelphia welcomed about 12 percent of the immigrants arriving in the United States. By then, New York's advantages were taking over the immigrant trade, and in the period between 1830 and the Civil War, Philadelphia handled only about 4 or 5 percent of the total number of immigrants—well behind both New York and New Orleans.[23]

Philadelphia demonstrated how one port might benefit from a specific practice of chain migration, where subsequent migrations from a particular place of origin followed their predecessors along the same route. Irish migration to Philadelphia in the eighteenth century had generated a particular settlement of people from Londonderry, the northernmost county in Ireland. An operator of sailing ships, McCorkell & Co. of Londonderry, established regular service between the two ports, and by 1850 was carrying as many as 2,500 emigrants a year to Philadelphia. What particularly fueled this migration stream was the receipt of remittances from the Irish in Philadelphia by relatives and friends in Londonderry. One estimate was that the firm received 25,000 pounds for prepaid tickets in one year. By this time English, Irish, and Welsh immigrants dominated immigrant travel to Philadelphia; the number of Germans was only about 6 percent of the total arrivals.

Arrival in Baltimore

The port of Baltimore developed as an immigration gateway mostly after 1820. One reason for the influx of immigrants was the growth of the trade in Chesapeake Bay tobacco from the port of Baltimore to Germany, and in particular to Bremen. German emigrants at Bremen could board ships which had brought tobacco for the European market and were soliciting passengers for the return voyage. Other ships brought Irish passengers from Liverpool and other ports, but between 1820 and 1860 the Germans were clearly the most numerous immigrants to Baltimore. The influx made Baltimore one of the most German cities on the Atlantic coast in the antebellum period. About one quarter of the city's population was German-born or German-descended by 1860.[24]

However, most immigrants arriving in Baltimore, rather than staying there, regarded the city as offering an attractive route to the West, and to the Ohio Valley in particular. Baltimore was closer to that region than any of the other East Coast seaports, although ships bound for that city had to make their way up the Chesapeake Bay to reach it. After 1815, Baltimore's road to Cumberland, Maryland, was extended further westward as the National Road, the first fed-erally funded highway to the West. The well-engineered road, with a crushed-stone surface, was completed to Wheeling on the Ohio River in 1818. Baltimore merchants then looked forward to gaining preeminence over New York and Philadelphia in the western trade. When the Erie Canal raised the stakes in competition for that trade, Baltimore merchants in 1828 organized the Baltimore and Ohio Rail-road, known as the first railroad in America to use steam locomo-tives. That route would not reach the Ohio Valley until 1853. But the National Road remained by far the best route into the interior for wagons and stagecoaches. Baltimore also became involved in canal-building up the Susquehanna Valley, which led to central Pennsyl-vania and connected to Pennsylvania's Main Line. Although failing to achieve Baltimore's goal of having the most favorable route to the West, these various public works offered common-labor construc-tion jobs for many of the arriving immigrants.

Antebellum Baltimore had long-established immigrant-aid socie-ties to assist newcomers. Its society of the Ancient Order of Hiber-nians, founded in 1803, worked to arrange both housing and employment for the Irish. The German Society of Maryland, founded in 1783 to protect indentured immigrant servants, adjusted to the new immigration of the nineteenth century, particularly by provid-ing employment services for the Germans. Baltimore was a rapidly growing city in the antebellum period, offering a wide variety of jobs, both skilled and unskilled. Another attractive element of the port of Baltimore was the city's position as the first Catholic diocese in the United States, making it the acknowledged American center of the Catholic Church in those years. Through the port of Balti-more, many religious orders brought members to the New World to open schools and hospitals which served the growing immigrant populations.

Arrival in Boston

The port of Boston was not among the foremost in the migra-tions that occurred before 1845. While it rivaled other U.S. ports for commercial traffic handled, it lagged behind as a port attractive to immigrants. Boston offered less convenient passage to the West than did New York, New Orleans, Philadelphia, or Baltimore. It did have the advantage of being closer to Liverpool than the other American ports. Before the flood tide immigration of the late 1840s and early 1850s, immigrants arriving in Boston were mostly British and Irish, the latter mostly from northern Ireland. The yearly influx in the 1820s did not exceed 3,000; it reached 4,000 in 1837; and in the early 1840s it ranged from 5,000 to 8,000 per year. In the famine years, the annual immigration rate rose to nearly 30,000 in 1849.[25] Immigrants to Boston's port included many who had come first on timber ships to the Maritime Provinces of Canada, then had gone by coastal steamers to Boston. Those who arrived on the docks of East Boston in the earlier years, if they had some means remaining, made their way inland, particularly to the rising factory towns further west in Massachusetts. Others, following the frequent advice of guidebooks that Boston offered little opportunity, sought the growing cities and farms beyond the Appalachians.

For those who lacked the means to travel further, as was true of an increasing number of Irish, there was little help provided; the immigrant aid societies of that city were weak and ineffective, certainly not equal to the task of dealing with the increasing numbers during the 1830s and early 1840s. Those who arrived on the docks penniless and without assistance were forced to take the first available jobs they could find, which were unskilled common-labor jobs in the streets, on the docks, or in the mills. When the poverty-stricken immigrants of the famine years began to arrive, they too would find little opportunity, and would add to the numbers of immigrants in the lowest social class. In the second half of the nineteenth century, some of the Irish of Boston began to ascend to the middle class and acquire economic and political power; they were then able to provide both remittances and job-offers to friends and relatives leaving Ireland. As such, the process of chain migration would help to make Boston a more attractive destination.

Arrival in Canada

Before 1834 more emigrants coming from the British Isles arrived in Canada than arrived in American ports. This was partly due to British policies which encouraged settlement of emigrants in other parts of the British Empire. Another reason was that in earlier years, the cheapest fare for passage across the Atlantic was in the timber ships which crossed the ocean to Britain and Ireland with cargo from Canada and returned with a cargo primarily of emigrants. In the early 1830s, the cost from Ireland to Quebec was about half the cost of travel from Liverpool to New York. But these ships also became known for their poor accommodations, unhealthy conditions, and brutal captains and crews. The rising trade between Liverpool and

New York in particular began to offer competitive rates to emigrants, and the Canadian emigrant trade declined slowly after 1834.

The majority of the migration through Canada came up the St. Lawrence River to Quebec City. In 1832, the Parliament of Lower Canada designated Grosse Isle, an island thirty miles below Quebec, as the quarantine station for arriving immigrants. Its establishment coincided with the cholera epidemic that struck later that year, and many of the emigrants afflicted by the disease perished in the hospital. There was another cholera epidemic in 1834, and an even more disastrous onslaught of typhus in 1847: in that year, the British government later reported, 3,452 immigrants died at the quarantine station, and another 6,585 in hospitals after leaving quarantine.[26] In the years after 1832, about 11,000 immigrants were buried on the island. Grosse Isle continued to be the principal Canadian immigration reception point into the twentieth century.

From quarantine, the immigrants could go to Quebec, to Montreal, or to other cities along the St. Lawrence. The number of Irish in Canadian cities grew in the early nineteenth century, and, as in the United States, the influx was increasingly of Catholic Irish. By 1844, the Irish comprised 6.3 percent of the population of Lower Canada (Quebec). Fewer newcomers from Ireland were Protestants, and the Irish-born Catholic population increased, as was happening at about the same time in the United States. Canada, however, had a greater proportion of its Irish-born taking up residence in rural areas, in contrast to the generally urban settlements of Irish in the United States. In the 1820s and 1830s, many Irish tenant farmers seeking better farms of their own settled in the rural areas along the frontier of the St. Lawrence Valley.

By the 1840s, however, for many new immigrants Quebec was simply a stop on the way into the interior. A boat trip through the Great Lakes could bring these immigrants to other points of settlement in Upper Canada (Ontario), but for many the more appealing destination was the growing area of the American Midwest. An alternative route was from Montreal southward through the Lake Champlain corridor and the Hudson Valley, which would bring immigrants to New York and other eastern cities.

The second most frequented immigration port in British North America was Saint John, in the Atlantic province of New Brunswick. In the second quarter of the nineteenth century, the vast timber resources of the interior of the province became the resource for the timber ships traveling to Ireland and Britain. The return trip of these ships became the cheapest route to America, especially for immigrants sailing directly from Ireland. The rough timber ships and their equally rough crews also made it the most uncomfortable journey. Estimates are that 150,000 Irish arrived in Saint John between 1815 and 1867. In the center of the harbor lay the Partridge Island immigration station, established in 1785. It became another place of quarantine, and the first hospital for arriving immigrants was established there during a smallpox epidemic in 1830. The quarantine was also the site of many deaths during the typhus epidemic of 1847.

Saint John became by the middle of the century the most Irish city in Canada; by 1851, according to the census of that year, over half the heads of household were persons born in Ireland. Notwithstanding the impact of the Irish on the province, it is estimated that over two-thirds of the arriving immigrants found their way quickly to the United States. The port offered very easy access to New England ports by coastal steamships, and many of the Irish immigrants populating the New England cities by mid-century had arrived by way of New Brunswick.

DIASPORA IN AMERICA

From their port of arrival, the growing waves of immigrants—those who were not remaining in the coastal cities—moved out along the principal lines of communication to the west and into a rapidly expanding America. In the early 1820s the term "the West" meant primarily the Appalachian region and the Ohio, Mississippi, and Missouri River Valleys beyond. By the 1830s, settlements along the shores of the Great Lakes in both Canada and the United States were attracting immigrants. In the great land boom that sprang up in the mid-1830s, settlement moved outward from the great river valleys and into the interior regions of Ohio, Indiana, Illinois, and Missouri. Immigrants were attracted both to new farming country and to new towns. In the early 1840s immigrant communities took shape in Wisconsin, Minnesota, Michigan, and Iowa. The period from 1820 to 1845 also marked the beginning of the phenomenon of a secondary migration of immigrants; for example, from Pennsylvania to Ohio, from Buffalo to Chicago, and from the Ohio River Valley to Missouri. These movements of immigrant peoples and their children began a process that would take some families from the East Coast to the West Coast by several moves before the end of the century. Thus was chain migration carried out to its extreme over several generations.

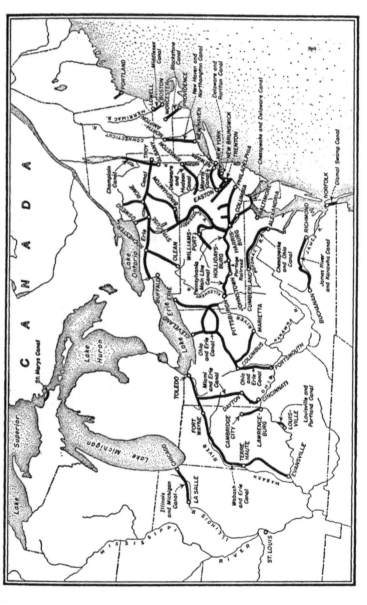

The U.S. river and canal system as developed by 1860. Before 1845, canals and other waterways were the principal network by which immigrants spread into the interior of the country. Immigrants provided much of the labor in building the canals, and settled in the towns developing along the waterways. From George R. Taylor, *The Transportation Revolution 1815–1860*, (vol. IV of the Economic History of the United States), 1st ed. (New York: Holt, Rinehart and Winston, 1951). Reprinted with permission of Wadsworth, a division of Thomson Learning: www.thomsonrights.com.

Those who knew their destination in the interior sometimes took a long time to get there. In 1829 and 1830, three brothers of the Morris family, all weavers fleeing the Industrial Revolution, left Lancashire, England for America. Their intent was to procure land in America and switch to farming, but only one of them, Thomas, was able to achieve this soon after arrival. He traveled to Ohio and bought land in Washington County, about fifteen miles from the Ohio River near Marietta. His brothers Andrew and William remained in the Philadelphia area, working in textile factories a few miles outside the city. Thomas continually encouraged them (as well as other family members still in England) to come and join him, but it was not until 1836 that Andrew, having lost his job when a factory closed, set out to achieve his goal of owning a farm. His brother William, who would follow Andrew in late 1837, described Andrew's journey by way of the Pennsylvania Main Line to Ohio:

They left Philadelphia on Sundy morning; got to Columbia that night, a distance of 82 miles by the railroad; got their things on board the boat before dark and slept on board that night. They started next morning about 10 oclock and got to Holydaysburgh [Hollidaysburg] on Thursday morning before day where they took the steam cars again and started about 8 oclock the same morning and at night they slept at a tavern on the top of the Alleyganey Mountains. They got to Johnstown on Friday about 3 oclock and in half an hour was under way on board another boat. They got to Pittsburgh on Sundy night about 8 oclock and slept on board. On Monday morning they got a passage in a steam boat to Marietta for 2 dollars each and the 3 children counted on[e] passinger. . . . They got to Marietta on Tusday morning at daylight. They got a wagon take them out to B[rother] Thomases for which they paid 6 dollers. It was 12 oclock when they left Marietta and they got to Thomases at 8 oclock that night. So you see they was 10 days on their jurney.[27]

Johann Pritzlaff, for another example, wrote to his parents and family in Prussia in April 1842 to explain where he had been since he left them in the spring of 1839. He had joined a group of Old Lutherans—dissenters from the state church of Prussia—on the voyage to establish a congregation in Wisconsin, where, they heard, land was still available at the government price of $1.25 an acre. They had gone from Hamburg to England by steamship, then to Liverpool where they embarked for America in July 1839. Their eight-week journey brought them to New York Harbor on September 6. As Pritzlaff wrote:

After we went from New York by steamship to Albany, and from there, partly by train, partly by canal boats that were pulled by horses, we finally arrived in Buffalo. . . . Those of us who were well-off went by steamship another 1100 English miles to Milwaukee and the area, in Wisconsin Territory, and the poor were forced to look for work in and around Buffalo; many of us went 15 German miles away from Buffalo to work on the canal. . . . After I had worked for one year in New York State, Herman Roggenbuck and I traveled to the state of Pennsylvanien [sic], because wages there were higher than in New York State. After we had worked there for 9 months. H. Roggenbuck moved back to his parents and his relatives in Buffalo. . . . Since I could not get the wages I had earned at the same time as my comrade, I was forced to stay there for another 4 months, when I then got my wages, and then I set out on September 29th 1841 and traveled partly by train and partly by canal boat to Buffalo and from there after a 3-day stay again by steamship (across Lake Erie, Lake Huron and Lake Michigan) to Milwaukee which is on the latter lake. . . . Great was the joy when I was reunited with my fellow countrymen and fellow-believers, many of whom have already bought land.[28]

As the routes of transportation—still mostly waterways in this period—were opened up to the interior of the country, immigrant communities sprang up along the way. Many new immigrants in fact were hired to build most of the canals in the construction boom that occurred in the 1820s and 1830s, and they moved westward as the canal system developed. The original stimulus, of course, was the Erie Canal, and immigrants were part of the workforce from the day it began construction in 1817. The canal, having distributed groups of immigrant workers all through western New York, was opened in October 1825. It was immediately hailed as a great success, particularly because it demonstrated that canal revenues would easily repay the state bonds which had been issued to finance its construction. Besides the construction workers themselves, the canal provided further employment for immigrants on the canal boats, as workers at the locks, and in the new towns springing up along the way. Soon after the Erie Canal was opened, plans began for its widening and for branch canals, and so the canal continued to provide jobs for newly arriving immigrants like Johann Pritzlaff over the next decades.

The example of the Erie Canal's success inspired other states and some private groups to undertake their own projects, such as the Pennsylvania Main Line, the Chesapeake and Ohio Canal, and the Illinois and Michigan Canal, to name several. As the flow of immigration rose in the late 1820s and 1830s, work on the growing canal system became reliably and readily available to immigrants, who were recruited by labor brokers directly from the transatlantic ships. In the days before heavy construction machinery, thousands of workers were needed to do the hand-shovel labor required. Although immigrants of all nationalities found work along the canal, the Irish became the most prevalent workers on the common-labor jobs. The work was hard and dirty, but workers finishing one segment of a canal could usually depend on more work further on. Those who tired of the work might stay in the towns and country-side newly opened up by the canal.

It was highly significant that the rising tide of immigration coin-cided with one of the great construction booms in American trans-portation. When a depression struck after 1837, it brought about a sharp decline in both immigration and canal construction. States which had begun building great canal projects reeled toward bank-ruptcy and were unable to obtain the financing needed to continue the work. Since the transportation boom had fueled much of the rest of the economy, jobs in other sectors became scarce. And the word quickly spread abroad that jobs for new immigrants were not so easy to find. As the economy recovered by the mid-1840s, some canal construction began anew, but the emphasis was changing to railroad-building. There, too, immigrants could find abundant work grading and laying the rails for the new railroads. The decade after 1845 would prove to be one of the great railroad-building eras of American history. By 1855 something like a network of rails had developed, at least in the North, and railroads were about to reach the Mississippi. The heyday of the canals had passed.

Earlier-developing cities which had attracted the westering immigrants were along the river systems—cities like St. Louis, Cincinnati, Louisville, and Pittsburgh. As immigration increased through the port of New Orleans, the migration of immigrants up into the river systems increased. When the Erie Canal opened up travel into the Great Lakes, Cleveland, Chicago, Detroit, and Milwaukee became centers of immigrant life. The rural areas near such cities offered attractive sites for immigrant farmers, particularly Scandinavians and Germans, as well as for Dutch immigrants, particularly in Michigan. The canals began to open up other possibilities, especially in the interior regions of Indiana and Ohio. As immigrants flowed into these places, they estab-lished, by the mid-1840s, centers of immigrant life that would attract others in the great wave of migration that followed. Chain migration would work to build many of these places into bustling centers of immigrant life in the great wave of immigration that occurred after 1845.

NOTES

1. *Illustrated London News*, December 21, 1844.
2. Eric J. Evans, *The Forging of the Modern State: Early Industrial Britain, 1783–1870,* 2nd ed. (New York: Longman, 1996), 432.
3. Terry Coleman, *Going to America* (Garden City, N.J.: Doubleday Anchor Books, 1973), 56.
4. A. C. Buchanan, *Emigration Practically Considered* (London: Henry Colburn, 1828), 87, as found in Edwin C. Guillet, *The Great Migration: The Atlantic Crossing by Sailing-Ship since 1770* (New York: Thos. Nelson, 1937), 57.
5. Marcus Hansen, "The Second Colonization of New England," *New England Quarterly* 2 (1929): 544.
6. Deirdre M. Mageean, "Emigration from Irish Ports," *Journal of American Ethnic History* 13 (1993): 15.
7. Hermann Wätjen, *Aus der Frühzeit des Nordatlantikverkehrs: Studien zur Geschichte der deutschen Schiffahrt und deutschen Auswanderung nach den Vereinigten Staaten bis zum Ende des amerikanischen Bürgerkriegs* (Leipzig: Felix Meiner, 1932), 122–25.
8. Ibid., 17.
9. Dirk Hoerder, "The Traffic of Emigration via Bremen/Bremerhaven: Merchants' Interests, Protective Legislation, and Migrants' Experiences," *Journal of American Ethnic History* 13 (1993): 68–81 and Mack Walker, *Germany and the Emigration, 1816–1885* (Cambridge, Mass.: Harvard University Press, 1964), 87–93.
10. Wätjen, *Aus der Frühzeit des Nordatlantikverkehrs,* 113–15, 191–93.
11. Agnes Bretting and Hartmut Bickelmann, *Auswanderungsagenturen und Auswanderungsvereine im 19. und 20. Jahrhundert* (Stuttgart: F. Steiner, 1991), 25–30.
12. Michael Just, *Auswanderungen und Schiffahrtsinteressen* (Stuttgart: F. Steiner, 1992), 14–19 and Wätjen, *Aus der Frühzeit des Nordatlantikverkehrs,* 118.
13. Wätjen, *Aus der Frühzeit des Nordatlantikverkehrs,* 138–42.
14. Ibid., 142–44.
15. London *Times*, June 15, 1832, quoted in Guillet, *The Great Migration,* 90.
16. Coleman, *Going to America,* 151–59.
17. Robert G. Albion, *Square Riggers on Schedule: The New York Sailing Packets to England, France, and the Cotton Ports* (Princeton, N.J.: Princeton University Press, 1938), 202.
18. Robert G. Albion, *The Rise of New York Port, 1815–1860* (New York: Charles Scribner's, 1939), 345–46.

19. Anonymous, "A Steerage Emigrant's Journal from Bristol to New York," in *Chambers's Edinburgh Journal,* October 21, 1848; as quoted in Coleman, *Going to America,* 181.

20. Albion, *Rise of New York Port,* 221–22.

21. Testimony of Tobias Boudinot in a legislative committee report, as quoted in Friedrich Kapp, *Immigration, and the Commissioners of Emigration of the State of New York* (New York: Nation Press, 1870), 67.

22. Joseph Logsdon, "Immigration through the Port of New Orleans," in *Forgotten Doors: The Other Ports of Entry to the United States,* ed. M. Mark Stolarik (Philadelphia: Balch Institute Press, 1988), 107–8.

23. Fredric M. Miller. "Immigration through the Port of Philadelphia," in ibid., 51.

24. Dean R. Esslinger, "Immigration through the Port of Baltimore," in ibid., 67.

25. Oscar Handlin, *Boston's Immigrants: A Study in Acculturation,* 3d ed. (Cambridge, Mass.: Harvard University Press, 1979), 51–52 and Richard A. Meckel, "Immigration, Mortality and Population Growth in Boston, 1840–1880," *Journal of Interdisciplinary History* 15 (1985): 400.

26. Coleman, *Going to America,* 159. Coleman considers these figures incomplete.

27. Letter of William Morris to his brother in England, dated June 4, 1837, in Charlotte Erickson, *Invisible Immigrants: The Adaptation of English and Scottish Immigrants in Nineteenth-Century America* (Coral Gables, Fla.: University of Miami Press, 1972), 165.

28. Letter dated April 23, 1842, in Walter D. Kamphoefner, Wolfgang Helbich, and Ulrike Sommer, eds., *News from the Land of Freedom: German Immigrants Write Home,* trans. Susan Carter Vogel (Ithaca, N.Y.: Cornell University Press, 1991), 305–6.

4

Immigration at High Tide, 1845–1854

The year 1845 began a decade of great turbulence, both in the Americas and in Europe. Over those 10 years, societies on both continents experienced wars, revolutions, famines, epidemics, and rapid population growth. In North America, there was territorial expansion, a gold rush, an economic boom, the unprecedented expansion of the transportation network, dramatic improvements in communication and printing technologies, and the opening of new lands to settlers. As always, conditions such as these gave rise to complex movements of peoples, and brought about momentous changes in the lives of the people involved.

The effects of this migration were felt in European societies, in the booming transatlantic movement of ships, and ultimately within American societies, most especially in the United States. There also occurred the first significant movement of peoples from Asia to the United States. The population of the United States increased by seven million, by 1854 reaching about 35 percent above the 20-million level of 1844. These numbers included slightly more than three million immigrants who arrived during that period, with 1.3 million from Ireland, and just under a million from the German states.

Those newly arrived in America during this decade generally found the economic prospects to be encouraging. In the boom times, at least, jobs were available and new farming country was being opened up. Many newcomers, however, came with very few resources and had to find a place to settle immediately. In the major ports of entry, such as New York, there was considerable competition for jobs. As the established immigrant communities in the cities of the North were flooded with new arrivals, new immigrant enclaves were springing up in the West. Cities in the South where few immigrants had gone before now began to have significant populations of the foreign-born. The presence of the foreign-born, their ethnic and religious diversity, and their frequent state of poverty became much more visible to the native-born, and anti-immigrant feelings were on the rise. The emerging nativism would lead to social and political conflict in the early 1850s, and would become fixed as a more-or-less permanent theme in American society and politics. Life was different for the newly transplanted immigrants, but life in America would be different for everyone else as well.

How the many different social and economic changes of the period affected immigrants' lives defies easy explanation. But looking closely at some of the individual immigrants' experiences before and after their arrival can give us some understanding.

THE IRISH AND THE GREAT FAMINE

During the autumn of 1845, a new blight began to appear on the potato plants of Ireland. First noticed in the eastern part of the island, by October it was spreading westward and threatening to afflict the entire island. The causes of the disease, more ruinous than other blights Irish farmers had experienced in the previous decades, were not known. It was widely believed to have originated in America, where it had been seen the previous year. People blamed bad seed potatoes, various insects and worms, the use of guano manure fertilizer imported from South America, air pollution from industry or from steam locomotives, and even gas emitted by the newly developed sulphur matches.

The actual cause was a fungus, *Phytophtora infestans*, which was initially seen as a minute, whitish growth on the leaves of the infected plants. The tiny filaments of the fungus released very light spores, which were easily spread by the wind, and then were washed down by the rains into the ground where they could infect the potatoes themselves. Leaves of the infested plants turned black and shriveled, and the potatoes themselves became completely rotted.

The partial failure of the potato crop in 1845 sent shock waves through Ireland, since many of the poorest farmers and cottiers were solely dependent on the potato for their sustenance. But the crop failure was only partial, and Ireland produced about three-quarters of the normal amount of potatoes in that year. Hopes that the blight would disappear in the next year were dashed, however, and the crop of 1846 was a total failure. Many were discouraged from even planting potatoes in the following year, but in fact the meager amounts harvested in 1847 showed no signs of the blight. This encouraged widespread new planting of the potato, but the blight struck again, and 1848 saw a major failure of the crop. Potato crops recovered in subsequent years, but the blight remained a permanent threat for the rest of the century, and potato production, no longer relied upon by peasants as the sole source of nutrition, dropped drastically from pre-famine levels.

The Famine's Consequences

The long-term consequences of the famine were drastic changes in the life and economy of Ireland. Many thousands of Irish peasants and farm-workers abandoned the land or were driven from it. Marginal small-acreage farms were consolidated into larger holdings, and many lands formerly planted with crops were converted to pasturage. Increasing amounts of agricultural products were destined for export to the English economy. Crop diversification lessened the reliance on the potato. Landlords relied less on tenants and more on wage laborers. Agricultural employment declined steadily, and there was little compensating growth in urban and industrial employment. Emigration begun in the famine years continued steadily for the rest of the century, and the Irish population shrank from about 8 million in 1841 to 6.5 million in 1851 and to 4.4 million in 1911.

The long-term account, however, says little of the immediate impact of the famine on those who were caught up in the disaster. The famine is reckoned to have cost at least 1 million lives to starvation and disease; another 1.8 million Irish fled the country to North America; others went to England and Australia. For four years, a considerable portion of Irish residents were deprived of their usual supply of potatoes. Alternative sources of food were limited. The grain and livestock usually sold in the market, much of it exported to England, could be consumed, but this left no other income for the farmers, and many were unable to pay their rent. The landless cottiers might consume their own pigs, which they normally sold in the market, but doing so would leave them without their usual source of income.

Immediate hardship was felt especially by the poorest farmers and the landless cottiers, who had had little else to rely on except the potato for their food and for sales to cover their rent. Those who were able to scrape up some savings, or perhaps steal some money, might escape their debts and leave the country, fleeing either to England or to America. The years of the famine were full of grim tales of starvation, violence, abortive revolution, family desertion, crime, and heartlessness toward the deprived.

Relief Efforts

What passed for public relief in the 1840s was meager, and came generally too little and too late in the unfolding disaster. The established relief system provided regional workhouses, set up by the British Parliament in the Poor Law of 1838. The workhouses were intended to provide housing and food to the most impoverished, who were required to live in them and to labor on public works such as roads and bridges. The districts comprising a single workhouse union were required to support the workhouse with taxes collected from the landholders. This meant that an area where nearly everyone, whether landlord or tenant, was already without income was required to finance its own relief. One result was very strict restrictions on who might seek relief from the workhouses. In 1847 Parliament added an even more stringent requirement: anyone holding more than a quarter of an acre of land was required to relinquish it in order to be eligible for relief.

Evictions

This requirement removing impoverished tenants from the land accelerated a process that many landowners had already been pursuing in the decades before the famine—namely, the reduction of the number of tenants on estates and the combination of landholdings into more efficient parcels, which could be tilled by hired workers or used as pasture. Some landlords both before and during the famine would offer money to their tenants to emigrate, some even chartering a ship to carry them to the United States, Canada, or Australia.

However, some landlords (many of them absentee landlords), themselves without income and unable to pay any taxes, simply pressured the tenants to leave because they had not paid and could not pay the rent. Cottiers who were paupers could legally be evicted by being paid a sum, usually one to three pounds, after which they had to give up possession of their cabins, which were immediately leveled when the inhabitants vacated them. Tenants who were not able to pay the rent on their land were, on the demand of the landlord, issued a "warrant to distrain," which compelled them to leave. Any crops and cattle on the property could be seized by this warrant. Next, a "bill of ejectment" was issued by a court, compelling tenants to surrender and vacate their cabins. The bill would be enforced by police or military troops, driving inhabitants out into the road if necessary, whereupon their cabins would be tumbled.[1]

Estimates vary as to the number of evictions that took place during the famine. In 1841, the census had counted about 685,000 land holdings in Ireland. Of these, 135,000 were less than one acre.[2] Police and court records, which may yield underestimates, reflect nearly 145,000 evictions during the period from 1846 to 1854. The total number of people evicted was estimated at 579,000, out of a population of around seven million.[3] Many former tenants wandered the roadways of Ireland, sometimes huddled in makeshift huts along the way. The many who found no relief and no place to go added to the numbers heading to the ports to emigrate on whatever ship might take them.

Starvation and Desperation

For those who stayed, there was starvation and disease. Relief measures were slow and inadequate, and authorities in England, out of touch as they often were with Irish affairs, were accused of being insensitive to the plight of the starving. The workhouses which originally were expected to provide employment were hard put to raise enough taxes locally, as they were required to do. In 1845 and 1846, Parliament did vote for more money to fund public works, but administrators were begrudging in the distribution of the money. By 1846, about 30,000 workers were engaged in public projects in Ireland. The government of Sir Robert Peel believed that direct relief by importing food to Ireland was the best answer, and ships were chartered to bring Indian corn from America to feed the hungry. But those without work could not buy the grain, and many who were unfamiliar with the yellow corn refused to eat it. Peel's cabinet was replaced in 1846 by another under Lord John Russell. Russell believed relief should be provided by the local workhouses, but agreed also to supply imported food, which was to be distributed and sold by private interests. Distribution of the food was uneven, and many regions went without any food supply. By late 1846 there was extreme distress and mounting starvation. Lord Russell's government reluctantly agreed to fund new public works, but made it necessary for each project to receive approval from London, thus slowing the relief process. Eventually 700,000 were put to work, many of them no longer required to live in the workhouses, but food prices were still so high that many who were employed were unable to purchase food. Finally the government agreed to provide free food through committees outside the work-house system. About three million Irish, comprising 40 percent of the population, were receiving public support, usually through soup kitchens. Voluntary agencies, many organized by Quakers, and support from American Irish also contributed to relief. By the end of 1848, over a million Irish had died from either starvation or diseases brought on by lack of nutrition.[4]

The Progress of Famine in the West

The famine was particularly hard in the west of Ireland, where the soil was poorer, reliance on the potato was heavy, and the population was greatest. An example of how hardships of the time led to pressures for emigration can be seen in the village of Kiltimagh and its surrounding electoral district of Killedan, which were in County Mayo. Mayo county had one of the greatest population densities in Ireland, with well over four hundred persons per square mile. Kilti-magh, about seven miles to the southwest of Swinford, lay within the Swinford Union (one of 130 unions set up by the Poor Law of 1838).

In January 1846, the Board of Guardians of the Poor in Swin-ford sent a memorial to the Lord Lieutenant, the appointed ruler of Ireland, asking for relief funds to avert the deprivation already becoming apparent. The board had thought that the potato blight in 1845 had damaged only part of the crop, but now, as they opened up pits where potatoes had been stored, they found that two-thirds of them were useless. "Our hopes are frustrated and we much fear a great scarcity and consequently dread a famine unless the Gov-ernment shall afford prompt and effective assistance."[5] The relief that came was in the form of employment funds to pay the destitute who were in the union's workhouse and who were obliged to labor on public works. These individuals could then pay for food being imported, particularly Indian corn from the United States. But by September this relief system was clearly not working; there was insufficient money to pay the workers, and the supply of corn meal had been exhausted. The residents of Kiltimagh reported that there was no relief coming from either the local landlords or the Swinford Union. In their own petition to the Lord Lieutenant, they begged for relief by employment on the public works: "The number of persons daily snatched away, both by the pestilence and by the effects of hunger, is rapidly increasing. . . . The most wretched of us, being now driven to desperation by the effects of hunger and disease, are beginning to disregard the admonition of the most peaceable."[6] The relief committee at Swinford admitted that the whole program was a failure.

In January the Inspector General's representative at Swinford echoed the reports from the relief committee: "[Y]ou would be horrified could you only see the multitude of starving men, women and children, who daily and hourly swarm the town, soliciting with prayers and tears one meal of food. . . . The people appear to be paralysed from starvation. They tell me they must use their little seed for food, and when that is used they say 'they must lie down and die.'"[7] The threat of violence was growing; desperate men, women, and children reportedly had attacked the carts carrying the corn meal from the mill to the market. The chairman of the relief efforts at Swinford confessed to the Lord Lieutenant that all local efforts were exhausted, and that unless aid came from the outside, the cases of starvation would grow.

By early 1847, starving tenants were being driven off the land. The *Mayo Telegraph* published a letter from "a Kiltimagh man," describing ejectments from the estate of the Earl of Lucan, in the village of Treenagleragh, two miles from Kiltimagh:

All the oats belonging to three of the most destitute in the parish have been seized and canted by his lordship's driver and subsequently ejectment decrees have been obtained against them. . . . It was by his lordship's special directions the notices to quit were served on those parties. . . . The persons thus treated are Anthony Duncan, John Kelly and Widow Kilgallin. Again, what think you of the time that had been fixed for exacting the last November rent? During the late frost, deep snow and storm![8]

Later that spring the parish priest of Killedan, Father John Brennan, reported that from October 1, 1846 to April 1, 1847, 650 deaths had been reported in the parish, 400 of them due to the famine. In the same period the previous year, the death toll had been 80.[9]

During the same year there were efforts at private relief. The most active agency was the Central Relief Committee formed by the Society of Friends (i.e., the Quakers), which solicited funds both in Ireland and abroad. The committee concentrated its efforts in the west of Ireland, and established soup kitchens and provided money, clothing, and food to various parishes. The government also acted to provide soup kitchens. During the year 1847 there were reported 367 deaths in the Swinford union's workhouse, many of them from typhus. It was the disease as much as the starvation that caused the year 1847 to be regarded as The Famine Year or Black '47.

That same spring, the rate of emigration from the area rose sharply. Those who had some means for passage headed for the ports. Despite the reports of deaths from typhus which came back from Grosse Isle near Quebec and from other American ports, many from the west of Ireland felt they had no alternative but to emigrate. In September 1847, in reviewing the previous year, the Finance Committee of the Swinford Union told the Lord Lieutenant that during the previous winter, "Influenced by terror and dismay, leaving entire districts almost deserted, the better class of farmers in numbers sold their property at any sacrifice and took flight for America, and the humbler classes left the country in masses hoping to find a happier doom in any other region."[10]

While the potato crop of 1847 seemed to be free from the blight, the harvest was very lean. The government nevertheless declared the famine to be at an end and canceled most of the work-relief programs. To qualify for relief, it was now necessary to declare oneself a pauper and to give up any land held in excess of one-fourth of an acre. In early 1848 the number of paupers grew, and there were too many of them to be housed in the workhouse, which could only accommodate 700 people. The workhouse was threatened with a contagion of "spotted scarlet fever of the most malignant kind."[11] Increasingly there was no place within the district to go for help, and the pressures to emigrate grew.

The blight returned in 1848; the potato crop was worse than in any other famine year. Reports of starvation increased. Evictions and ejectments also continued. In Kiltimagh, in June, Lord Lucan again evicted the poorest tenants from his lands for lack of paying the rents. As the parish priest there, Father Daniel Mullarkey, reported in the *Freeman's Journal:*

On the 14th instant, the sheriff with a strong force of the police, arrived in the townland of Treenagleragh, parish of Killedan, county Mayo, with strict orders from the landlord, Lord Lucan, to execute the law by evicting the poor inhabitants. The townland is now made the theatre of many a melancholy and heartrending scene. The whole townland, I may say, presents the appearance of a battlefield the day after the fight—nothing to be seen but the shattered ruins of what were so lately the abodes of men. No less than thirty-three families, numbering in all one hundred and forty-five human beings, have been thrown on

Mourners accompany the coffin of a victim of the Irish famine through the streets of Skibbereen, County Cork. From *Illustrated London News*, February 13, 1847. Courtesy Swarthmore College Library, via Bryn Mawr College Library Special Collections.

the world. It would be impossible for me, Sir, to give you a full and fair description of the wretched and deplorable condition of these unfortunate creatures, stretched along ditches and hedges—many of them children and decrepit old parents—falling victims to cold and hunger and destitution.[12]

From Swinford it was reported that "three-quarters of the entire population are now reduced to utter destitution."[13] Both the Catholic priest and the Protestant minister at Kiltimagh begged the Quaker relief agency to send more food. Mortality increased in the workhouses, and, in the early winter, plans were made to export to Australia many of the orphans aged 14 to 18 who were living in the workhouses. By May 1849, Father Mullarkey of Kiltimagh was urged by his parishioners to write an impassioned letter to Lord John Russell, Britain's prime minister. He spoke of both the suffering in his parish and of the failure of the relief system, still based upon the workhouses and financed only by taxes upon the lands in the district:

This is partly the wretchedness to which we are reduced—our towns, our villages, in distemper, in disease; friends turn from friends either by death or emigration; some running to the poorhouse, some crying for relief. Dead bodies without a covering, and thousands without shelter, all occasioned by cruel landlords and defective legislation. . . .

What is to become of them? If they go to the poorhouse the landlords are empowered to tumble their houses and seize their crops, both themselves and their descendants become for ever beggars, and will continue to entail additional misery, and wretchedness on those who may survive the dread calamity that now afflict[s] us all.[14]

Little was done to provide more relief. A grant of funds by Parliament to the workhouse unions in February 1849 was the last from that source. The potato crop of 1849, still smaller than those of pre-famine days, was relatively free from blight, and British officials concluded that the famine had run its course. Queen Victoria visited Ireland in August to affirm that the famine had ended; she traveled by yacht between the eastern ports of Belfast, Dublin, and Cork, and saw little of the countryside.

The crop of 1850 was better, but the economic devastation of the previous years did not disappear completely, and the numbers of emigrants continued to mount, reaching a peak in 1852. The census of 1851 revealed that in the preceding decade the population of the parish of Killedan had declined by nearly 20 percent, from 6,410 to 5,152, as a result of both deaths and emigration.[15] There were 169 fewer houses than a decade before. Many other districts saw greater losses. The famine was over, but emigration continued in the years afterward. From fear of disease and starvation, from complete abject poverty, from lack of housing, from sheer desperation, many from Kiltimagh had taken flight, leaving behind what few possessions they had remaining, heading to the nearest port, there to take ship for America if they could, and if not, to flee across the Irish Sea and hope for some livelihood and whatever relief they could find.

A Desperate Swarm

For seven years as the famine waxed and waned, the tide of emigrants fleeing Ireland continued. From the countryside, people without relief from starvation and those evicted from their homes headed for the nearest port, some of them pushing handcarts filled with their remaining earthly possessions, hoping to find some way to board an emigrant ship. There were also workers from the few industrial areas, mostly the linen factories in the North, who suffered the loss of jobs during the economic panic of the same years. The emigrants of necessity sought the cheapest routes and the lowest fares. Ports in the West of Ireland which had not been so frequently used in the previous decades now offered passage on lumber ships returning to Canada or grain ships arriving from America with relief provisions. Steerage rates were generally lower than those in the pre-famine years. From Londonderry, the northernmost port in Ireland, McCorkell & Co. charged fares of $12–15 to Saint John, New Brunswick; $17.50 to New York; $20 to Philadelphia; and $25 to New Orleans. Irish ports could not provide enough ships bound directly for America, so many migrants chose to take the steamers to Liverpool. The poorest might get no further. Lacking any means to take a transatlantic ship, they filled the slums of Liverpool and other English cities and sought whatever factory and common-labor jobs they could find. Others more fortunate boarded ships for Canada or the United States. Since the most available and least expensive ships were bound for Saint John and New York, these locations became the destinations for many.

SOCIAL AND POLITICAL UNREST IN EUROPE

On the European continent, the early 1840s saw the culmination of many of the economic and social tensions which had been developing slowly ever since the Napoleonic Wars. In the German states in particular, growing population pressures, the beginning stages of the Industrial Revolution, the decline and stagnation of small village life, and the fragmentation of small farms, combined to bring the economy and society to a critical state by 1845.

Agricultural Distress and Its Consequences

The states of southwestern Germany, already a large source of emigration, were struck in 1845 by the potato blight, which was felt in other parts of Europe as it was in Ireland. It was the marginal small farmers there who were particularly affected, since they had the heaviest reliance on the potato, both for food and for income. But the crop failure would affect other sectors of society as well. The potato blight struck at a time when the price of food was generally increasing. A contributing factor was an outbreak of wheat rust, another fungus, which reduced wheat crops in central Europe. Greater market demand also contributed to the rising cost of food. In 1846, the second year of the Irish famine, Britain repealed its Corn Laws (which imposed tariffs on agricultural produce imported from outside Britain), thus opening its markets to produce from the continent. The new competition for foodstuffs worked to raise European prices drastically. As in Ireland, the failure of the potato crop in 1845 was partial, but in 1846 it was nearly complete. The hot summer of that year also produced the worst grain crop in decades. Within a short time the price of basic foodstuffs doubled.[16] By 1847 there was a full-scale recession, and there were food riots in Silesia, Berlin, and many other German states, as well as in France.

There was no catastrophic famine on the continent as there was in Ireland. For one thing, the agricultural economy was more diversified, and not so heavily dependent on one crop. For another, the harvest of potatoes and grain recovered in 1847, and remained plentiful for the next several years. Food prices declined, although they would rise again in the mid-1850s. Also, the effects of the food shortages were moderated by effective intervention from many of the German states, which opened soup kitchens, subsidized the importation of food, and prohibited food exports. The contrast with the slower response of the British government in Ireland was striking.

Economic distress in the countryside was felt by people other than the farmers. The artisans and shopkeepers in the country villages found no market for their wares, and many of them gave up and made their way to German industrial areas or to America. The market for manufactured goods also shrank, leading to layoffs and unemployment in the factory towns and great cities. Wage levels also declined for those who kept their jobs; the average wage in Germany declined by about 20 percent during the 1840s.[17] The increasing numbers of unemployed workers and individuals on public relief increased sharply in 1847 and 1848. The growing numbers of the discontented would be an important factor in both emigration and in the revolutions.

Even before revolutions broke out in 1848, the flow of German emigrants to America had begun to rise, from around 20,000 in 1844 to 74,000 in 1847. In contrast to the middle-class types that had characterized most German emigration since the 1820s, the migrants increasingly came from the lower economic strata. The sources of migration were now more often found in the northern and eastern parts of Germany. The failure of grain crops in 1846 was felt particularly in the eastern provinces. On the great estates there, farm workers were mostly wage laborers with no claim to the land, and landlords were finding ways to remove surplus laborers from the land as they consolidated their estates.

Conditions were such as to make emigration easier and to create competition for the emigrant trade. Seaports in Belgium and the Netherlands competed with Hamburg and Bremen, and Liverpool still claimed to offer the cheapest route of emigration. Newly built railroads offered cheap fares to various ports. Ship owners also joined the competition for the emigrant business. For those turned loose from the land or from their occupations, the decision to emigrate was made easier. Those who still had some claim to a piece of land might choose to wait a little longer, until depressed land values would rise again and help to finance their emigration.

Some states and communities offered subsidies to emigrants. They were faced with the problem of supporting them at home, and the cost of emigration was cheaper than continuing to provide relief for the unemployed. In August 1846, a group of emigrants arrived in New York City from the Hessian province of Stackenburg. They were penniless, unable to travel further, and immediately became burdens upon the city. They had been sent by the town of Grosszimmern, which had simply used its poorhouse funds to send the most desperate, undesirable, and allegedly criminal elements to America. The German Society of New York, completely unable to provide help to such a number, wrote an angry letter to the government of Hesse, leading to public denunciations and a heated exchange. Nativist elements in the United States cited this event as a prime example of the deleterious foreign influence, and the public image of German emigration was severely damaged.

The Revolutions of 1848

Economic historians afterward would look at Europe's economic problems of the 1840s as growing pains that were part of the rapid transition of the economy to one of greater industrialization, wider-reaching commerce and trade, and more efficient agricultural production. But the end result of this transition could not be foreseen at the time by those who were displaced, starving, unemployed, or left homeless in the process. That the reaction of the unfortunate could lead to political unrest was not surprising. Although the economy was in some recovery by 1848, there was much dissatisfaction remaining among those affected by the recession. The principal stimulus to revolution, however, would come from other elements, especially those among the professional and upper middle classes, such as lawyers, journalists, merchants, university professors and their students, and, of course, politicians.

There had been slowly developing dissatisfaction in the German states, Prussia, and the provinces of the Austrian Empire over the lack of true constitutional and representative government. During hard times, this dissatisfaction easily translated into stronger political opposition to the established regimes, including the Austrian and Prussian monarchies. Calls for a broader franchise, stronger legislatures, and constitutions were heard across Europe. Significantly, the author of *Democracy in America*, Alexis de Tocqueville, arose in the French Chamber of Deputies in January 1848 to call for reform and a wider franchise, lest more radical elements turn dissatisfaction into revolution. Republicanism, perceived by many European intellectuals in the model of the American experience, became the watchword of the advocates of reform. To this would be joined another ideal, that of nationalism, particularly in the German states, where those who aspired to greater power were frustrated by the patchwork of divided and absolutist governments.

In late 1847, various efforts to reform governments had met with stiff resistance from autocratic regimes. In early 1848, things took a more violent turn. In February, street demonstrations turned to uprisings in Paris, and King Louis-Philippe of France abdicated. Responding to the pressure of the crowds, the French Parliament proclaimed a republic. This sudden success of the republican movement inspired similar actions elsewhere. Insurgents manned the barricades in Munich, Vienna, Budapest, Venice, Cracow, and Berlin. In what would be known as the March Days in Berlin, Prussia's King Frederick William yielded to the crowds behind the barricades, declaring that he would lead the German people and that Prussia would be "merged in Germany." His bow to nationalism as well as reform inspired renewed efforts toward republicanism and nationalism across the German states. The result was a revolutionary assembly, organized by liberal elements from many German states, which met at Frankfurt am Main in late May 1848. The Frankfurt Parliament, comprised mostly of educated and professional elements, held painstaking debates and constructed a constitution, which it announced in March 1849. The constitution created a federal, united Germany (which excluded Austria); an elected parliament with great control over government administration; and a hereditary emperor, whose power was limited to a veto that could suspend but not reject legislation. The Parliament elected King Frederick William of Prussia to be the emperor of the united Germany. But within a month the king refused to accept the crown and the constitution, since both came from a popularly elected body and therefore denied the divine right of kings. The Parliament disbanded, and the effort for a united Germany had clearly failed.

The Refugees of 1848 in America

Over the next year, revolutionary efforts in the states within the Austrian empire also failed, and a strong reaction against the revolutionary participants followed. Thus began the emigration of a famous but very diverse group of people displaced by the revolutions. Some had taken part in the Frankfurt Parliament. Others had led armed rebellions in various states. Some had been imprisoned when suspected of planning revolutionary efforts. As the reaction strengthened, the tide of émigrés grew. Some fled to Switzerland or England, then eventually found their way to America. Some hesitated for a while, hoping for a new effort to achieve nationalism and republicanism, but that never took shape. Slowly a disorganized group of refugees known as forty-eighters began to establish themselves in America. The group included former professors, lawyers, journalists, government officials, engineers, intellectuals, and many ordinary farmers and workmen who had been caught up in the revolutionary tide.

The forty-eighters, most of whom had not planned to go to America, were often perplexed about how they would fit in or what they could do to support themselves. Some waited, hoping for a revival of revolutionary efforts in Germany, and hoping as well that Americans would rally to assist the cause. By late 1850, however, it was becoming clear that the reaction was firmly in control in Europe and that the Americans were entirely distracted by the booming territorial and economic expansion that was just unfolding in their own country. Many of the refugees of 1848 then had to accept the reality of a long-term stay in the American Republic.

Most had to struggle to overcome the difficulties posed by this unexpected change in their lives. Lawyers found they had to learn English and a whole new legal system. Journalists were left to ply their trade within the German-language newspaper press, which, fortunately for them, was rapidly expanding at the time. Others found trades or places of employment within the German communities, whose reception of the refugees was not always warm. Eventually some of the newcomers would begin to enter the political realm, often raising questions about the traditional politics of German-Americans and becoming a disruptive force within the American political parties, which would soon be troubled by further disruptions during the 1850s.

There were no typical forty-eighters. They were too diverse a group for that. The most famous of them all was Carl Schurz. As a young student still in his teens at the University of Bonn, he had been influenced by the nationalist professor Gottfried Kinkel and had joined the revolutionary forces when revolution broke out in 1848. He took part in several encounters as a lieutenant of revolutionary forces, especially in the Grand Duchy of Baden. When the revolutionary forces there were surrounded by the Prussian army in the town of Rastatt, Schurz escaped through a sewer and fled to France. His return to Germany under a false passport was for the purpose of rescuing his former professor Kinkel, who had been jailed by the Prussians in the fortress of Spandau near Berlin. Schurz, in a dangerous undertaking, bribed a guard, freed Kinkel, and escaped with him on a rope lowered from the roof of the prison. The two then found their way to England, where Schurz remained as a teacher for two years.

In 1852, seeing that there was no longer hope of a revolution in Germany, Schurz came to America. He lived for four years in Philadelphia, then went to join the growing Wisconsin German communities, settling in Watertown. By 1857 Schurz was able to become a citizen and began to participate in American politics. The new Republican party offered an opportunity to become involved in the slavery controversy then transforming politics on the national scene. Having achieved some status in the Wisconsin party, Schurz supported Abraham Lincoln in the election of 1860 and went on to organize the immigrant vote for the party in that crucial election. He would be rewarded by being appointed minister to Spain, but would return a year later to serve as a general in the Union army in the Civil War. After the war he turned to journalism, becoming editor of a St. Louis-based German newspaper in 1867. As a Missouri resident, he served a term as a U.S. senator, and also allied himself with the Liberal Republican movement against Ulysses Grant in the election of 1872. Upon the election of Rutherford Hayes to the presidency in 1876, Schurz was named Secretary of the Interior. In 1880 he returned to journalism as editor of the New York-based *Evening Post.* He continued to be involved in reform politics, and in his later years wrote and lectured extensively. Schurz's spectacular rise in American politics was due to a number of factors, including his willingness to adjust to the American system, his command of the English language, his ability to act as a spokesman for German citizens (not all of whom accepted his leadership), and his strong sense of the realities of American politics.

There were only a few hundred genuine forty-eighters—that is, members who had actively participated in the European revolutions and had been forced to leave after revolution failed. Their varied careers and exploits defy easy categorization. Some, like Schurz, would apply military skills gained in the revolutions to the American struggle during the Civil War—such as Franz Sigel, who had been a military leader of the revolution in Baden. After coming to America in 1852, he avoided politics and taught in schools in New York and St. Louis, but then was drawn into the conflict at the outbreak of the Civil War and became one of the most famous (and controversial) generals of the Union Army. Others entered the world of German-American journalism, like Georg Schneider, who developed Chicago's *Illinois Staats-Zeitung* into a leading force in the new Republican party, and served as a consul in Denmark during Abraham Lincoln's presidency. Most forty-eighters would tie themselves to the Republican party after 1854, but some, like Oswald Ottendorfer, who became the editor of the powerful *New Yorker Staats-Zeitung,* would continue throughout his career as a supporter of the reform elements of the Democratic party. There were women forty-eighters, too, such as Anna Mathilde Anneke, wife of a revolutionary officer in Baden, who had published feminist tracts there and who would go on to establish a feminist newspaper, the *Deutsche Frauenzeitung,* in Milwaukee. Others would find pursuits in realms other than politics, such as Friedrich Hedde, a lawyer and journalist in Schleswig-Holstein. Hedde became a pioneering developer in the new Nebraska Territory, founded the town of Grand Island, and eventually became an agent in Germany promoting settlement in Nebraska. Some forty-eighters would eventually return to Germany. Karl Griesinger, for example, who published a satirical periodical in Stuttgart, turned his satirical work to current political events during the 1848 revolution and was imprisoned for high treason in the fortress of Hohenasperg. He was released when an amnesty was declared, and decided in 1852 to settle in New York; however, unable as a writer to adjust to the American environment, he returned to Germany in 1857 and published works about America for German consumption. Another young intellectual and writer, Christian Essellen, came to America in 1852 and tried to practice journalism in several cities. He took his struggling literary journal *Atlantis* with him; in it he published serially his own epic poem, *Babylon,* which was based on the 1848 revolutions. His career was cut short when he died in 1859 at the age of 36. Many of the forty-eighters simply settled in a German-American community, took up their old professions, and joined the German social organizations that were developing wherever Germans congregated. Seldom in American life has such a small group of immigrants made such a profound impact on the life of an ethnic group.

AMERICA: EXPANDING BUT
NOT ALWAYS WELCOMING

The rising tide of emigration over the decade after 1845 brought newly arrived immigrants to the ports of the East Coast and to New Orleans, spread inward through the waterways and along the newly built railroads, and added increased foreign population to communities both old and new. The annual influx of Germans, which had been numbered at 15,000 in 1841, reached 74,000 in 1847; mounted to 145,000 in 1852; and peaked at 215,000 in 1854. The Irish, who had numbered about 38,000 newcomers in 1841, counted 106,000 arrivals in 1847; 221,000 in 1851; and 102,000 in 1854. British immigration to America remained more stable. From 23,000 in 1847, British immigrants mounted to 55,000 in 1849; declined to 41,000 in 1852; rose to 59,000 in 1854; and remained above 45,000 annually until 1858.

From 1854 to 1855, total immigration dropped by over half, from 428,000 to 201,000. By that time, the dynamic forces that had propelled the European emigrants in the previous decade were beginning to change. The European economy was improving; the severe problems of food shortage were passing; and political peace, albeit the product of reaction, was returning. In America, however, the economic boom was noticeably weakening. By late 1854 there were many business failures and bankruptcies. Unemployment, especially among the working class, was growing. In 1854 the Crimean War, which brought together England and the major powers of the continent against Russia, caused those powers to restrict the emigration of those who were liable for military service, and raised the costs of shipping. But another influence causing Europeans to decide against emigration was the news being relayed across the waters in late 1854: the long-smoldering animosities among Americans against immigrants, which had been growing with the tide of new arrivals during the previous decade, had finally reached heated and even violent heights.

The Rise of Nativism

Nativism—the fear of immigrants and the opposition to their influence in American society—was not a new phenomenon. The anti-Catholicism that was one of the principal elements of nativism had flourished in largely Protestant America since its colonial origins, and it stretched back at least as far as the English Reformation. By the second quarter of the nineteenth century, as Catholics, most of them Irish, began to become a more visible element in the growing country, anti-Catholicism became linked especially to the defense of republicanism. Immigrants, especially "priest-ridden," illiterate Catholics, were said to be unsuited to democracy and liable to undermine the entire political system with their corrupt ways. During the 1830s, nativist writers began to speak of insidious Catholic plots to take over the United States. The supposed villains behind this alleged conspiracy were European missionary societies that encouraged the emigration of Catholics to the New World. This was one of the principal themes of Samuel F. B. Morse, an artist later to become famous as the inventor of the telegraph, who in 1835 published *Foreign Conspiracy against the Liberties of the United States,* exposing the supposed "papist plots" in considerable detail. Others, like Lyman Beecher in *A Plea for the West* (1835), raised the fear that the immigrants pouring into the Mississippi Valley during the considerable wave of expansion then taking place were about to become the majority there and displace the republican ideals supported by American Protestantism. Beecher bemoaned the "rapid influx of foreign emigrants, unacquainted with our institutions, unaccustomed to self-government, inaccessible to education, and easily accessible to prepossession, and inveterate credulity, and intrigue, and easily embodied and wielded by sinister design."[18] The sinister designs, in Beecher's view, emanated from the papacy and from the despotic governments of Europe.

But probably more influential in the American popular mind were the salacious tales depicting the lustful lives of priests and the debauchery occurring in convents. Most famous of these was Maria Monk's *Awful Disclosures of the Hotel Dieu Nunnery of*

Montreal (1836), with its accounts of the author's abuse in the convent by priests and nuns, and of her escape after having been made pregnant by a priest. Despite clear evidence that the whole story was a fabrication and that the author had never been in that convent at all, the book, which Maria Monk had been encouraged by a group of Protestant clergymen to write, took on a life of its own and became the largest best-seller of its time. Perhaps 300,000 copies were in print by the time of the Civil War.

Nativism also aimed at targets other than Catholicism. The movement saw itself as one part of the more general social reform movement of the time. Its various and sometimes conflicting aspects included feminism, peace reform, educational reform, prison reform, Sabbatarianism (a movement to preserve the sanctity of Sunday), anti-Catholicism, and temperance reform. These objectives, emanating in complex ways from Enlightenment ideals and evangelical religion, aimed at purifying the American Republic and ridding it of outmoded European traditions. Thus, nativist reformers feared European immigrants as threats to the existence of the entire republic, because they failed to live up to the ideals of the Enlightenment and evangelical Protestantism, customarily indulged in alcoholic drink, profaned the Sabbath with their noisy celebrations, and debased the democratic process by providing masses of votes for political machines. These accusations were lodged at Germans as well as Irish, and could even extend to the more radical Germans from the revolutions of 1848. The immigrants repaid the insults of the reformers in kind. The Germans called them *Mucker*—bigots or hypocrites. Some of the reformers began to turn toward antislavery views. Lyman Beecher's sermons argued that both the presence of immigrants and the presence of slavery were threats to the future of the West. Immigrants complained that these zealots wanted to free the black people but enslave the immigrant with hostile laws and regulations. It was no wonder that the foreign-born did not join the abolitionist movement in large numbers.

Nativism Takes a Violent Turn

As the number of new immigrants rose during the 1830s, tensions between the foreign-born and nativists increased, and violence over the issue of immigration became more common. A signal event was the destruction of an Ursuline convent in Charlestown, near Boston, in August 1834. Aroused by some heated sermons in Boston by Lyman Beecher, a mob, intent upon investigating rumors of imprisoned nuns, descended upon the convent. When entry was refused by the mother superior, the mob stormed the building and set fire to it. As emotions rose, political alignments began to reflect the divisions over immigration. When the Democratic party was assailed for exploiting immigrant votes, the immigrants themselves (and particularly the Irish) tightened their relationship with the party. The opposition party, the Whigs, began to harbor more of the nativists, and the process of polarization continued. From 1834 to 1844, rioting and conflict between Irish and nativist gangs was a regular feature of elections in New York and Philadelphia. By 1844, an openly nativist party, the American Republicans, won the municipal elections in New York City.

Nativist agitation was also reaching its peak in Philadelphia at about the same time. In late 1842, the Catholic bishop there, Francis Kenrick, echoing a complaint heard earlier in New York City, protested that the Catholic children attending public schools were obliged to listen to readings from the Protestant Bible, with no opportunity to hear the Catholic version. The school board decided to allow children to use either Bible. Militant Protestant groups took this decision as evidence that the Catholic Church was dictating educational policy with the objective of eliminating Protestantism from the schools. By March and April 1844, tensions were mounting when the nativist American Republican party determined to hold a meeting in Kensington, an industrial suburb heavily populated by Irish Catholic workers. An Irish mob gathered and broke up the meeting. Defiantly, the American Republicans announced their intention to meet again in Kensington on May 3; they were again driven away by an Irish mob. The new nativist paper, the *Native American,* beat the drum to persuade nativists of all sorts to attend a new rally on the sixth of May. Several thousand turned up, only to be dispersed by a heavy rain; but as they marched toward an indoor meeting-place, shots rang out and a nativist was mortally wounded. Again an Irish mob dispersed the nativists. On the seventh of May, the nativists gathered in the center of the city, marched into Kensington, and in the ensuing brawls over thirty Irish homes and an Irish fire company, the Hibernia Hose, were burned to the ground before militia intervened. The rioting, now out of control, resumed the next day, when nativist mobs once again invaded the Irish district, this time setting fire to two Catholic churches, St. Michael's and St. Augustine's. Both were completely destroyed by fire. At least fourteen people (on both sides) were killed in the riots.

Contemporary drawing of the nativist riot in the heavily Irish suburb of Kensington near Philadelphia, May 1844. The nativists are shown on the left, wearing tall beaver hats. At least fourteen people died in two days of rioting. From *A Full and Complete Account of the Late Awful Riots in Philadelphia* (Philadelphia: John B. Perry, n. d. [1844]). Courtesy McGarrity Collection, Villanova University Library.

A period of uneasy calm followed in the aftermath of the May riots, but more violence flared up in early July. Nativist mobs gathered at another Catholic church, St. Philip Neri, in the nearby suburb of Southwark. There were reports that rifles had been brought into the church to be used for its defense. On July 5 a nativist mob assembled outside the church, demanding that the weapons be given up. The sheriff arrived, and, to placate the crowd, brought about the surrender of some of the firearms and stationed guards in the church. The crowd remained, however, and the next day the sheriff returned and brought in militia units. He finally persuaded the crowd to disperse. But when it was discovered that one of the militia units left in charge of the church was an Irish unit, the Hibernia Greens, the crowd reassembled, this time bringing cannons and laying siege to the church. Although an agreement had been reached to remove the militia and replace them with a group set up by the nativist leaders, the crowd rebelled and ransacked the church. The crowd failed in its attempt to set fire to the building. The continuing mayhem was halted only when the governor sent a strong force of militia to evict the nativists from the church. This was accomplished only after a night-long battle. By the morning of July 8, the official count of casualties was 14 dead and 50 wounded. Many suspected that the toll was considerably higher.

Nativism Turns to Political Organization

While many feared that the nativist violence would spread to other cities, the aftermath of the Philadelphia riots saw a quieting of nativist passions, as many who had held nativist views decried the resort to rioting and violence. Perhaps one reason for the decline was that the nativist agitation in Philadelphia (and elsewhere) had brought together two elements, the middle-class reformers and the working-class natives. The workingmen's antagonisms against the foreign-born were fueled by competition for jobs, especially in hard times. The native-born workers in the nativist riots were often joined by other immigrant groups of longer standing, such as the Protestant Irish and English. However, in the late 1840s competition for employment diminished as the economy expanded and new territories opening up in the West provided more opportunities.

But the more ideological forms of nativism grew in the late 1840s, as the tides of emigrants from Europe grew. With a renewed fear of the death of American republicanism, reformers began to resort to government intervention to subdue what they perceived to be the most obnoxious elements of the immigrant culture. While it was nearly impossible to stop or restrict the flow of immigrants into the country, advocates for reform began to propose ways to restrict the voting power of new immigrants, thus preventing the use of the foreign-born as so-called voting cattle of urban political machines. Before the Fourteenth Amendment to the Constitution, citizenship rights were in the hands of the individual states. Thus some reformers called for state laws postponing the acquisition of voting rights after naturalization; a common proposal was that 21 years must pass before the immigrant could vote.

Other legislative initiatives aimed at discouraging the supposed deleterious habits of the immigrants, particularly their violation of the Sabbath and their customary heavy drinking. The temperance movement, previously a crusade mostly of evangelical preaching, turned to legislation to impose its standards upon the immigrants. The first such law to appear was in Maine in 1851, where the production and sale of alcohol was generally prohibited. The so-called Maine Law led to similar moves in other states, and remained a live issue throughout the 1850s. Another initiative against the immigrant culture stemmed from Sabbatarianism, the Puritan tradition from colonial days of keeping the Sabbath holy, which was now enforced in many places by Sunday closing laws. In larger cities such laws were passed requiring all retailers of alcohol to close on Sunday (the only day of rest for most working people). The Irish saloons, often condemned as dens of iniquity, and the German beer halls were threatened by such laws in many municipalities. Inveighing against the hypocrisy of the temperance reformers who held a rally in New York City in September 1849 supporting Sunday closing laws, the New York *Irish American* complained:

Whilst wines and brandies are imported, sold and consumed by the rich; whilst the "upper ten" guzzle, and swill, and get drunk with impunity, the working man's lips are to be padlocked, the liquor stores shut up, and the beer cask spilled into the channel. . . . [D]o not make one law for the rich and another for the poor.[19]

The Germans often responded to such opposition by moving their Sunday activities to beer gardens just outside the city limits. Legislation aimed at the immigrant lifestyle probably had little effect in discouraging new immigration, but it certainly had its effect on the political allegiances of the immigrants during the turbulent times of party realignments in the mid-1850s.

In the early 1850s, the American party emerged as the first national party to put forth an anti-immigrant platform. The party was based upon a coalescing of various anti-immigrant organizations, some of them secret organizations like New York's Order of the Star Spangled Banner. Its prohibition of members' revealing the order's activities led to the popular name "Know-Nothings," which was eventually applied to the American party itself. The party's brief flowering and subsequent decline in the mid-1850s had its influence in the growing sectional party conflicts, and influenced the direction of immigrant politics as well.

Historians have attributed the rise of nativism in the 1830s and 1840s to the nation's difficult adjustment to the rapid growth of the country and to industrialization. Both the middle-class reformers and working-class native-born Americans feared the disappearance of older and simpler ways of life. Small towns and villages, with long-held Protestant values and styles of life, seemed to be yielding to more diversified cities and towns, populated by the tide of immigrants, as Lyman Beecher had warned in his *A Plea for the West*. Industrialization displaced old-time artisans and small shops; there was little room for them in the great factories now appearing. Immigrants flowing into the Northeast provided cheap labor for its factories, displacing native workers such as the factory girls of the old New England textile mills. Immigrants in their restless search for a place in American society seemed to symbolize disorder, cultural decline, and an uncontrolled threat to the democratic ideals of the republic.

MANIFEST DESTINY AND THE ERA OF EXPANSION

The swelling of the tides of incoming immigrants coincided with the culmination of Americans' fascination with the doctrine of Manifest Destiny, an almost religious faith that God had given the United States a mandate to expand its republican sway across the continent, and even elsewhere in the world. Manifest Destiny found concrete expression during the 1840s in the movement to annex Texas; the acquisition of California and the Southwest in the wake of the Mexican War; and the settlement of the so-called Oregon Question through a treaty with Britain (1846), which gave the United States all of the Columbia River region south of the 49th parallel. The result was an increasing westward flow of the population into recently developing areas of the Midwest and on into the newly acquired regions toward the Pacific. The railroads, now technologically improved, began to replace the waterways as the most efficient means of transportation, and were facilitating the growing flow of commerce between east and west. One of the greatest waves of railroad-building in the country's history occurred between 1848 and 1854, opening up previously undeveloped areas in the upper Mississippi Valley to settlement and spawning new cities and towns located away from the major waterways. Immigrants, once the primary source of labor for the nation's canals, began to apply their labor to the building of the new rail lines. Immigrants bent upon taking up a farm poured into the public lands which were being made accessible by the railroads. New states were admitted to the Union, including Iowa in 1846, Wisconsin in 1848, Minnesota in 1858. Immigrants who lived in the older communities of the East now were drawn to the greater opportunities offered by the new towns springing up in the West.

As the railroad network expanded to the Mississippi River by 1854 and pushed onward across Missouri to the Missouri River by 1859, the lure of the faraway Pacific grew steadily. In the 1820s and 1830s there had been a trickle of pioneers passing down the Oregon and Santa Fe Trails. Some adventuresome immigrants had been among them. In the early 1840s the Oregon country, particularly the Willamette Valley, began to attract a steady stream of migrants. In 1847 the Mormons fleeing Illinois began their settlement of the Great Salt Lake Valley, in the false confidence that they would be far from the governmental reach of both Mexico and the United States. The coming of the Mexican War, the acquisition of California and the Southwest, and the discovery of gold in California would change the picture of Western settlement dramatically. All of these events would also affect the fate of many of the swarms of immigrants entering the country at the same time.

THE MEXICAN WAR

In early 1846 the United States declared war on Mexico. The war stemmed from the 1845 annexation of Texas, which had been an independent republic since its revolution against Mexico in 1836. Mexico had never recognized Texas's independence, and when Mexican troops crossed the Rio Grande into territory claimed by the United States and now defended by an American army, the skirmish that resulted on April 25, 1846, caused President James K. Polk to ask two weeks later for a declaration of war. Historians since have surmised that Polk was intent upon claiming more territory in the Southwest, even California and its Pacific ports, but in any event American troops were marshaled to invade Mexico, both through New Mexico and by an invasion from the sea at Vera Cruz.

Immigrants in the Army

Immigrants had been a major component in the enlisted ranks of the army long before the outbreak of the war. Recruiting of enlisted men was centered in the northeastern cities and towns and drew heavily on members of the wage-earning classes, especially those who might be out of work because of declines in the economic cycle or hard times in the factories. Immigrants were a large proportion of people in such circumstances. In the 1840s, many immigrant laborers on the canals lost their jobs as canal construction began to decline, and found their way into the army. And the peak of the immigrant tide in the late 1840s brought many in the immigrant ships who saw few other options when they arrived. An estimated 40 percent of army recruits during the 1840s were immigrants. A prohibition against recruiting the unnaturalized was frequently bypassed, and in 1847 the prohibition was removed. When immigrants were rejected by the recruiters, it was usually for the reason that they could not speak English. As the midcentury tide of immigration reached its peak in 1850 and 1851, immigrants accounted for over 70 percent of recruits coming into the regular army.[20]

Life was hard in the army. Privates were paid $7.00 per month, plus $3.50 for clothing. Food was supposedly provided, but soldiers in the field often had to forage for their own. Military posts were far removed from the rest of society, and the everyday regime of the peacetime army was unremitting drudgery. Officers, often intent upon proving their superior status, imposed harsh discipline. Flogging, still a legal means of discipline in the 1840s, was frequent. The rate of desertion was high. Some estimates were that as many as 30 percent of recruits deserted during their term of service. Immigrants enlisted in the army directly off the arriving ships, in the hopes that the army would pay for their transportation to the West, after which they would soon desert. Many soldiers saw desertion as the only way out of an enlistment contract that called for a five-year term of service. Discipline was meted out quickly upon any soldier suspected of planning desertion.

For Catholic immigrant soldiers, a particular grievance was the anti-Catholic culture that pervaded the military, especially the officer corps. Soldiers were routinely required to attend religious services, and the chaplain was almost invariably Protestant. A soldier serving with Zachary Taylor's army along the Rio Grande in the months before the war complained that although about two-thirds of the troops were Catholic, the enlisted men were compelled "to attend the services of a Presbyterian minister, whose words are mainly directed to insulting, calumniating and abusing the Catholic Church."[21] Some Catholic soldiers along the border, and later within Mexico, went off to attend Mass in the local parishes of the Mexicans, raising accusations of disloyalty. After war was declared, President Polk appointed two Catholic priests to serve as chaplains with the army in Mexico.

Militia and Volunteers

At the outset of the war President Polk sent out a call to the states for 50,000 volunteers to add to the regular army forces. The standard source of volunteers in the early republic had been the universal militia system, in which every adult male was eligible for military service and could supposedly be mustered up in times of necessity. That universal system had, however, fallen into disuse in the years after the War of 1812. While theoretically males could still be called up for service, annual musters had become infrequent, a relaxation of rules encouraged perhaps by the thirty-year lack of any significant military threat to the country. In some places service requirements had been replaced by a penalty fee. During the early 1840s, Massachusetts, Vermont, New York, Maine, Ohio, and Connecticut all abolished compulsory militia service. In place of the universal militia there began to emerge volunteer groups, which were based on more restricted political, social, or ethnic constituencies. These units were usually drawn from the lower classes, but were often organized and commanded by elite members of the community. Some states supported militia members with payments. The units often functioned as social clubs whose main activity was to parade in public festivities, often in ornate dress uniforms that would have little use in actual combat. By the 1830s and 1840s some militia units were clearly nativist in their makeup, and regarded themselves as having police functions to protect the republic against the unruly and disloyal immigrants. In response, immigrant leaders organized their own units, clearly identified as Irish, German, and French. The immigrant militiamen looked upon their militia service as validation of their status as citizens and their right to bear arms in their own defense. Richmond, Virginia, for example, had both the Irish Montgomery Guards and the German Virginia Rifles. They mustered and paraded not only on the American holidays (such as July 4) but also on the days of ethnic celebration—St. Patrick's Day for the Irish, Friedrich Schiller's birthday for the Germans. Since militia groups were organized around both nativism and ethnicity, the potential for conflict among them was considerable. After nativist mobs attacked a German festival outside Richmond in June 1855, the Virginia Rifles took on the regular duty of guarding German picnics, festivals, and other social outings.

After the declaration of war, President Polk called for volunteers, and the response came from both established militia units and new ones specially organized to take part in the war. Among the volunteers overall, the proportion of immigrants was probably lower than in the regular army. But there were some significant foreign-born units, including a number of German companies from Missouri and the mostly Irish Jasper Greens from Georgia. The Jasper Greens notoriously became involved in an ethnic brawl with another Georgia unit, the Kennesaw Rangers, in Mexico in August 1847. Volunteer units being raised in eastern seaboard cities found many willing recruits among the recently arrived immigrants. An American volunteer, recounting the extensive false promises and frauds being perpetrated by recruiters, described his New York regiment as consisting "of about eight hundred rank and file, three hundred Americans, the balance Dutch, Irish, French, English, Poles, Swedes, Chinese, Indians, &c, there were not one hundred men and officers even born in the City of New York in the whole regiment."[22]

The Story of the San Patricio Battalion

Even before the declaration of war, some American immigrant soldiers had already deserted to the Mexican side. When General Taylor established his position on the north side of the Rio Grande, a number of immigrants began to leave the post and flee to the Mexican army on the opposite bank. Desertion had been encouraged by broadsides issued by the Mexican officers in early April 1846, three weeks before the first shots were fired, promising good treatment to the foreign-born from the American army and transportation to the capital city of Mexico. Thus began a series of desertions that went on throughout the war, encouraged by other inducements advertised by the Mexican authorities. Typically, the Mexicans assured the immigrant Catholics that they would be better treated in the Catholic culture of Mexico. Few deserters actually received all the promised benefits, and many who were enrolled in the Mexican Army found the conditions there worse than in the U.S. Army.

Some of the deserters actually fought for the Mexicans against their former American units in early May 1846, when Mexican artillery shelled the American forces of General Taylor across the river from the town of Matamoros, just south of the Rio Grande. Not long after, some deserters were organized by Mexican officers into a Foreign Legion, with recruits who were of several different nationalities, but a majority of whom were probably Irish. The prime force in gathering together the deserters was the Irish-born John Riley (sometimes spelled Reilly), who had entered the United States from Canada in 1843, worked in Michigan, and then enlisted in the American army in 1845. Among the early deserters from Taylor's troops, Riley, formerly an enlisted man, was made a lieutenant in the Mexican Army and organized a company; it later became a battalion, and Riley was eventually promoted to the rank of major. The Mexicans designed for the battalion a green flag with a harp and shamrock on one side and a representation of St. Patrick on the other; thus the unit became known as the San Patricio Battalion.

The battalion acquitted itself well for the Mexicans in the major battles of Monterrey, Buena Vista, and Cerro Gordo. As the forces of General Winfield Scott approached the capital of Mexico City in September 1847, the San Patricios were decimated in the battle of Churubusco, and 85 of them, including Riley, were captured. Swift justice was meted out to the deserters, and 50 of them were hanged. Riley and five others were spared the noose, for the reason that they had deserted before the actual declaration of war and not in wartime, and therefore the death penalty could not legally be imposed. Riley was whipped severely and branded on his cheeks, then imprisoned. He and 15 other San Patricios were released from prison in June 1848 and discharged. Riley returned to the Mexican army and served as lieutenant colonel for a reorganized San Patricio unit for the next two years. In 1850 he was discharged from the Mexican army, whereupon he disappeared from the records, although it is thought that he returned to Ireland. The San Patricio Battalion was honored for its bravery in the military annals of Mexico, but the American nativists of the time marked the unit's record as convincing evidence of the untrustworthy and dangerous character of the foreign elements.

Consequences of the War

The war came to an end after the capture of Mexico City in September 1847, with the signing of the Treaty of Guadalupe Hidalgo in early February 1848 and its ratification by the U.S. Senate in March. In the treaty, Mexico agreed to the annexation of Texas with its Rio Grande boundary, and also ceded to the United States a vast territory in the Southwest, including both New Mexico and Alta California (the later state of California). The United States in turn agreed to a payment of $18.25 million to pay for the acquisitions and to settle many claims against Mexico by American citizens. The acquisition of California and the Southwest opened up greater opportunities for an expanding America, and not the least for the immigrants who were just entering the country in the mounting wave of the late 1840s.

GOLD RUSH CALIFORNIA AND THE IMMIGRANTS

When the Mexican War ended, John August Sutter had already been established for 10 years on a large grant of land in the Sacramento Valley. The Swiss-born Sutter (originally named Johann Augustus Suter), his dry-goods store failing, had left Switzerland, fleeing his creditors and abandoning his wife and five children, and had found his way to the United States in 1834. There he migrated to the Western frontier, and for a few years took part in the fur trade conducted out of St. Louis. He found frontier life to his liking and in 1838, again fleeing his past and his creditors, made his way to California, which was at that time still a part of Mexico. Sutter, a tireless entrepreneur, but also an adventurer, self-promoter, and charlatan, arrived in Monterey and succeeded in persuading the governor of California to allow him to establish a frontier colony in a remote section of the Sacramento Valley. He named the outpost New Helvetia (meaning "New Switzerland"), and in 1841 received from the Mexican governor the grant of a rancho of over 75 square miles on a site later to become the city of Sacramento. Sutter's Fort, as it would commonly be called, became the basis of a vast and successful enterprise, developing fur trading along the northern frontier of California, but also raising crops and cattle and providing a defensive post against the unfriendly Indians to the north. The colony gathered together a ragtag population of drifters, fur trappers, former soldiers, friendly Indians, immigrants, and wandering Americans who came down the California Trail from the United States.

In late 1847, John Sutter hired James Marshall, a millwright, to construct a sawmill for him on the American River near its junction with the Sacramento. On January 24, 1848, nine days before the signing of the treaty ending the Mexican War, Marshall found gold particles in the bed of the millrace. Despite efforts by Sutter to keep the information secret, the word spread, and when it reached San Francisco, the rush to the gold sites began. Sutter's Fort and the surrounding area were overrun with prospectors who ignored Sutter's previous claims to the land. Squatters pillaged Sutter's crops and slaughtered his cattle. Sutter was unsuccessful in defending his Mexican land grant in extended litigation in the 1850s. Eventually he fled to a smaller farm in the Feather River Valley. He never prospered from the gold find.

The first rush to the mines came from California and along the Pacific Coast, but by the end of 1848 the news had spread to the East Coast and abroad, President Polk had mentioned the gold discovery in his annual message to Congress, and samples of the gold were being displayed at the War Department in Washington. A huge migration was underway, numbering perhaps 300,000 so-called Argonauts by 1854. Among them would be many immigrants recently arrived in the United States, and many others who would come directly to California from all parts of the world. The shortest (but most expensive) journey from the East Coast, about one month, was by ship to Panama, then across the isthmus, and by another ship to California. Others went by ship around Cape Horn, or overland from Missouri River towns along the western trails, through the valley of the Great Salt Lake, and on to California.

The Whole World Rushes In

California before the gold rush was already accustomed to a great diversity in its population, even in the days when the "foreign-born" were from the United States and the Spanish-speaking Californios, small in number, were the "natives." The ports of California, as they became key points in the trans-Pacific trade, had been attracting merchants, traders, land speculators, and laborers from many lands. And the frontier areas had been attracting their share of immigrant adventurers, like John Sutter, and like the Martin Murphy family, with their vast landholdings.

But as the rush to reach the gold-diggings began, immigrants from many countries joined in. Sailors from all nations deserted their ships in San Francisco Bay to head up the Sacramento River to the mining country. Throughout 1848, eager adventurers heard the news in Hawaii, Peru, and Mexico and rushed to the scene in California. By the end of the year, a wide variety of miners were spread across the western slope of the Sierra Nevada, beginning the makeshift camps that sprang up willy-nilly. The next year, 1849, a flood of eager Argonauts arrived both overland and by sea from the East and from foreign countries. Not all were able to stake a claim and establish a site for placer mining, and many did not know how to mine for gold. Some of the immigrants with mining backgrounds from Cornwall in England, from Wales, from Saxony in Germany, and even a few from Italy and Spain, brought some technical expertise from which others might learn.

Fewer than half the Argonauts, however, actually went into mining. The others set up rooming houses and restaurants, brought in provisions for sale, offered legal services, worked as teamsters, and built the ramshackle buildings of the mining camps. The rapidly burgeoning population of California did not allow for a great deal of sorting out of immigrant groups amid the turmoil. In 1848, when the Mexican War ended, there were about 14,000 people other than Indians in California. By the end of 1849, there were nearly 100,000; by 1852, around 250,000.[23] About one-third

of the people arriving during the Gold Rush years were classified by the U.S. census as foreign-born. These included Peruvians
and Mexicans, many of whom had previous mining experience.
Many of the Mexicans came overland from Sonora into the more
southern areas of the gold fields, south of Sacramento. The earlier stages of the Gold Rush included many Indians from nearby
tribes who hastened to take advantage of the opportunities for
placer mining, which did not require heavy equipment. However,
racist prejudices would ultimately operate to exclude the Indians.
Immigrants of British origin often came by way of New Zealand
or Australia, where some had been imprisoned in the British penal
colony of Botany Bay. In France, great enthusiasm in 1849 over the
news of the gold discovery had led to a larger than normal emigration to America. In the gold fields, the French often associated
themselves with the Spanish-speaking migrants. The Germans and
Irish, although still subject to some of the nativist prejudices they
experienced in the East, mingled more easily with the American-
born, even eventually forming a common cause with them against
the Latin Americans, the Indians, and the Asians.

A street scene in San Francisco in 1850 shows the great diversity of
"Argonauts." The gold rush brought foreigners from around the globe—
Asians, Latin Americans, Europeans—in search of wealth in the mines.
From *Illustrated London News*, December 28, 1850. Courtesy Swarthmore
College, via Bryn Mawr College Special Collections.

Enter the Chinese

Before the Gold Rush, there were very few Chinese in the United States. The years of the Gold Rush brought a sudden upsurge in Chinese migrants to California. Within a decade, the society of California (which became a state in 1850) was considerably affected by the influx of these racially different Asians. In 1849 about 325 Chinese were among the thousands of forty-niners responding to the lure of gold—the Chinese called California *Gam Saan* (meaning "Gold Mountain"). Another 450 arrived in 1850, and the numbers mounted to 2,716 in 1851 and over 20,000 in 1852.[24] The new arrivals from Asia were overwhelmingly male; no more than 5 percent were women, and those mostly prostitutes. The Chinese—like many other immigrants in the gold fields—thought of themselves as sojourners, destined, they hoped, to make their fortune and return to China, where they could bask in the increased wealth and status that they would find in Gold Mountain.

The Chinese arriving in the Gold Rush came in great majority from one small rural area, the Pearl River Delta in southeast China, near the port cities of Canton (later "Guangzhou") and Hong Kong. The Province of Kwangtung (later "Guangdong") was by 1850 very accustomed to emigration. Emigrants from the region had been going for many years to Southeast Asia, Indonesia, Malaysia, and Latin America. The demographic and economic forces at work in Kwangtung were not unlike those that had propelled many emigrants from European countries in the same years: growing population, limited availability of land, disruptions from civil wars and internal violence, and a developing market economy tied to ports increasingly involved in international trade. People along the Pearl River had ready access to information about America, because the famed American China trade that had developed in the early nineteenth century centered at Canton. Seamen, artisans, agricultural laborers, and some entrepreneurs began to seek their fortunes in far-off regions.

Some Americans talked of the trade in "coolies," indentured servants transported in conditions near slavery to work in places like the tropical plantations of Latin America and the Caribbean. But those who came to Gold Rush California were not coolies. Most were free agents who came under the credit-ticket system: they paid for their passage to Gold Mountain with money borrowed from brokers, who then could demand repayment, usually at very high interest rates. At a time when common labor in California commanded ten times the wages that the same labor commanded in South China, the high interest rate did not seem burdensome. The peasants and workers who came under the credit-ticket system were able to seek their own employment, either in the mines or in businesses in the towns and cities, where there was a considerable demand for labor.

Because of the demand for their labor, the Chinese were welcomed initially in San Francisco and in other towns as well. But problems developed when they began to claim mining rights in the gold country. When larger numbers of Chinese began to arrive after 1852, they often took up placer mining claims, where they searched for gold by sifting through the gravel of stream beds. Other miners had abandoned placer mining, instead taking up prospecting for claims for quartz mining, where the ore lay inside rocks under the earth. Mining camps where placer mining was the main activity saw the numbers of Chinese workers grow, and many such camps had a majority of Chinese. Because the arriving Chinese bought out many of the placer-mining claims being abandoned by other miners, they were welcomed. Eventually, however, rivalries and prejudices would develop that would force the Chinese into social isolation.

Gold Rush Nativism

The Gold Rush occurred within a setting of general American nativism, and also amid a wave of American supernationalism that accompanied the enthusiasm of the era of Manifest Destiny. The American victory in the war against Mexico had won California, and thus, it was asserted, Americans should be the ones to benefit from that victory. To this argument was added a strong feeling of rivalry based on ethnic differences, born in the scramble to acquire the best mining claims.

Some of the first to arrive in the gold fields in 1848 were miners from Mexico, Chile, and other areas of South America; Native Americans; and blacks, who came from both the United States and other countries. While at that time there were plenty of possibilities for prospectors, the greater flood of migrants that came in 1849, perhaps numbering 90,000, changed the situation. This group included many from foreign ports, both in Europe and in America. Arriving miners quickly developed jealousies against the ethnic groups they found in the mines, and by force of numbers quickly developed means to exclude them. These exclusionary efforts were based primarily on the associations formed by miners to fill the regulatory vacuum left by the lack of any state or federal legislation. Through these associations in each mining camp, the miners themselves could formulate the rules for claiming and exploiting the gold mines. These rules were in many ways equalitarian and democratic, as befitted the rough equality of the mining frontier, but also were written to work against those groups that were deemed to be unfit for participation in a democratic society.

Those groups with more pronounced racial and ethnic differences were made the object both of exclusionary laws and regulations and of outright physical intimidation. In 1849 many mining camps began to pass resolutions demanding that all foreign elements leave. There was little protection against the consensus of these rough mining-camp communities. The European migrants who were beginning to arrive in 1849 often were subjected to the same pressures, although increasingly the Irish, English, and Germans, who began to develop sheer force of numbers, became aligned with the native-born Americans against the other ethnic groups. The adversaries included the French, who were often seen as tied to the Spanish-speaking groups and were regarded as clannish and exclusive.

In April 1850, the California territorial legislature enacted the Foreign Miners' Tax, requiring all foreign miners to pay a tax of $20 per month, a sum beyond the reach of most of the placer miners. In practice the tax was mostly collected from French- and Spanish-speakers, although potentially it could be collected from any foreigners. The law seemed to put the California government on the side of the violent anti-foreign elements already showing themselves in the mining camps. The law was harshly enforced by tax collectors who could keep $3 of every $20 collected. Collectors were often aided by vigilantes who could take over the claims abandoned by those who could not pay the tax. By 1851 most Spanish-speaking and French-speaking miners were driven away from the mines. Many of the French retreated to San Francisco, where they provided restaurants, department stores, and various services to the rapidly growing city.

In 1851 the legislature, responding to objections by those who had hired immigrant labor and who had supplied the immigrant colonies, replaced the original miners' tax with a reduced tax of $3 a month (at a time when the typical Chinese placer miner might earn $6 a month). As the influx of Chinese increased in 1852, they would become the principal payers of the tax. The tax was increased several times, and it provided a significant portion of state income until 1870, when it was found unconstitutional by the California Supreme Court.

Perhaps an even more restrictive blow to the rights of Chinese was the court decision by the California Supreme Court in the 1854 case of *People v. Hall.* George W. Hall had been convicted of murdering a Chinese; the principal testimony for the prosecution was from other Chinese. When the case was appealed to the Supreme Court, the Court overturned Hall's conviction, and ruled that the Chinese were subject to the existing California law stating that the testimony of blacks, mulattoes, or Indians against a white person could not be accepted in court. This exposed Chinese people to many acts of fraud or violence to which they could not make an effective contest in court. In addition, from the time of their arrival, the Chinese were deemed not to be eligible for citizenship under the 1790 U.S. Naturalization Act, which allowed only whites to become citizens. The presence of Chinese as immigrants was beginning to add racial theories to pre-existing nativist ideology. Despite these restrictions on their freedom, the Chinese continued to increase in the California population, and began to gravitate to other areas outside the mining regions.

A CHANGED IMMIGRANT WORLD

In the decade that ended in 1855, the conditions under which Europeans were emigrating and the conditions that they found in America had changed greatly. The Irish famine, economic depressions, and political unrest had encouraged greater numbers to make the decision to go to America. Many people with limited resources had nowhere else to go. News of opportunities in the industrializing cities, the expanding farmlands of the Midwest, and the gold fields of California all encouraged many to leave their homelands. The flood tide of immigrants would not reach such a high number again until the 1880s.

The transatlantic voyage had also become more regular and predictable, even if not always easier. The tide of immigrants brought more ships into the trade, and encouraged the building of larger ships for the immigrants. By 1855 ships over 1,500 tons powered by steam, an increasing number of them of iron construction, were becoming available. There was increased rivalry among steamship lines, who had begun to compete for steerage passengers. The growing emigrant trade at Liverpool stimulated lower fares, and by the late 1850s the fare for steerage passengers on steamships was often lower than it was for sailing ships. With improved technology in steam engines and the adoption of screw propellers, the time consumed by the voyage had been shortened to less than two weeks, and the feeling that return to the homeland was nearly impossible had begun to fade. More emigrants could think of themselves as sojourners. By 1861, over 30 percent of immigrants to New York would travel on steamships.[25]

There continued to be hazards in the voyage and abuses of ship passengers, although government attempts were being made to regulate the trade. In New York, always the principal entry port for immigrants to the United States, a Board of the Commissioners of Immigration was formed in 1847, charged by the state of New York with improving the conditions of the arriving immigrants. The board immediately took over the administration of the existing hospitals for immigrants, and in 1855 opened a reception station at Castle Garden, near the Battery at the lower end of Manhattan. Castle Garden would remain the principal receiving point for immigrants until the opening of Ellis Island in 1892. Castle Garden was

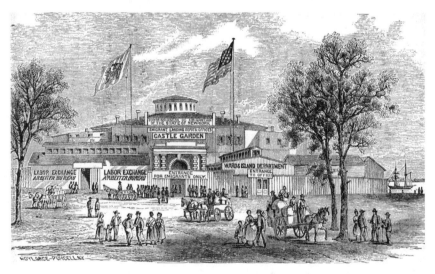

Castle Garden Emigrant Depot. In 1855 the New York state authorities, seeking to reform the process of immigration, opened a central immigration station at Castle Garden near the Battery at the southern end of Manhattan Island. It remained the principal receiving point for immigrants until the establishment of Ellis Island in 1892. From *Haverty's Irish-American Illustrated Almanac* (New York: P. M. Haverty, 1871). Courtesy McGarrity Collection, Villanova University Library.

somewhat successful in controlling access to the newly arrived by runners who attempted to steer newcomers to lodging or transportation, thus reducing the instances of fraud and abuse of newcomers just off the ship.

The economic boom that swept the country between 1848 and 1854 produced new opportunities for arriving immigrants. Not the least of these, of course, were the beckoning gold fields of California. But there were also the rapidly extending railroad lines, which offered construction labor and opened up new agricultural areas to development. The transition from water-oriented to rail-oriented transportation fostered the development of new cities and towns in the West, many of them with new immigrant communities. Older communities would be transformed by the arrival of the new flood of migrants. In many places the growing numbers of the immigrant population would allow them opportunities to establish themselves more firmly, organize, preserve their cultures, defend their ways against nativists, and work their way into the fabric of American life.

NOTES

1. Michael Galvin, *Black Blight: The Great Famine, 1845–1852: A Four Parish Study* (Middleton, County Cork, Ireland: Litho Press, n.d. [1995?]), 295–96.

2. Dean M. Braa, "The Great Potato Famine and the Transformation of Irish Peasant Society," *Science and Society* 61 (1997): 212.

3. Tim P. O'Neill, "Famine Evictions," in *Famine, Land and Culture in Ireland,* ed. Carla King (Dublin: University College Dublin Press, 2000), 48.

4. Kerby A. Miller, *Emigrants and Exiles: Ireland and the Irish Exodus to North America* (New York: Oxford University Press, 1985), 282–85.

5. Liam Swords, ed., *In Their Own Words: The Famine in North Connacht, 1845–49* (Blackrock, County Dublin, Ireland: Columba Press, 1999), 26.

6. Ibid., 86.

7. Ibid., 104.

8. Ibid., 150.

9. *The Nation,* June 5, 1847, quoted in Peter Sobolewski and Betty Solan, eds., *Kiltimagh: Our Life and Times* (Kiltimagh: Kiltimagh Historical Society, n.d.), 58.

10. Swords, *In Their Own Words,* 224.

11. Ibid., 281.

12. Ibid., 331.

13. Ibid., 317.

14. Sobolewski and Solan, *Kiltimagh: Our Life and Times,* 65, 67.

15. Ibid., 65.

16. Mack Walker, *Germany and the Emigration, 1816–1885* (Cambridge, Mass.: Harvard University Press, 1964), 72.

17. Jonathan Sperber, *The European Revolutions, 1848–1851,* 2d ed. (New York: Cambridge University Press, 2005), 24 (graph showing real wages).

18. Lyman Beecher, *A Plea for the West* (Cincinnati: Truman and Smith, 1835), 49.

19. *New York Irish American,* September 9, 1849 (in Balch Institute collections, Historical Society of Pennsylvania).

20. Paul Foos, *A Short, Offhand, Killing Affair: Soldiers and Social Conflict during the Mexican-American War* (Chapel Hill: University of North Carolina Press, 2002), 23.

21. Ibid., 26–27, quoting *Truth Teller* (Cincinnati), April 16, 1846.

22. Albert Lombard, *The "High Private," with a Full and Exciting History of the New York Volunteers* (New York: n.p., 1848), quoted in George Winston Smith and Charles Judah, eds., *Chronicles of the Gringos: The U.S. Army in the Mexican War* (Albuquerque: University of New Mexico Press, 1968), 19–20. The "Dutch" referred to in Lombard's account were probably mostly German.

23. Rodman W. Paul, *Mining Frontiers of the Far West, 1848–1880* (New York: Holt, Rinehart and Winston, 1963), 15. Paul points out that census figures of both 1850 and 1852 were flawed and allow for only rough estimates.

24. Ronald Takaki, *Strangers from a Different Shore: A History of Asian Americans,* rev. ed. (Boston: Little Brown and Co., 1998), 79.

25. Raymond L. Cohn, "The Transition from Sail to Steam in Immigration to the United States," *Journal of Economic History* 65 (2005): 472.

5

Developing Immigrant Communities, 1820–1855

When the great immigration tide of the 1850s subsided, the foreign-born population of the United States had become more visible, often gathering in ethnic communities which offered a welcoming culture for those still in the process of adjusting to a new land. Older ethnic communities which had been languishing for lack of newcomers were revived by new arrivals who sought protection and help from their fellow countrymen. However, the newcomers also had the potential for straining the existing resources of the older ethnic communities, and sometimes challenged their established leaders and created new internal divisions. In the West, new communities of immigrants formed rapidly as railroads created new opportunities for settlement.

Although Americans frequently thought of the immigrant communities as exclusive and densely occupied by only one immigrant group, there were very few places, at least in the cities, where that was actually the case. The larger cities of the mid-nineteenth century were still walking cities, where public transportation was scarce and expensive, and people of modest means generally lived within walking distance of their workplaces. Thus different classes and ethnic groups might be mixed together, although the poor and the well-off were not usually next door to each other. Immigrant communities should therefore be thought of not as neighborhoods defined by a geographical boundary, but rather as commonly held cultures, where people of similar ethnicity are in communication with one another, even while distributed around a city and its environs. What outsiders might have called the "German district" or the "Irish neighborhood" would be the area where most of the institutions of that ethnic group were found, usually a centrally located place to which all of the same ethnicity might go. Even within those districts, the particular foreign-born residents and their children seldom counted for more than half of the population. In rural areas, immigrant activities might be centered around a church or in a nearby town.

HOUSING

Class and wealth status, more than ethnicity, tended to determine the location and quality of immigrant housing. In New York City and other ports of entry, the poorest immigrants, those who could not move on to other places, took housing in the older urban districts close to the docks. These might also be close to their workplaces, as for example when the Irish took jobs along the waterfront or in the warehouses and factories nearby. The increase of immigrants in New York led in the 1830s to the subdividing of older housing in lower Manhattan, to allow for more people to be packed into the confined quarters. By the 1850s property owners would build new housing divided up into equally constricted living quarters—the first of Manhattan's tenements. These were brick buildings of as many as five stories designed to provide living space for as many people as possible. The typical lodgings for a family might consist of a main room eight by ten feet, and a bedroom six feet by ten. Stairways were steep, passageways dark and narrow, and many rooms had no windows and little artificial light. As the historian Tyler Anbinder observed, "The thought of carrying young children, groceries, or pails of water up three, four, or even five flights of these steep, dark stairs filled many a housewife with dread."[1]

The most desperate might find housing in garrets or in basements, which were notoriously dank and disease-ridden. In the growing cities to the west, where there was often newer housing stock, poorer immigrants often overcrowded the available housing or resorted to shanties built on the outskirts. Immigrants who were of the skilled-labor group or of the middle class, which included a larger proportion of Germans and English, might find simple housing near their place of work. Artisans and storekeepers might occupy housing behind or above their stores or shops. For those newly arrived, and for single men of longer-term residence, there were the innumerable boardinghouses, often operated by proprietors of similar ethnicity, in places close to their work, where they shared meals, rooms, and sometimes beds. Although immigrants in time tended to move outward from the central commercial district, the outer fringes of the cities, undesirable because of their locations, were often populated with the shacks of poor squatters. In New York, for example, the area above 59th Street was occupied by the shanties of both Irish and Germans, who would eventually be displaced when the land was taken over to build Central Park in the late 1850s. The outskirts of Chicago and other Midwestern cities were occupied by poor German settlers who made their livings by raising produce for sale in urban markets.

The immigrant communities in the larger cities served as distribution centers for immigrants seeking other frontiers. New York was the prime example of this, and many who arrived there in the immigrant ships were on their way elsewhere within a day or two. Others would remain because of the need to find immediate employment, and then, after weeks or years, find their way west. Chain migration and the network of friends and relatives in new places often drove this migration. Thus the community and its institutions, while appearing very stable to outsiders, was really a sort of revolving door with a frequent renewal of the immigrant population within.

In rural areas, especially the newer regions being developed in the West, immigrants' destinations tended to be determined by new towns springing up along the transportation routes, and by the availability of land, which could often be bought from the federal land offices. There were some heavily German small towns and rural communities, usually the end result of chain migration from specific regions of Germany, but not as many as would develop in the 1860s when railroads which received land grants from the federal government began to market them to specific immigrant groups in Europe. Generally speaking, housing built in these new communities tended to reflect the housing patterns of the American host culture. A few heavily ethnic towns, such as the German settlement of Hermann, Missouri, managed to re-create some of the look of a German village, but usually with construction of brick or other local building materials. The half-timbered construction that was still common in nineteenth-century Europe, with heavy wooden beam structures filled with some lighter material, was found only in a few communities, such as those in Ohio populated by Amish groups clinging to traditional ways. Given the much greater availability of lumber and the presence of many local sawmills, the common American practice of frame construction prevailed.

TIES THAT BIND: IMMIGRANT INSTITUTIONS

While some immigrants lived as close neighbors to one another, the more important elements in building their communities were the organizations that tied people together across geographical space. Every arriving immigrant group developed a network of social organizations, churches, cultural institutions, political clubs, and interest groups which responded to the needs felt by recently arrived immigrants. While these institutions were often seen by outsiders as holding immigrants away from the general American society and offering segregated refuges, in actuality many of them had a more urgent purpose in helping the newly arrived countrymen

Architecture in styles brought from Germany is found in the largely German town of Hermann, Missouri. Shown here is the house built by Carl Strehly in 1842–1843, which also housed a print shop in the basement where the German-language newspaper *Licht-Freund* was published. To the right is the tavern and wine cellar built between 1854 and 1857. Historic American Buildings Survey, Library of Congress Prints and Photographs Division.

find jobs, deal with government authorities, understand the different economy of the new country, and learn the new language. In other words, besides being instruments of cultural preservation, these organizations were also instruments of acculturation to American society. The ethnic societies were most vital in times of heavy immigration; in time, their work in introducing new immigrants to America would become less relevant to subsequent generations born in America, and they would dwindle as they became primarily institutions for preserving cultural and ancestral ties.

Among the Irish

Since colonial times, there had been Irish organizations in the seaboard cities of America, like the Friendly Sons of St. Patrick, organized in Philadelphia in 1771 and in New York in 1784. Even during the 1700s these charitable societies celebrated St. Patrick's Day with a parade and an annual dinner. The early societies were composed of both Protestants and Catholics, although in the early republic the Protestants tended to dominate—in part because the membership was drawn mostly from a wealthy elite. The societies followed a tradition of not discussing political or religious questions in their meetings. As Catholic Irish newcomers began to outnumber Protestants during the 1830s, and as religious antagonisms began to develop between them, separate institutional structures began to emerge. The more extreme Protestant group, the Orange Order, which had antecedents in Ireland, took shape in America in the 1820s and 1830s. Outright clashes occurred between Orangemen and Irish Catholics in New York in 1824 and in Philadelphia in 1831. The anti-Catholic character of the Orange Order sometimes placed them in alliance with the nativists. The Catholic Irish developed their own institutions, like the Ancient Order of Hibernians, originally a secret society, which emerged in the 1820s and operated under a variety of names. While the group was well-known for its confrontations with nativists and Orangemen, it also served as a mutual-insurance society offering sick and death benefits to the poorer classes of Irish. Unlike the traditional societies such as the Friendly Sons of St. Patrick, the newer Irish societies were avowedly Catholic and also increasingly advocates of an independent Irish nation. The earlier societies persisted, those in New York holding their elaborate annual dinners in elite places like Delmonico's Restaurant and the Astor House—but this was far from the world of the typical Irish immigrant.

By the 1840s the most important institution in the Irish communities was without doubt the Catholic Church. The Catholic Church in Ireland had been for many years the center of resistance to British domination, with the local parish priest—often a literate among many illiterates—the acknowledged leader of the village. Priests and parishioners had a common experience in the campaign in Ireland to achieve basic civil rights for Catholics, which was partially achieved in the Catholic Emancipation Act, passed by Parliament in 1829. It was only natural that the church and its clergy would play a similar role in defending the Irish against the hostilities of the new American environment.

The American Catholic Church at the beginning of the nineteenth century was under the control both of colonial families, mostly from Maryland and of English background, and of missionaries, mostly French, who were active in the West. The onrush of Irish immigrants beginning in the 1820s soon changed the picture. Irish immigrants overwhelmed the older parishes and started new ones. American bishops were forced to plead with bishops in Ireland to send clergy to help them. Since Ireland had an oversupply of priests, many came to lead American parishes filling with Irish newcomers. Amidst this drastic transformation of the American Catholic Church, the emergence of a dominant Irish hierarchy was a foregone conclusion.

In 1842 the Irish-born John Hughes was appointed bishop of New York; he would become archbishop in 1850. He immediately took up the task of representing Catholicism and the Irish to the city and the rest of America. He established a system of parochial schools; debated nativists; encouraged religious orders (many of them of Irish origin) to found colleges, hospitals, and orphanages; and encouraged mutual-assistance societies through the parishes. In 1858 he laid the cornerstone for an impressive new Gothic cathedral named for St. Patrick at 50th Street and 5th Avenue. It was envisioned as a symbol of the Irish Catholic presence in America.

While Hughes did not see himself as promoting Irish ethnicity (instead emphasizing the immigrants' need to adapt to American society), the institutional network he created was seen by Irish immigrants as a protector of their interests. At the same time, other Irish bishops throughout the United States were following the example of Hughes. The network that tied the Irish community together across the country was to a large extent the work of priests, bishops, and nuns. This network, then, served the purpose of preserving the faith, but it also eased the problems of assimilating into the new society.

The other principal institution forming the world of the new Irish immigrants was the saloon, a male-dominated locale. The ubiquitous drinking places, denounced by proper American society as dens of iniquity, drunkenness, and immorality, were not merely places of refuge for the hard-working laborers. They also functioned as centers of communication, as job bureaus, and as political clubs. In a day when masculinity seemed to matter, the saloons provided places for boasting, story-telling, gambling, and even brawling.

Drinking places could be established with little capital, offering opportunities to those who were eager to go into business. Many local Irish politicians began as tavern-keepers or as constant patrons of the saloons, tied as they were to specific neighborhoods. In Andrew Jackson's day the Democratic party had discovered the Irish saloon as a source of votes, while the opposition Whig party sealed itself off from the Irish votes by its frequent appeals to nativists and temperance reformers. In the saloons, entertainment evocative of the old country could be heard, protest movements could be organized, prize fights could be promoted, and political patronage could be sought. From the customer base of the local saloon, militia companies were recruited and volunteer fire companies were formed.

A voting place on Pearl Street in the Five Points district of Manhattan, November 1858. The artist from *Harper's Weekly* seemed shocked that the polling place was in the back room of an Irish saloon. From *Harper's Weekly*, November 13, 1858. Courtesy Bryn Mawr College Special Collections.

The costs, of course, were often alcoholism, impoverishment, and ruined families.

The saloons were almost entirely male preserves; only women of questionable character could be found there. For their part, Irish women generally became by default the lay caretakers of the church, supporting it with pittances from their own hard work and organizing frequent fairs to help build and maintain the church structures. The famine era was still a time when many males had infrequent ties to the church, and that laxity in Ireland carried over to the United States. The 1850s saw the beginning of a devotional revolution both in Ireland and throughout its diaspora, during which evangelization would increase church-adherence; but until then the men would dominate the saloons and the women would take care of church life.

Among the Germans

The Germans, the second largest immigrant group in 1850, had a much more complex social and institutional structure. Many of them did not identify themselves as Germans, but rather as emigrants from any of the numerous independent states of Germany— as Rhinelanders, Bavarians, Badenese, Prussians, or Saxons, to mention a few. Some even linked their identity more narrowly to the hometown from which they had come. While the Irish were on average about 80 percent working class, the Germans were much more diversified in their class structure, and included a large number of middle class men, as well as professional men and men of considerable wealth. Two of the richest men in the country in the 1840s, John Jacob Astor and August Belmont, were German-born. Religion was yet another source of differentiation among the Germans; they included Catholics, different Protestant sects both Calvinist and Lutheran, a significant Jewish minority, and an often-outspoken group of irreligious and freethinkers, who quarreled among themselves as often as with the established religious groups.

These varied sources of identity for the German immigrant—their places of origin, social statuses, and religions, to name the most evident—led to an intricate system of organizations and institutions. The Germans, like other national groups, had all-inclusive groups dating from the eighteenth century, such as the various German Societies, formed in Philadelphia in 1763, in Baltimore in 1783, and in New York in 1784. In the nineteenth century, these societies adhered to their original purposes of helping indigent immigrants, but also began to take up objectives of cultural preservation, celebrating ethnicity in annual dinners and celebrations. To a great extent, however, the new immigrants bypassed the older societies with their limited elite memberships and formed newer organizations of their own.

The older established German Protestant churches from the eighteenth century still existed in eastern states like Pennsylvania, Maryland, and Virginia, although many of these churches had yielded to the second and third generations by establishing English services, sometimes even abolishing services in German. Newcomers often turned to founding their own churches. In areas of the developing West, where there were often no German churches, recently arrived ministers from Germany began to establish them. In rural areas, efforts to establish one often resulted in a united church, ministering to both Lutheran and Reformed (Calvinist) adherents, and offering a sort of compromise from both traditions. These united churches were often modeled on the established state churches that existed in places like Prussia and Saxony. In time, however, when strong-minded pastors from one or the other tradition came along, dissidence might grow among the members, leading to the establishment of separate Lutheran and Reformed churches. Dissent among Lutherans developed with the arrival during the late 1830s and early 1840s of conservative Lutheran groups from Saxony and other areas of eastern Germany. Unwilling on doctrinal grounds to join with existing Lutheran synods, some Old Lutherans organized the Missouri Synod in 1847. This group would carry on the conservative tradition among German Lutherans. As the tides of Germans swelled in the late 1840s and early 1850s, division and dissent grew among German Protestants. So did the number of freethinkers, including some of the forty-eighters, who disdained all institutional religion and brought disharmony into many localities.

Somewhere between one-quarter and one-third of German immigrants professed Catholicism (statistics are lacking, and estimates varied). They had established some Catholic parishes in Pennsylvania in colonial days, but the numbers of German Catholic parishes multiplied after 1820 in the Ohio and upper Mississippi valleys. In the rapidly developing West, the Irish bishops dominated the new dioceses, but the Swiss-born priest John Martin Henni, who had been active in the diocese of Cincinnati, ministering to its Germans and establishing a German-language newspaper, became the first bishop of the frontier village of Milwaukee in 1844. By the time

Wisconsin achieved statehood in 1848, Germans were pouring in and Henni was becoming a national spokesman for the German Catholics. Across the nation, the German-language parishes created a network of parish organizations and mutual-assistance societies for German Catholics.

Religion, which was a strongly uniting force among the Irish, was a divisive element among the Germans. Attempts to unite all German Americans for some social or political purpose usually came to naught. Loyalties based on class, religion, or provincial origin always seemed to prevail. These competing and overlapping identities led to a bewildering array of voluntary organizations, the famous *Vereine,* that formed much of the fabric of German-American life. *Verein* meant something like "union," but not just in the sense of a labor organization, although some of those did exist. The word implied the uniting or bringing together of people for some common interest. Some organizations were tied to churches; many were secular. There were literary societies which kept up with German cultural developments. Every German community of any substance fostered at least one singing society, and the Germans were instrumental in introducing musical culture to places where there had previously been very little. Dramatic societies fostered a German theater, and in the larger cities these developed into professional theaters. There were *Schützenvereine* (shooting clubs) that held Sunday target practices and competitions. Professional societies and clubs were formed by physicians, pharmacists, and lawyers. Most abundant were the mutual-aid societies, which offered insurance, providing sick benefits of a few dollars a week and a small death benefit. Many of these were organized on the basis of religion or provincial origin, and usually held social gatherings bringing together people of similar background.

While the varied social organizations of the Germans were already on a firm base before the increasing migrations of the late 1840s, the number and complexity of them increased greatly during the period of high migration. The best-known of the new organizations were the Turner societies, which were first established by political refugees in America in 1848, and which developed rapidly in the years before the Civil War. These societies had a previous tradition in Germany, where they originally emerged after the end of the Napoleonic wars. The name *Turner* implied the gymnastic origins of the societies, which embodied the physical culture theories of the "Turner father," Friedrich Ludwig Jahn. But the societies in Germany also reflected the spirit of the Enlightenment, especially republicanism and German national unity. These ideals were perceived as threats by the rulers of the German states, and in fact the societies were banned there from 1839 until 1842. When republicanism and national unity seemed lost in the wake of the failed revolutions of 1848, the refugees of 1848 sought to rekindle the spirit of the Turner movement in America. The first Turner society in America was founded in Cincinnati in 1848. The name of the national organization founded in 1851, the Socialist Turner Union of North America, reflected their radical ideology. Most Turner societies supported antislavery opinions in the years before the Civil War, and served often as auxiliaries to the rising Republican party. In time, however, many local organizations would mute the radical aspects of the Turner movement as they sought a wider following within their communities. The societies' gymnastic and physical education activities were often what attracted other members, as well as their role as social centers offering cultural events, lectures, and ethnic celebrations. Just after the end of the Civil War, the Socialist Turner Union was renamed the Turner Union of North America.

German-American men, following in the nineteenth-century traditions stemming from the Enlightenment, were attracted to fraternal orders and secret societies. In the early nineteenth century, some joined American lodges like those of the Masonic order and the Odd Fellows. But beginning in 1819 there were established German-speaking Masonic lodges affiliated with those in Prussia. By the 1840s, fraternal orders that were purely of German-American origin began to appear. Among these were the Sons of Hermann, established in 1849 by former members of an Odd Fellows lodge, and the Order of Harugari, founded by freethinkers in 1847. German Jews established the fraternal B'nai B'rith in 1843. The Harugari name derived from a mythic pagan priest who had opposed Roman rule in Germany. More often appealing to the working-class Germans, it was one of the most successful of the fraternal orders, and counted over three hundred lodges by the early 1870s. These societies were advocates of German nationalism, and rallied in some of the first American demonstrations of support for the revolutions of 1848. The orders often played a leading role in the ethnic celebrations of local Germans.

The German immigrants also had their less formal social institutions, particularly the beer taverns and beer gardens that were an integral part of every German community. Their functions in the community, however, differed from those of the Irish saloons. The German beer taverns were easily accessible social centers for the whole family, and women and children were welcome at the Sunday gatherings, which often featured music, dancing, and other entertainment. Political discussion, while not unknown, was pushed to the side by celebration. The thought of women and children being present in these drinking places shocked many Americans, but in fact the Germans reflected a long tradition of moderation in the use of alcohol, and moderation was often enforced in the German taverns. The Germans also had local "groceries" that served as drinking places mostly for working-class German males.

The elaborate institutional structure of the Germans added to their visibility in American society, and was the envy of other immigrant groups. But although they seemed to demonstrate a high degree of German solidarity, in effect they also offered means

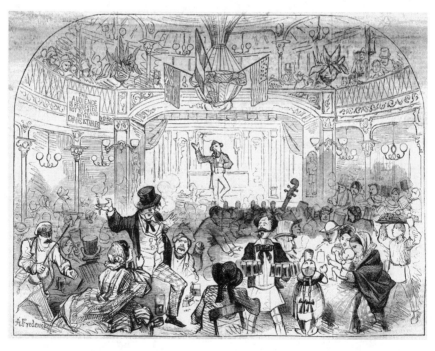

Sunday evening in a German beer garden, New York City. The artist draws attention both to the supposedly riotous behavior and to the presence of families with children. *Harper's Weekly*, October 15, 1859. Courtesy Bryn Mawr College Special Collections.

for Germans to differentiate themselves from one another and to quarrel with one another.

Varieties of Ethnic Communities: Two Extremes

The need of an immigrant group to establish a tight-knit community varied according to the need to deal with the differences between immigrant culture and American culture. It also varied according to the degree of nativist pressure applied by the host society. The example of the British is that of the loosest and most ephemeral community. Given the similarity of the English language and culture with the rest of American society, there was little need for institutions to help with the transition.

The British, of course, had their ancestral societies, which by the early nineteenth century were attended by Americans of several generations' descent from their forefathers. There was a St. George's Society for the English, the St. Andrew's Society for the Scots, and the St. David's Society for the Welsh. These had existed in the eastern port cities since the mid-eighteenth century. Like other such national societies, they were largely elite, upper-class groups, although they still held to their older mission of assisting impoverished new immigrants.

As for the role of the church, the newly arrived British immigrants could easily find a church similar to that of their homeland, which would welcome them and provide somewhat familiar surroundings. These might be Episcopal, Presbyterian, Methodist, or other evangelical churches. There was no particular pressure for the newly arrived immigrants to create churches for themselves. In the cities and other localities where there was a concentration of skilled British workers and mechanics, they often became active in labor organizations, but these groups were not particularly ethnic-based and often cooperated with native-born American workers. While new British immigrants no doubt felt some sense of loneliness because of the cultural differences between themselves and Americans, they only began to develop institutions of cultural preservation after several decades. The Welsh immigrants, concerned about the loss of their distinctive language, did establish cultural groups and singing societies, but these often waned as the language disappeared from common use among them.

The British, with no strong need for organizations of their own, developed the least substantial network of immigrant societies. The historian Charlotte Erickson called them "invisible immigrants," and, speaking of the British immigrant farmers particularly, remarked: "It is difficult to imagine circumstances more propitious to the rapid assimilation of an immigrant group than these British immigrants met in rural America."[2]

At the other extreme of community structure was the incipient Chinese society just developing in California, most notably in San Francisco but also duplicated to some extent in the mining towns. Given the pressure that developed from Americans against the Chinese community, the emerging Chinatown in San Francisco became highly concentrated within the boundaries effectively set by Americans; the Chinese district, northeast of the business district and centered on Dupont Street (later Grant Street), would remain the core center of Chinese life for the next hundred and fifty years. Sealed off from the rest of San Francisco, it remained an area where the mostly male, frequently transient Chinese population provided for its own needs, whether they be restaurants, lodging, imported merchandise from across the Pacific, medical help, or illicit drugs and prostitution. It also was an area that other Americans often feared to enter. In the 1850s, there was no attempt to construct buildings in an Asian style; with the exception of the headquarters of the principal Chinese societies, the buildings were like most others in San Francisco. The idea of inviting a tourist trade lay fifty years in the future.

This highly introverted community did need to organize itself for defense against the rest of American society. Although initially some leadership was exerted by prominent Chinese merchants, disillusion with their supposed complicity with American authorities led to the establishment of the first of the secret societies or Triads, organizations which had a long previous history in China. In America these were known as "tongs," and the one organized in 1850 in San Francisco was the Kwong Duck Tong. Its membership was always rather small, and it functioned more as an underworld gang, ruling the Chinese community by extortion, intimidation, force, and vigilante tactics. Other tongs would follow, but other more active organizations arose to regulate the inner workings of the Chinese community. These were the *hui-kuan*, social organizations based on regional origins in China. They also had their predecessors in the cities of China. Since perhaps 90 percent of the Chinese in San Francisco in the 1850s were from Kwangtung province, the *hui-kuan* began to differentiate themselves into organizations from specific districts within the province. In 1853 the four principal regional organizations established a federation known as the Four Great Houses—later to become the Five Great Houses, and then the

Chinese miners in a California mining camp, 1857. Chinese in the gold fields were usually relegated to placer mining sites already exploited by others. From *Harper's Weekly*, October 3, 1857. Prints and Photographs Division, Library of Congress.

Six Great Houses. Other social organizations would follow, often based upon commonly held surnames.

The *hui-kuan* served many functions within the community. They established headquarters that served as social centers and included temples. The leaders, many of whom were Chinese merchants, represented the Chinese community to the American authorities and to other businessmen. They represented Chinese in legal actions against the nativists. They mediated disputes within the community, saw to it that debts were collected, and recruited new members from among those arriving on the docks. They extended their activities to the mining camps, where they built dormitories for the Chinese miners and provided other services. Although tongs continued to exist and new ones would be established, especially in the 1860s, they would never gain the membership or the influence of the *hui-kuan*, which served as agents of stability to a very fluid and changing Chinese population.[3]

Between the two extremes were other ethnic communities of the smaller immigrant groups. The rural communities of such groups as Swedish, Norwegians, and Dutch often centered upon churches,

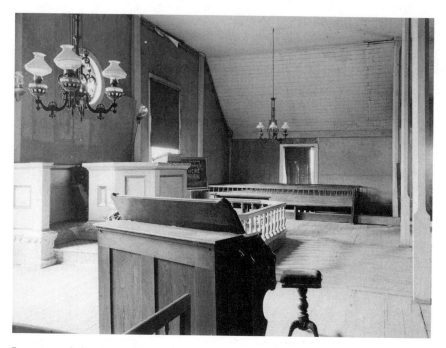

Interior of the Swedish Old Colony church at Bishop Hill, Illinois. The colony was founded by Eric Janson, a dissenter from the established Lutheran Church of Sweden, who led a group of some 1,100 Swedes to settle in Illinois in 1846. The colony served to attract other Swedes to the Midwest in subsequent decades. Historical American Buildings Survey, Library of Congress Prints and Photographs Division.

and other organizations were often related to the church. Each of these populations had a considerable element of religious dissenters, who had come in part because of alienation from the established church in their homeland. Thus the churches, as in the case of the Germans, served to be a divisive factor within the group. The emigration of Dutch Calvinists in the 1840s was in many ways carried on under church auspices. Congregations and related emigration societies in Holland helped to organize overseas migration, and the new congregations provided encouragement for others in the homeland wanting to follow along the path of chain migration. While these individual communities were homogeneous, there remained strong religious differences among the Dutch generally. Catholics, although only about 18 percent of the Dutch emigrants, occupied distinctly different communities in the American context.[4] A division among American Dutch Calvinists occurred in 1857, when they split into the older Reformed Church body and the newer Christian Reformed Church, the latter reflecting more conservative Calvinist traditions brought from the homeland.

Likewise, the Italians in their few urban communities like New York and Philadelphia gathered around churches set up for those speaking Italian. Although most of the Italians of this period came from northern Italy, some divisions among them based on regional origin began to appear even before the Civil War.

DRAWING TOGETHER: CELEBRATIONS AND FESTIVALS

Although immigrant communities were often torn by divisions and conflicts, there were occasions when efforts were made to draw a community together. This most often could be done by celebrations and festivals, where ethnic symbolism could be used to create at least a superficial sense of unity. The European immigrant groups, especially the Catholic ones, were often culturally attuned to festivals that occurred on Sundays and saints' days. Celebrations on Sundays in America inevitably conflicted with the more sober American version of Sunday, rooted in New England Puritanism. Thus government intrusion into Sunday became a sore point for most new immigrants. Eventually, the European tradition of Sunday observances would prevail, especially in the growing cities of the post-Civil War era.

The most important general celebration in the early Republic was the Fourth of July. Nearly every town and city drew together their forces to celebrate Independence Day, which generally included a parade, a series of patriotic speeches, and fireworks. Over the years participants attached various meanings to the celebrations. By the 1840s reformers and abolitionists in the North used the parade to demonstrate for their causes. In the South, a defense of the slave system came to be an expected part of the day's rhetoric. It was not surprising that by the 1840s nativist societies were also demonstrating on the Fourth of July in favor of their version of the pure and undefiled Republic—one without the immigrant. The immigrants, of course, responded, with nearly every society they could muster joining in the parade, carrying banners declaring their loyalty to the Republic and its promise of freedom. These were perhaps the only occasions where all immigrant groups acted in concert, except possibly when they gathered publicly to protest temperance and Sabbath-law reforms.

The Irish came to hold the most conspicuous public ethnic celebration, Saint Patrick's Day, March 17. St. Patrick's Day observances
in America dated to the late eighteenth century, when the occasion
was usually celebrated with a dinner of an elite society like the
Friendly Sons of Saint Patrick. In the first decades of the nineteenth
century the celebration took on a somewhat more elaborate form,
but remained—like the Irish-American population itself at that
time—largely middle-class in its character. A Mass was followed by
a parade, typically a short procession to some hall or meeting place
where there were lectures, patriotic speeches, a dinner, and end-
less toasts. The arrival of many thousands of famine immigrants
changed the character of the Irish-American population and the
nature of the celebration. While a Mass continued to be at the beginning of almost every observance, the celebration went far beyond
the honoring of the Irish patron saint, and, as the Irish-American
population was greatly augmented by the famine migrants, Irish
nationalism and anti-English sentiments increasingly became major
themes. In 1849 about 1,500 participants, mostly from the traditional
ethnic societies, took part in the New York parade. Over the next
decade the observance in New York grew spectacularly, and by the
end of the Civil War, thirty to forty thousand marchers were taking
part each year. Similar developments in other cities had made the
celebration a nationwide event. The parade had become the central
attraction, pushing the speeches and dinners into the background.
The banners, speeches, and songs increasingly emphasized the
Irish-Americans' identity with both Catholic faith and Irish nationalism.

The New York parade of 1857, observed by many thousands,
demonstrated the new character of St. Patrick's Day. The procession made its way past a reviewing stand at City Hall Park, and
then up Broadway. In the lead were the Irish Dragoons, followed
by nearly two dozen other Irish militia groups. Then came numerous benevolent societies and workingmen's associations, escorted
by honor guards from the militia. Included were the Laborers'
Union Society, two branches of the Ancient Order of Hibernians,
the Father Mathew Benevolent Society (named for a temperance
reformer), the Quarrymen's Protective Union, the Workingmen's
Union Protective Society, the Montgomery Protective Society, the
Hibernian Benevolent Society, the Roman Catholic Society, and
the Longshoremen's Society, followed by many carriages. Said the
reporter from the *New York Times*, "There was music *galore* and of
the right sort."[5]

In the evening, there were celebratory dinners of many societies, including the Hibernia United Protective Society, the Young Friends of Ireland, the Hibernian Society, and the Doran Guard. All of these featured speeches, toasts, and songs celebrating American patriotism and Irish identity and national pride. At the 73rd annual dinner of the Friendly Sons of St. Patrick, held at the Metropolitan Hotel, the speaker of greatest note was Thomas Francis Meagher, the fiery Irish nationalist who had escaped to America after having been sentenced by the British to exile in Tasmania. Apparently mindful of the more conservative nature of the Friendly Sons, he avoided discussion of Irish nationalism or criticism of British rule, and confined his speech to the glories of Irish culture, with tributes to Irish soldiers, statesmen, poets, and artists. He concluded with a call for unity among Irish people, "where men of different religions—men of different political schools, men of different pursuits and walks in life—meet together on a common ground . . . and there, in a wise and glorious spirit, flinging to the winds all provincial and sectarian prejudices, recognize the common land of their nativity."[6]

Meagher's speech did exemplify the superficial quality of most ethnic celebrations, where divisions and conflicts among a group could be covered over with appeals to unity based on certain cultural elements common to all. Nevertheless, among the Irish the dominant themes of Catholicism and nationalism would prevail. The American St. Patrick's Day celebration was becoming something far different from the traditional observances in Ireland.

For the Germans, finding a basis for unity was more complicated, given the provincial identifications of many of the immigrants in America. The principal basis for unity was a common language, but even then the German Americans spoke many different dialects, which served to accentuate their differences. Given religious divisions, the celebration of a patron saint did not serve to bring Germans all together. Efforts in the mid-nineteenth century to organize a German day that would rival St. Patrick's Day often made use of some cultural figure. The most common celebration was perhaps Schiller Day, centered on the October birthday of the famed poet Friedrich Schiller; there were elaborate celebrations on the centenary of Schiller's birth in 1859. This observance, however, never gained the currency among Germans that St. Patrick's Day did among the Irish. Other attempts to find a symbolic gathering point came later: in the 1880s, commemorations of the German settlement of Germantown in Pennsylvania in 1683; and in the twentieth century, festivities honoring the American Revolutionary general Friedrich Wilhelm von Steuben.

However, many local German communities had celebrations organized by one particular *Verein*—a provincial group, a singing society, or a Turner society, in which most other members of the community could join. The Sunday festivities of several groups might turn into a general celebration. Sometimes competitions were organized by gymnastic groups, singing societies, or shooting societies from various towns and cities, helping to establish a wider network among German-Americans. These various festivals typically attracted the participation of whole families, and most of them were conducted with the assistance of that great common denominator of Germans, lager beer.

The Christmas season and its celebrations were looked upon by Germans as their own contribution to American culture, and it can be argued that the American Christmas owes much of its character to the German influence. In colonial days, Christmas in America was generally limited to a religious holiday. In Calvinist New England, only a church service was allowable, and extravagant celebrations were frowned upon. But the Germans of Pennsylvania were celebrating Christmas in their way in the late eighteenth century, with observances stretching from St. Nicholas's day to Epiphany, including the common practice of a decorated evergreen Christmas tree. Christmas trees were finding their way to the public markets of Philadelphia in the early nineteenth century, and the newer immigrants arriving after 1820 also brought the practice with them. However, the more widespread American custom of decorating Christmas trees found its way from Germany to America by way of England. After Prince Albert of Saxe-Coburg married Queen Victoria, he installed a Christmas tree with decorations during the 1841 holiday at Windsor Castle. In 1846 the *Illustrated London News* published a picture of the royal family's tree, and Americans as well as English were quick to follow the fashion.

COMMUNICATING: THE IMMIGRANT PRESS

Americans, possessing a high degree of literacy and a growing interest in politics, had by the second quarter of the nineteenth century developed a general habit of newspaper reading. Newly arriving immigrants usually lacked such a habit, having come from places where politics was closed to common people and newspapers were considered a pastime for the elite classes. Nevertheless, many newcomers adjusted to the American custom, as they learned the advantages of keeping current with matters in the old country and in the new. The political parties that emerged in the heated politics of the Jacksonian period recognized the possibilities of using the press to educate the immigrants. Ambitious politicians were expected to support foreign-language papers just as they subsidized the English-language ones. Educated and professional people among the immigrants quickly noted that the press was a way of exerting leadership over a group that sometimes lacked leaders.

The immigrant newspapers were affected by the same influences that were changing English-language journalism in America at the same time. New technologies for producing and distributing newspapers were developing rapidly. In the late 1840s, telegraph lines were being strung across the country, providing immediate news to the newspapers, and daily newspapers were becoming more common. New steam-operated rotary presses enabled the printing of larger numbers of newspapers, and the expanding rail network facilitated their widespread distribution. Newspapers were becoming a factor in the lives of all Americans, and the immigrants were no exception. While America had had some foreign-language newspapers in the late eighteenth century, they became much more common after 1830.

The Germans established many more newspapers than did any other immigrant group. After the period of the Napoleonic Wars, when immigration was at a low ebb, the pre-1800 German press that remained served mostly areas settled by the eighteenth-century Germans. Beginning around 1830, the German press began to expand into new areas as immigration picked up. What would become the largest and longest-lasting German newspaper, the *New Yorker Staats-Zeitung,* was founded—like many others—to support a political party, the Jacksonian Democratic party, in the New York municipal elections of 1834. Supported by party leaders at its inception, it never deserted the party. The 1830s also saw the founding of many other important German-language papers. The arrival of many literate middle-class Germans, and especially of educated and professional men fleeing the failed revolutions of 1830, provided new leaders who found a future in journalism. Many of the cities with growing German populations acquired papers during the 1830s: the Cincinnati *Volksfreund,* the Philadelphia *Alte und Neue Welt,* the Cleveland *Germania,* the Buffalo *Demokrat,* and the long-standing mainstay of German journalism in the West, the St. Louis *Anzeiger des Westens.*

The flood of German immigration after 1848 brought more readers, and more refugee intellectuals who found their place in the expanding realm of journalism. Estimators counted about 70 German newspapers across the country in 1848; there were at least 89 by 1851, and the number had expanded to 144 in 1860.[7] Many of the large-city papers had become dailies, and new papers were being founded in smaller towns that were centers of German settlement. The large contingent of forty-eighters who had become editors in those years would continue to dominate German-language journalism until nearly the end of the century. They would play an especially important role in persuading many Germans to follow a new political course in the hectic political party upheavals of the 1850s.

The German newspapers readily gained a following among the mostly literate German population. Although they regularly presented news brought to America by ship from the European homelands, their more important role was to introduce newcomers to American society and politics. They brought news from other German communities across the country by publishing "exchanges," excerpts from other newspapers that copied their news in return. They informed their readers about where new lands and jobs were becoming available. They put the German population in touch with German merchants who sold familiar items and with American merchants who sought their trade. They could offer an immigrant readership to politicians who sought immigrants' votes. The newspapers also reflected the divisions among German immigrants: there developed radical newspapers, Catholic newspapers, Lutheran newspapers, and magazines and papers devoted to various special interests. The German newspaper network served to tie together the widespread German communities, even as they exposed the conflicts and differences within them.

The Irish never could surpass the profusion of German newspapers. This was partly because many of the Irish masses were illiterate, but also because those who were literate could easily read the mainstream English-language newspapers. The Democratic party's principal journals knew the value of catering to the Irish vote and were careful not to offend the Irish population.

When Patrick Lynch, formerly a newspaperman in Ireland, undertook to begin the *Irish American* in New York in late 1849, he noted the need for an Irish paper and refused to believe that the Irish were "not intelligent" enough to support one. "The Germans, with a population about half that of ours, have four daily papers. . . . the Franco Americans, two; the Italians, one."[8] Lynch's solution was to make his paper a weekly issued on Sunday for those who were completely occupied with labor for the other six days of the week. "Three cents on a Sunday morning will never be missed by him who earns six dollars in six days."[9]

Lynch's efforts did produce a paper that would become, within ten years, the largest-circulating Irish newspaper in the nation. His method was to try to appeal both to Irish Catholics and to those who supported Irish nationalism. He particularly concentrated on publishing the latest news from Ireland, sorted out county-by-county to allow readers to find the news most relevant to them. But he also followed the course of the Irish nationalist movement with broader political articles from Ireland.

For many Irish, however, the preeminent paper was the avowedly Catholic *Boston Pilot*. This weekly had been founded as a church-related paper by Bishop Benedict Fenwick of Boston in 1829. It took on the name *Pilot* in 1836; the name was taken from a Dublin newspaper that was the chief organ for the Irish Repeal movement (which advocated repeal of the Act of Union with Great Britain and the reestablishment of a separate Parliament for Ireland). In 1838 Patrick Donohue, an advocate of Repeal, took over as editor and controlled the newspaper until his death in 1891. Donohue shaped the paper to serve the needs of Irish Catholics across the United States, and succeeded in developing a national circulation. The paper persistently carried anti-nativist material, and reported on abuses of the Irish Catholic population by hostile forces. It ran columns of news both political and personal from Ireland. A special function of the paper was to track down Irish immigrants who had lost contact with friends and relatives. Each weekly issue carried a "Missing Friends" column, in which appeals from those seeking the lost persons were published, at a cost of one dollar for three insertions. The advertisements for Missing Friends mirror the disorderly and chaotic nature of the Irish diaspora, especially during the famine years.[10]

The New York Catholic-oriented newspaper comparable to the *Boston Pilot* was the *Freeman's Journal*, founded in 1841. Soon after its inception it became a supporter of Archbishop John Hughes in the controversy over the reading of the Protestant Bible in the public schools. In the view of the nativists of the time, the paper became a symbol of the Catholic influence in politics. A rival paper more strongly supportive of Irish nationalism appeared when Thomas D'Arcy McGee fled from the failed 1848 revolution in Ireland to New York. He founded the *Nation*, which spoke strongly in favor of Irish liberation, as well as advocating for the welfare of the Irish immigrants in America. In 1857 McGee was invited by the Irish community in Montreal to start an Irish newspaper there, the *New Era*. He entered Canadian politics and became known as one of the architects of the movement that achieved Canadian confederation in 1867. During the same time, he turned against Irish nationalism and became a stronger defender of Catholicism and British rule. His attacks upon the Fenian movement, a radical Irish nationalist group then emerging in North America, are the likely cause of his assassination in Ottawa in 1868. Other Irish nationalists expanded the world of Irish-American journalism in the 1850s and introduced many Irish immigrants to the cause of Irish nationalism.

The demographic and technological factors which led to the expansion of Irish and German newspapers at mid-century also were instrumental in fostering newspapers for other immigrant groups. The settlement of a new wave of Dutch settlers in Michigan and Wisconsin in the late 1840s led to the establishment of the *Sheboygan Nieuwsbode* and *De Hollander* (of Holland, Michigan). The political conflicts of the 1850s would produce more Dutch newspapers. Among the Scandinavians, the Norwegians saw their first American newspaper, *Nordlyset*, founded in Norway, Wisconsin, in 1847. In 1855 the Swedes in Galesburg, Illinois, welcomed the newspaper *Hemlandet*, begun as a Lutheran church newspaper but eventually broadening its scope and its distribution. It moved to Chicago and continued publication until 1914. Eventually it would find an antagonist in a more secular newspaper, *Svenska Amerikanaren*, founded in Chicago in 1866.

The French Americans had a long history of newspaper publishing dating back to the late 1700s. The 1800s saw a variety of newspapers founded in Louisiana and catering to its French-speaking population. New immigration also gave birth to *Le Courrier des Etats Unis* in New York in 1828, and the French who joined in the gold rush started *L'Echo du Pacifique* in San Francisco. Both those papers would last into the twentieth century.

The Chinese in California were producing newspapers just a few years after their gold-rush arrival. The first was the *Golden Hills News* of 1854. Like many others to follow, its text was produced in Chinese characters handwritten by brush, then printed by lithography. Several others followed in the 1850s, including the *Chinese Daily News* in 1857, a daily produced in America before any daily paper had been produced in China itself. Despite a high degree of illiteracy among the Chinese, the newspapers found a readership for a while because of the concentration of their readers in San Francisco, Sacramento, and the mining camps.

Newspapers were instruments of assimilation for new immigrants; they educated them about life, society, and politics in America. Reading the newspapers was itself an act of assimilation, the acquisition of a cultural habit that had been unknown to them in the old country.

TOURING SOME IMMIGRANT COMMUNITIES AT MID-CENTURY

Thirty years of immigration had created in America a great variety of immigrant communities. Although formed by the desire of a group to preserve some of the culture of the land of origin, these communities were also shaped by the conditions and history of a particular place in America, by the pragmatic needs of a group to establish itself in a new environment, and by the demands and pressures of the host society. Some ethnic communities might be harmonious, others driven by conflicts and divisions. Some might have a complex of ethnic institutions, others might have only a few. Every major city was different, with varying component ethnic groups which interacted with each other and with the native-born population in various ways.

The Port Cities

The major port cities served as gateways to America for new immigrants, and also offered links to the interior. Most had served as entryways for immigrant populations since colonial days, and housed some ethnic institutions which dated from the eighteenth century. The immigrant communities served very transient populations, with some staying only a few days, some for years. Some of the permanent institutions offered assistance to newcomers, helping them to find jobs and lodging, either temporary or long-term. The turnover within the immigrant communities meant that while their structures might be more-or-less permanent, their character sometimes changed as newer immigrant arrivals replaced earlier constituents who moved on.

New York, consistently after 1820 the largest port of immigration with the largest population of foreign-born, reflected this turbulence. By 1850 the number of foreign-born was about 235,000, amounting to about 47 percent of the city's population. The sheer size of the immigrant population encouraged subdivision of the immigrant institutions; there was plenty of room for separate organizations for both Irish Catholics and Irish Protestants, for Irish nationalists and those who opposed them, for German Lutherans and German Catholics, for Bavarians and Prussians, and for many other subgroups as well. With each individual free to find a compatible institution, achieving unified action remained difficult.

By 1850 most of New York City's population was still concentrated on the lower end of Manhattan Island, below 34th Street. Much of the immigrant population remained in the older districts below 14th Street. Only the more fortunate ones were able to move into the more recently developed sections to the north. As commercial activity, industry, and warehouses continued to grow in lower Manhattan, the heavily immigrant population was crowded together in subdivided older houses and in tenements newly built to house as many as possible. In lower Manhattan as elsewhere, there were few exclusive neighborhoods for any immigrant group; Irish, Germans, and others were likely to be living in close proximity. However, the Germans predominated in areas east of the Bowery—which had, early in the century, been the city's most fashionable street, but which had now deteriorated into a commercial district heavily geared to the immigrant trade, with many cheap boardinghouses and saloons. Between the Bowery and the East River and above Division Street were the heaviest concentrations of German-born immigrants: they composed 34 percent of the 1855 population of the 11th Ward, near the East River waterfront. In the 10th Ward, near the intersection of the Bowery and Division Street, were located the more prominent German institutions: churches both Catholic and Protestant, a thriving German theater district, a Turner Hall, and numerous other gathering places. The 10th Ward's population was about 30 percent German-born. The German district also included the 13th and 17th wards, and was becoming known as Little Germany (*Kleindeutschland*). New York in 1855, with about 154,000 German-born and their children, had the third largest German population of any city in the world—behind only Berlin and Vienna.[11]

Across the city generally, the Irish constituted the largest ethnic group, making up about 28 percent of its population in 1855, not counting children born in the United States. About one in every twelve Irish-born in the United States could be found in New York City.[12] The Irish, despite many examples of upward mobility, were still primarily concentrated in the laboring class. The New York

State census of 1855 counted 19,783 foreign-born laborers in the city; 17,426 were Irish, 1,870 were German. Out of 746 listed as musicians, 528 were foreign-born; of these, 274 were German, 95 were Italian, and 57 were Irish.[13]

The heaviest concentration of Irish was in the wards to the south and west of Little Germany, including most of the waterfronts along both the East River and the Hudson at the lower end of Manhattan. The 6th Ward, just west of the heavily German 10th Ward, was the district most heavily populated by the Irish; they numbered 34 percent of the population.[14] It included the most disreputable slum in the city, "Five Points," located at the conjunction of Cross, Anthony, and Orange Streets (later Park, Worth, and Baxter Streets, respectively). However, the largely common-labor employment of the Irish brought them into dwellings in all quarters of the city, including the waterfront, the northern outskirts, and the manufacturing districts. The Irish Catholic churches followed them; between 1840 and 1860, 23 new Catholic parishes were founded, 15 of them Irish, along with 7 German churches and 1 French.[15] The other principal institutions of the Irish community, the saloons, were distributed throughout the city, offering a useful base of operations for many Irish ward politicians. By mid-century, the Irish involvement in the city's politics had developed sufficient influence to recruit larger numbers of Irish policemen—about 27 percent of the police force in 1855.[16] Their presence in the Irish neighborhoods helped to tie the institutions of municipal government more closely to the immigrant community.

Nearly every American immigrant group of the era had some institutional presence in New York City—through churches, mutual-aid societies, and cultural groups. There were contingents of French, Poles, Italians, Greeks, and even a few Chinese—indeed, 38 Chinese men were recorded in the 1855 census. But all also had contact with the whole range of other ethnicities. New York surely qualified as the nation's largest "melting pot," long before the term became common.

Philadelphia had been the largest port of entry for immigrants in the colonial period, although its relative status declined after the 1820s, while New York quickly rose to become the leading port of entry. New immigrants to Philadelphia now most often came by way of New York, attracted by the thriving industry of the Quaker City (in which the Quakers were now a distinct minority). But the earlier passage of both Germans and Protestant Irish through the city in the eighteenth century had formed immigrant communities based on churches and on societies to protect newcomers.

The newcomers of the second quarter of the nineteenth century, however, generally created a new institutional structure. The venerable German Society of Pennsylvania, increasingly an organization of descendants, had made English its official language in 1818, and had ceased using German in any of its records by the late 1840s. Newcomers would begin to take over the organization and revive it in the 1850s, and the Society would return to the use of German in the 1860s. The eighteenth-century German churches had mostly abandoned German-language services by 1830, and the newer immigrants were creating their own churches, both Protestant and Catholic. Philadelphia remained an organizational center of Lutheran and Reformed churches, and through them spread its influence into German communities elsewhere. Philadelphia's Catholics acquired a German-speaking Bohemian-born bishop, John Nepomucene Neumann, who served from 1852 until his death in 1860 (he would be declared a canonized saint in 1977). He labored heavily to serve all ethnic groups equally, founding an orphanage for German children, learning Gaelic to better relate to the Irish community, and establishing the first parish in America especially for Italian immigrants.

As new German immigration picked up toward mid-century, the Germans developed a great diversity of social and cultural groups. Philadelphia had been the birthplace of the German-language press in colonial days; by 1850, it had two German newspapers, the *Demokrat*, founded in 1839, and the *Freie Presse*, founded in 1848 by freethinkers. By 1850 there were 5 German singing societies in Philadelphia. In that year they joined with 10 other singing societies from along the eastern seaboard to organize a *Sängerfest*, the first of many annual festivals that would form the basis for an intercity federation of singing societies, the *Sängerbund*. The associations formed by German cultural and social societies across the nation were developing by the middle of the century into a national network linking immigrants together, and creating a shared German consciousness that gradually weakened their previous provincial identities.

While Germans had once dominated the immigrant population of Philadelphia, the Irish were taking the lead in numbers by 1850. The second largest city in the country, with a population (including the suburbs) of over 400,000 in 1850, Philadelphia counted just under 30 percent of its population as foreign-born. But 60 percent of the foreign-born were now Irish, and the number was growing with the famine migration. The leadership of the colonial and early nineteenth-century Protestant Irish, once politically and economically influential, had given way to the Catholic Irish. Philadelphia had become known as an intellectual center for Irish Catholics, largely due to the leadership of the Irish-born Mathew Carey (1760–1839), a prolific author and one of the most prominent book publishers of the time.

The strongest uniting element among Philadelphia's Irish was the struggle against the nativists; the memory of the riots of 1844 was still fresh. Nativism still endured at mid-century and was a driving force in the reorganization of the city and its merging with Philadelphia County in 1854. That consolidation provided for a united police force that could deal with immigrant unrest, and the first mayor elected under the new municipal framework was a member of the new American, or Know-Nothing, party. In the turbulent political world of the 1850s, the continuing nativist threat was welding the Irish more closely to the Democratic party. The burgeoning Catholic parishes and the many mutual-assistance organizations of the Irish also served as protections for a beleaguered group. The Irish community in Philadelphia could be seen as an example of a community built upon conflict.

Baltimore, with about 21 percent foreign-born in 1850, was not as heavily populated by immigrants as the other port cities, but was nevertheless a city of considerable ethnic diversity. A latter-day scholar described the nineteenth-century city as "a patchwork of nationalities and establishments stitched together by a complex thread of economic and demographic change. It consisted of white native, German, Irish, other foreign groups, and blacks. . . . Some neighborhood clusters of one group appeared here and there, but heterogeneous mixtures of various ethnic groups were more common."[17] Within this patchwork, the Germans clearly dominated as the most numerous foreign-born element. The reason was that the tobacco trade with Germany through Baltimore's port brought back many immigrants on ships returning from German ports such as Bremerhaven. The German-born population included many Catholics, and the Catholic churches served as social and cultural organizations. The nation's leading German Catholic newspaper, the *Katholische Kirchenzeitung*, was published in the city. The Germans, with a long-standing presence, had a well-developed middle and upper class, whose neighborhoods were spreading to the north and east of the center of the city, along with German savings banks, churches, and cultural institutions. The larger concentrations of Irish were in the southern part of the city, although they could be found in all quarters.

Baltimore was a city torn between north and south, and Maryland was a slave state. The city also had a considerable number of free blacks, around 32,000 in 1850. The influx of new immigrants in the early 1850s, many of them working class, created a greater competition for jobs, which drove some of the free blacks out of the city; their numbers declined to about 26,000 by 1860. Meanwhile, the number of the city's foreign-born rose by about 50 percent, from 35,000 in 1850 to 52,000 in 1860. The result was tense and sometimes violent relations between blacks and working-class whites. The upsurge in the immigrant population also developed a strong Know-Nothing reaction in the city, targeted as elsewhere particularly against the working-class Irish Catholics.

If Baltimore was seen as a city dominated by Germans, Boston was clearly in the hands of the Irish. By 1855 about 30 percent of Boston's population was Irish-born, and only one percent German-born. The city in the early nineteenth century had not been a very prominent port of immigration, but the famine years in the late 1840s brought large numbers of the most impoverished Irish to New England. Many of them had come by way of the Canadian maritime provinces or by way of New York. During the famine immigration, the poorest and most desperate Irish migrants came in the lumber ships to Saint John, New Brunswick, then traveled down the coast to Boston and other cities. The lowly state of the Irish by the 1850s made them the special targets of nativist attacks. The city served as a point of distribution for immigrants going into interior New England, especially those who were becoming the workforce of the textile mills there after 1840. But the lack of easy connections to the West (in comparison with other port cities) left many stranded in Boston. The arrival of so many at mid-century crowded them into tenements, concentrated in the city's North End, with poor health conditions and high infant mortality.

The Catholic Church in Boston had grown only slowly in the first four decades of the nineteenth century, but during the 1840s it was expanding under the pressure of the arriving immigrants. In 1846 Boston acquired a new American-born bishop of Irish parentage, John B. Fitzpatrick. In the ensuing decade a number of new parishes were built to serve the Irish, and priests from Ireland were sought to staff them. It was the various mutual-assistance and charitable organizations founded by the church that bore the brunt of relief efforts for the many indigent Irish.

The tide of famine immigrants began to increase the Irish numbers in the city's electorate, with many of them acquiring naturalization in the early 1850s after five years' residence. Their votes were now sought by both native-born and Irish-born political leaders. Political reformers (many of them Whigs) began to seek ways to restrict the political influence of the Catholic Irish. In 1854 a new state constitution that would have restricted legislative representation of those in the city in favor of those in country towns was roundly defeated with the overwhelming opposition of the Irish. This set the stage for a resurgence of nativism and a sharpening of the division between the mostly Irish Democratic party and the loose coalition of reform forces—many of which would eventually wind up in the new Republican party. The ethnic-political polarization that would underlie Boston politics for most of the next century was now underway. The Boston Irish were far from having political control of the city in the 1850s; the first Irish mayor would not be elected until 1885.

New Orleans in the second quarter of the century became the second largest port of immigration. Its society, based on earlier populations of French-speaking Creoles, had accepted a variety of other cultures during its growth. There were many so-called New French—French-speaking immigrants who came after the War of 1812—including many from the West Indies as well as France itself. There were also Germans and English, many of them involved in the cotton and sugar export trade which were important aspects of the city's economy. There were also many Irish, who were the largest single foreign-born group, although they did not constitute a majority of the immigrant population.

Only a small percentage of immigrants arriving in New Orleans chose to stay in the city. It is estimated that in the period from 1820 to 1860, over a quarter of a million Irish arrived; yet the number of Irish-born actually in the city in 1860 was a little over 24,000. Immigrants of every type quickly found their way north up the Mississippi River. Many bypassed the southern states entirely, avoiding competition with slaves for employment. Others disliked the hot climate, and many had a justifiable fear of the scourge of yellow fever, which afflicted not only New Orleans but also other southern cities. In a particularly deadly epidemic of the yellow fever in New Orleans in 1853, an estimated 12,000 people died. Over one-third of these were Irish, and many Germans died as well.

New Orleans reached its peak as a port city of immigration during the early 1850s. In the second half of the decade, the number of new immigrants passing through the port dropped drastically. The reason was the development of new railroad routes from the eastern ports to the Mississippi River and beyond, which gave immigrants faster and cheaper access to the Upper Mississippi Valley.

The most turbulent period in the city's development had been the 1830s, just as the Cotton Belt was opening up across the Gulf states and new areas in the Midwest were attracting settlers and sending their produce down the Mississippi. By 1840 the city had increased to over 100,000 people, and was at that time the third largest city in the United States. The arrival of newcomers had its effect on the black population of the city, both free and slave. Facing competition for work from immigrants, many blacks left the city, and their proportion of the population declined. This trend continued through the 1840s and 1850s, as high cotton prices caused planters to pull their slaves out of the city and new and more restrictive segregation laws helped to drive free blacks away. There were many instances of violent conflict between Irish and free blacks, with the Irish generally prevailing.

The Irish did not succeed, however, in taking over the Catholic Church in New Orleans as they did in many other dioceses. While the French bishop (later archbishop) Anthony Blanc, who presided over the diocese from 1835 to 1860, welcomed the Irish, founded new churches for them, and encouraged the development of Irish Catholic societies, this was not enough to offset the more relaxed French-Creole culture that still dominated the Catholic population. At Blanc's death the clergy was still in a majority French, and the authority of the bishop still weak. In contrast to the dioceses in many other American cities, the archdiocese in New Orleans would not have an Irish bishop until 1918.

The Way West

As newly arrived immigrants made their way west along the rivers and canals after 1820, immigrant communities began to develop in cities located along the routes. They often became centers serving subsidiary immigrant communities in a surrounding area, and were points of departure for immigrants finding places of settlement further on. Thus there developed a network of immigrant communities linked together by chain migration, family ties, church organizations, and communications through the press and mail. This gave the larger urban immigrant communities a fluid and changing quality similar to what was found in the major ports of entry.

Cincinnati, rapidly becoming known as the "Queen City of the West" in the years after the War of 1812, became also a cultural center for the Germans. Immigrants arrived there overland from the eastern ports but also increasingly by traveling up the Mississippi and Ohio Rivers from New Orleans. This migration was facilitated in particular by the introduction of the steamboat into western waters after 1820. Several tributaries flowed into the Ohio River near Cincinnati from both north and south, providing access to the newly opened lands being settled in the late 1820s and 1830s. This conjunction of trade routes leading out of the hinterland helped to make Cincinnati the center for slaughtering and packing salt pork, which was then exported down river and through New Orleans. By 1840 the city's reputation, reflected in its nickname, "Porkopolis," was well established, and about 200,000 hogs were being slaughtered there annually. In that year the German-born immigrants of Cincinnati, together with their children, comprised nearly a third of the population.

The heaviest concentration of Germans was in the neighborhood to the north and east of the Miami and Ohio Canal. Many of the growing city's industries, including meat-packing, brewing, and furniture making, were near the canal. These enterprises were employers of many of the Germans. The nearby neighborhood, to the east and north of the canal, came to be known as "Over-the-Rhine," the canal standing in for the Rhine River. In 1840 slightly less than half the population of Over-the-Rhine was German, but most of the German social and cultural institutions were developing there. They included German churches, both Protestant and Catholic; the German Catholic church of St. Mary, built in 1842, was said at the time to be the largest church structure in the Ohio Valley. Here was also located the first Turner society in America, founded in 1848 by the revolutionary Friedrich Hecker. Here as well were the singing societies, German theaters, and mutual aid societies, as well as the beer taverns. This concentration of organizations gave Cincinnati the most fully developed German community in the country. But like other German communities, it reflected great diversity and many inner divisions.

Among the Germans attracted by the thriving commerce of the Queen City were many German Jews, who considered themselves members of the German community. Most of the German Jews belonged to the Reform Jewish movement then developing in Germany and finding adherents in the United States. Although English Jews had organized an Orthodox congregation earlier, the Reform Jews formed their own in 1841. In 1854 Rabbi Isaac Wise would take over leadership of the congregation and become the most significant leader of American Reform Judaism.

The Irish population in Cincinnati was half the size of the German community. Many Irish were employed in the river trade, serving as stevedores, canal workers, or teamsters. Others worked on the public works of the rapidly expanding city. The Irish lived in all parts of the city, near their workplaces, but the largest concentration was along the riverfront and near the public landing. Irish Catholic churches proliferated in the 1830s and 1840s, and there were many saloons to serve the Irish as well.

St. Louis, with its strategic location near the confluence of the Missouri and Mississippi Rivers, became by 1850 the economic and cultural center of a region populated by many immigrants. The Germans were numerous in several counties on the eastern side of the Mississippi in Illinois, including in the town of Belleville, where many so-called Latin Farmers—German intellectuals fleeing the failed 1830 revolutions—had settled during the 1830s. To the west along the Missouri River, many communities of German ethnicity had been founded, the earlier ones attracted by Gottfried Duden's famous guidebook. The city and its environs developed as a German center with the rise of immigration through the port of New Orleans; those immigrants who were skilled workers, professionals, and middle-class entrepreneurs found their way to the largest city on the upper Mississippi.

The city's location made it a center for German churches. The Missouri Synod of Lutherans, organized in 1847, was centered in St. Louis. The Catholic Cathedral of St. Louis, the first U.S. cathedral west of the Mississippi, provided a center for Catholics of all ethnicities over a wide area. The bishop of St. Louis had established Saint Louis College (later to become St. Louis University) in 1818; in 1827 it was put under the administration of Belgian Jesuits. In the 1850s many free-thinking refugees of the 1848 revolutions came to St. Louis, attracted by the already vibrant German culture there. They took over leadership of the already liberal *Anzeiger des Westens*, a German daily newspaper read widely throughout the region. The presence of these diverse elements led to considerable ferment within the German community. Lutherans fought with Catholics, radical forty-eighters criticized all religions, and Germans clashed with Irish as well. All immigrants would contend with nativists in the heightened Know-Nothing tensions of the early 1850s.

By 1860 St. Louis was the eighth largest city in the nation, and its population was just under one-half foreign-born. Out of 161,000 inhabitants, over 50,000 were German-born and 30,000 were Irish.[18] Although the city, like other towns along the Mississippi, had had its Irish laborers all during the early part of the century, their numbers had grown as many famine immigrants arrived during the fifties, when the city nearly doubled in population. The Irish found traditional employment on the levees, but also in the growing mills and factories of the city, as well as in the construction of railroads just beginning to proceed westward. By 1860 there were eight Irish Catholic churches in addition to the earlier parishes shared with the French. The German Catholics had four churches. The area of the Kerry Patch, on the north side of the city and near the riverfront, traditionally held the largest concentration of Irish, but the immigrant flood of the fifties had spread them to the north and west. The Germans generally settled more in the southern part of the city. It was in that neighborhood that Eberhard Anheuser and his son-in-law Adolphus Busch began to brew lager beer in 1852.

Buffalo, at the western end of the Erie Canal, was a city created by that canal. In 1825, when the canal opened, its population was about 2,500. By 1860 the city housed over 81,000. Its commerce rested on the transshipment of goods between the Great Lakes and the Erie Canal. The grain coming from the expanding Midwest was the largest element in that trade. According to the historian David Gerber, "By the mid-1850s, Buffalo was the world's largest grain port. Three-fourths of all grain and at least one-half of all rolling freight shipped in the United States changed hands at Buffalo."[19] This thriving commerce provided thousands of job opportunities— working on the canal, unloading ships in the port, shoveling grain in the grain elevators, and serving in the offices of merchants and grain dealers.

As elsewhere, the Irish, who had initially arrived with the canal, held many of the common-labor jobs and were often housed in slum conditions and shantytowns along the canal or near the Lake Erie waterfront. About three-quarters of the Irish workers were unskilled, and employed in occupations which offered little opportunity for advancement. About 19 percent of Buffalo's Irish women were employed outside the home, largely as domestic servants for middle- and upper-class American families.[20]

As in other cities, the Irish community in Buffalo was very much centered on the Catholic Church and its associated societies. The first Catholic bishop of Buffalo, John Timon, American-born of Irish ancestry, took over leadership of the new diocese in 1847. He fostered literary societies, a church newspaper, and social welfare organizations. The few secular organizations not sponsored by the Church nevertheless were mostly composed of Catholics. These included two Irish militia groups, and chapters of the Sons of Erin and the Friendly Sons of St. Patrick, both of which organized the annual St. Patrick's Day Parade.

Bishop Timon, however, did not leave the Germans out of his concerns. Germans outnumbered Irish in Buffalo; in the 1855 state census, about 39 percent of the heads of households were German-born, as opposed to 18 percent Irish-born and 12 percent born in England, Scotland, and Canada. Many of the Germans of the heavy migration of the late 1840s and early 1850s had come from the southern, more Catholic, states of Germany. The proportion of German Christians who were Catholics has been estimated to be as high as 60 percent.[21] There were six German Catholic churches, which out of necessity were more or less autonomous within the diocese; Bishop Timon found a German vicar to oversee them, and sought German-speaking priests from German religious orders. The German Protestants had six Lutheran churches, attached to various synods. There were also two United churches, a Reformed church, and several smaller Calvinist congregations. The Protestant sects, when not contending with the Catholic Germans, were prone to quarrel with each other. The German-speaking Jews of Buffalo established a synagogue in 1848.

The typically diverse German population, spread across the city but concentrated on the east side, gave rise to a complicated network of social and cultural organizations, which divided the community into various subgroups reflecting differences of religion, class, and provincial origin. Germans of many types found compatible company in a host of singing societies, literary groups, recreational associations, and mutual-assistance groups. The leading German newspaper, the *Weltbürger* (which merged with the *Demokrat* in 1852), sought to unite the diverse groups under a common German spirit. The refugees of 1848, many of them more secular and radical, began to found their own institutions, including a workingmen's union and a *Turnverein*. The general turbulence of the time militated against the formation of any common German set of ideals. Although the forty-eighters arrived with their own heightened sense of German nationalism, which they attempted to transmit to a German-American community divided by provincialism, internal division continued to divide the German community, as would be seen in the heightening political controversy of the 1850s.

Chicago, at the western end of the Great Lakes, experienced even more spectacular growth during the decade of the 1850s. Its population rose from 30,000 in 1850 to 109,000 in 1860. The city's rapid growth stemmed from its fortunate place in the nation's developing transportation network. The completion of the Illinois and Michigan Canal in 1848 achieved the long-awaited water connection between the Great Lakes and the Mississippi, and opened a new outlet for trade from the prairies stretching south and southwest across Illinois. And in the great railroad-building boom of the early 1850s, Chicago had become the center of a network of rails that extended in all directions from the shore of Lake Michigan.

The foreign-born formed over half the city's population in both 1850 and 1860. Immigrants, especially Irish, had been attracted to the city since its founding as a village in 1833. By 1860 Chicago had become the fourth largest Irish city in America. Irish men who worked in building the long-awaited canal had established themselves in a neighborhood called Bridgeport, alongside the canal, where Irish laborers worked on the canal itself and also in the nearby factories and packing houses. The building of the railroads and the expansion of the city brought the Irish into many other neighborhoods, including a concentration just north of the Chicago River in the Seventh Ward. Chicago became a Catholic diocese in 1843, and its first bishop, the Irish-born William Quarter, founded an Irish parish, St. Patrick's, in 1846; he also oversaw the building of many Irish institutions, including other parishes, orphanages, a hospital, and schools. As in other cities, the Irish community was largely built around the Catholic institutions. From the earliest times Chicago's Irish had associated themselves with the Democratic party, and by the 1850s they were a dominant force in the party, linked especially to the powerful Democratic U.S. Senator Stephen A. Douglas. The party leadership used its patronage to bind the Irish voters closely to the party.

The Irish were Chicago's largest foreign-born group before 1850, but the Germans were beginning to surpass them by that date, when they accounted for about one-sixth of the city's population. The upsurge in German migration was especially strong during the canal and railroad boom around the middle of the century. The Germans tended to settle in the neighborhoods to the north of the Chicago River—an area even Americans referred to as the *Nord Seite*. In the Seventh Ward, which was located in the western part of the North Side, Germans and Irish were present in about equal numbers, and that fact played a role in the excited local politics of the 1850s.

Many of the German institutions were concentrated on the North Side. The number of institutions grew especially during the middle of the century, and there was a strong influence of the forty-eighters in many of them. The first German-language newspaper, the *Volksfreund*, began in 1846, but was succeeded in 1848 by the *Illinois Staats-Zeitung*, which would play a strong role in German-American affairs across the Midwest for the rest of the century. In 1856, ethnic German leaders, many of them forty-eighters, constructed an impressive *Deutsches Haus* on the North Side, to be a meeting place for all German organizations. Despite the efforts of the *Deutsches Haus* toward unifying the Germans, they remained divided on the usual bases of religion, provincial origin, and class.

At the middle of the century Chicago was just beginning to develop its role as a cultural and organizational center for the mostly rural Scandinavians who earlier had settled in Illinois and Wisconsin. The development of the city as a transportation center made it by the 1850s the point of distribution for new Scandinavian immigrants settling to the north and west and just beginning to reach into Minnesota. The Norwegians were the longer-established and larger element in Chicago; about 500 were in the city in 1850, and 1,313 were counted in 1860. The Norwegians had been in the city as early as 1836, and had worked on the Illinois-Michigan Canal as well as on the boats plying the Great Lakes. The smaller Swedish settlement numbered 816 in the census of 1860. The Swedes founded an Episcopal church in 1849 and a Lutheran church in 1853; in 1855 the principal Swedish newspaper was relocated to Chicago from Galesburg. The greatest number of the Scandinavians clustered on the north and northwest sides of the city. Norwegian and Swedish women were in considerable demand as domestic servants.

Milwaukee had emerged in the 1840s as a German center as the city grew rapidly, its boom in development resting largely on its claim to be a prime port of export of Wisconsin's grain through the Great Lakes. During the 1840s, the city had contended with Chicago for the grain trade; but during the 1850s it lost ground in the competition, as Chicago easily won out as the center of the railroad network that turned the grain trade in its direction. Milwaukee, however, maintained its status as the economic center of the new state of Wisconsin. By 1850, still a city of only 20,000, it had established itself as an attractive place of settlement for German immigrants. There were several reasons for this. In 1844 the new Catholic diocese of Milwaukee had been taken over by Bishop John Martin Henni, who had quickly established himself as the spokesman for America's German Catholics. He welcomed Catholics from both the United States and Germany with the promise of a friendly reception in Milwaukee. He made a European trip in which he appealed to Catholic missionary societies in Vienna and Munich to send priests and religious orders to Milwaukee, and to encourage emigrants to choose Wisconsin as their destination. Henni was aided by other boosters, both American and German, who sent out leaflets and copies of the Milwaukee German newspaper, the *Wisconsin Banner,* to be distributed in Germany. In 1852 Wisconsin even established a state-sponsored Commissioner of Emigration to encourage new arrivals in New York to come to Wisconsin (however, the post was abolished under nativist pressures in 1855).

Despite its reputation as a center for Catholics, Milwaukee's German community demonstrated a vibrant diversity of ideologies and religious viewpoints. By 1852 the city housed three different daily German newspapers, the *Banner,* the *Volksfreund,* and the *Seebote,* papers of widely varying and sometimes conflicting political and ideological persuasions. The Germans of Milwaukee prided themselves on the variety of cultural and social institutions they had established, and in the 1850s Milwaukee was already becoming known as the "German Athens." The city housed singing societies, a musical society that presented concerts, and various literary societies including the Workers' Reading and Educational Society. The arrival of forty-eighters produced various free-thinker groups, including a *Turnverein,* which fostered a wide variety of cultural and physical activities, even introducing the radical innovation of gymnastic classes for girls in 1855. Both Lutheran and Catholic churches organized German-language schools, and the free-thinking elements organized in 1851 their own *Schul-Verein,* which sponsored the German and English Academy. Although many Germans envisioned a growing ethnic unity as the city grew, there was instead continuing disunity. As Kathleen Conzen, principal historian of Milwaukee's Germans, remarked, "The sense of German common purpose forged in the mid-forties . . . effectively diversified into a series of more specialized sub-societies."[22]

There were fewer than half as many Irish in Milwaukee as there were Germans in 1850, and the proportion of Irish in the total population dwindled as the decade went on. By 1860 there were more foreign-born in the city's population than native-born. There were just over 3,000 Irish-born, but almost 16,000 German-born.[23] The Irish had been attracted to the city in its early growth period, reacting to the demand for common labor, and they remained a primarily working-class group. As elsewhere, their community was defined largely by the existence of the Catholic churches; Bishop Henni had taken care to make sure that they were served by churches separate from the German ones. There was also, of course, the alternative social institution of the saloon, countered to some extent by various Irish temperance societies, intent on improving the image of the Irish in America.

ETHNIC COMMUNITIES AND CULTURAL CHANGE

These examples of the varying urban immigrant communities of the 1850s afford some sense of the wide range of character and composition found in them. There were of course also smaller rural and small-town communities, often considerably insulated from the general American society and quite homogeneous in character. Most, like the urban communities of the 1850s, were still in the process of development and were showing no signs of decline. But ethnic communities, rural or urban, generally served the same functions: they helped to preserve some of the culture of the old country, but also served as mediating agents between the immigrant and the host society and its culture.

The sociologist Milton Gordon once described the typical immigrant community in this way: "a kind of decompression chamber in which the newcomers could, at their own pace, make a reasonable adjustment to the new forces of a society vastly different from that which they had known in the Old World."[24] These communities were in that sense very concerned not just with preserving cultures, but also with the inevitable cultural change. Immigrant communities would contribute many things to the American way of life, but immigrant cultures would also be changed in the process.

NOTES

1. Tyler Anbinder, *Five Points: The 19th-Century New York City Neighborhood That Invented Tap Dance, Stole Elections, and Became the World's Most Notorious Slum* (New York: The Free Press, 2001), 81.

2. Charlotte Erickson, *Invisible Immigrants: The Adaptation of English and Scottish Immigrants in Nineteenth Century America* (Coral Gables, Fla.: University of Miami Press, 1972), 64.

3. Eve Armentrout-Ma, "Urban Chinese at the Sinitic Frontier: Social Organizations in United States' Chinatowns, 1849–1898," *Modern Asian Studies* 17 (1983): 107–35.

4. Robert P. Swierenga, *Faith and Family: Dutch Immigration and Settlement in the United States, 1820–1920* (New York: Holmes and Meier, 2000), 156.

5. "St. Patrick's Day," *New York Times*, March 18, 1857.

6. Ibid. See also Kenneth Moss, "St. Patrick's Day Celebrations and the Formation of Irish-American Identity, 1845–1875," *Journal of Social History* 29 (1995): 125–48.

7. James M. Bergquist, "The German-American Press," in *The Ethnic Press in the United States: A Historical Analysis and Handbook*, ed. Sally M. Miller (Westport, Conn.: Greenwood Press, 1987), 136–37.

8. *New York Irish American*, September 9, 1849 (files in Balch Institute collections, Historical Society of Pennsylvania).

9. Ibid.

10. The Missing Friends column is the source of a database housed at Boston College, with names and information on more than 31,000 persons. The database may be searched online at http://infowanted.bc.edu/.

11. Stanley Nadel, *Little Germany: Ethnicity, Religion, and Class in New York City, 1845–1880* (Urbana: University of Illinois Press, 1990), 1, 173.

12. Hasia Diner, "'The Most Irish City in the Union': The Era of the Great Migration, 1844–1877," in *The New York Irish*, ed. Ronald H. Bayor and Timothy J. Meagher (Baltimore: Johns Hopkins University Press, 1996), 93.

13. Population figures derived from the New York state census of 1855, as tabulated in Robert F. Ernst, *Immigrant Life in New York City, 1825–1863* (New York: King's Crown Press, 1949), 214–19.

14. Ibid., 188–96.

15. Jay P. Dolan, *The Immigrant Church: New York's Irish and German Catholics, 1815–1865* (Baltimore: Johns Hopkins University Press, 1975), 13–16.

16. Diner, "'The Most Irish City in the Union,'" 97.

17. Joseph Garoznik, "The Racial and Ethnic Makeup of Baltimore Neighborhoods, 1850–1870," *Maryland Historical Magazine* 71 (1976): 401.

18. William B. Faherty, *The St. Louis Irish: An Unmatched Celtic Community* (St. Louis: Missouri Historical Society Press, 2001), 53.

19. David A. Gerber, *The Making of an American Pluralism: Buffalo, New York, 1825–1860* (Urbana: University of Illinois Press, 1989), 6.

20. Ibid., 128.

21. Ibid., 92, 163, 191.

22. Kathleen Neils Conzen, *Immigrant Milwaukee, 1836–1860: Accommodation and Community in a Frontier City* (Cambridge, Mass.: Harvard University Press, 1976), 189.

23. Ibid., 14.

24. Milton M. Gordon, *Assimilation in American Life: The Role of Race, Religion, and National Origins* (New York: Oxford University Press, 1964), 106.

6

Changing Immigrant Cultures, 1820–1855

Immigrants were forced to adapt to new and varying environments as soon as they arrived in America. Some had already had to abandon older traditional ways even before they left the old country, as they moved from the countryside to the city or from agricultural work to industrial employment. For many Irish, especially during the famine migration, there was little choice except to make the swift change from the Irish countryside to the American city. All immigrants had to face a drastically different way of life in America, which would challenge their traditional practices. In many ways, being Irish-American, Norwegian-American, or German-American would quickly become something different from being Irish, Norwegian, or German. It was perhaps easiest for the British immigrants to adjust, since they came to a culture already based on British antecedents and had no language barrier to face. For all, the gradual process of assimilation began as soon as they got off the immigrant ships.

URBAN WORKPLACES AND WORK-LIFE

For most arriving immigrants, the most urgent necessity was finding a job. The more fortunate had relatives or friends who could harbor new arrivals and help them find employment. Professional people and skilled laborers might find their abilities in demand, especially in times of economic expansion. Otherwise, they might have to settle for a job beneath their qualifications. Some would find their employment to be the first step toward a different place or a more promising job. Others might keep a low-status job for the rest of their lives.

In urban contexts, immigrants by the mid-nineteenth century provided the bulk of the unskilled and semi-skilled labor in regions outside the South; even in the cities there, they made up a significant proportion of the adult male workforce. Labor on public works, building construction work, jobs as teamsters and longshoremen, and other types of outdoor work often constituted the most readily available work for those newly arrived. Both Irish and Germans were found in such occupations, but the Irish were often in the majority and tended to continue to work in the same category without rising in status. In Milwaukee, a new and rapidly expanding city, the census of 1850 counted about twice as many Germans as Irish in the workforce. In that year, 55 percent of the Irish-born heads of households were employed in unskilled work, and only 17 percent were in the skilled trades. By contrast, 46 percent of the German heads of households were employed in skilled labor, and only 26 percent were unskilled workers. As for the British-born, 54 percent were in the skilled trades, and only 2 percent were considered unskilled labor.[1]

Similar situations could be found in other cities, both east and west. The circumstances of the lowest unskilled classes militated against their rising in the hierarchy of labor. There were few opportunities for learning new skills, they lacked any capital for running a shop or business of their own, and nativist prejudices often kept other doors closed to them. Many of the unskilled jobs were seasonal, and winter might find those workers in a fruitless search for employment. The numbers of immigrant inhabitants of the poorhouse tended to rise at such times.

In 1855, over half of New York City workers involved in the building trades were foreign-born. Half of those were Irish, and another quarter German. In that city Germans and Irish accounted for three-quarters of the workers in the clothing industry. The manufacture of ready-made clothing was just in its infancy in New York; the piecework was, in the language of the time, "put out" to both Irish and Germans. In the 1830s and 1840s this piecework was often done at home, where families stitched together the pieces that were cut in clothing factories, but by the 1850s it was increasingly being done inside the factories, and with the aid of newly introduced sewing machines. German Jews were included among those finding a foothold in the clothing factories. Meanwhile, the more skilled and experienced tailors, mostly Germans, found fewer employment opportunities for their skills as custom tailors, and often had to accept the less-skilled work of the factories. Boston also became a center of clothing factories, but workers' pay there was only about half the $8–10 weekly rate paid in New York. Generally, women in factory jobs were paid only half the wages earned by men.

Around the middle of the century the making of shoes was beginning to follow the same course as clothing, changing from production by individual shoemakers in their shops to factory production. This transition was facilitated by the introduction during the 1850s of a sewing machine that could handle the shoe uppers. By 1855 nearly all of New York's shoemakers were foreign-born—about half of them German and a third Irish. But those shoemakers who were individual craftsmen were meeting with competition from the factories, and often were forced into factory work or into another trade.

Germans found their way into the food industry in the second quarter of the nineteenth century, and by the middle of the century were coming to dominate it. Small bakeries and butcher shops set up to serve the German community began to attract customers from other sectors of the population. The large pork-packing operations in Cincinnati, the prototypes for the coming mass-production meat industry, were the employment places of many Germans. The Germans came to dominate the brewing industry, establishing over several decades small breweries which produced the German-style lager beer. The 1840s saw the founding of lager breweries in Cincinnati, Milwaukee, Boston, Chicago, and San Francisco. These produced a beer fermented with yeast on the bottom of the vat, in contrast to the earlier English ales which were fermented on the top. The German beers were then stored for a month or longer in cool places, usually underground caves (*lagern* means "to store" or "to lay down"). Many beer-drinkers in American society were converted to lager beer, and employment in the industry became increasingly German.

More Germans than Irish came to America as skilled artisans and craftsmen, and they came to predominate in certain crafts in American cities. They were often found as ironworkers, in furniture making and upholstering, and in smaller occupations like tobacconist, jewelry maker, watchmaker, glassblower, and musical-instrument maker. The Germans who arrived in the early

Christian Staehlin's Phoenix Brewery in St. Louis, during the 1850s. The brewery dated from 1825, but turned to the production of lager beer around 1840. Library of Congress, Prints and Photographs Division.

nineteenth century were accustomed to training by apprenticeship, even as that practice was declining in America. German craftsmen and artisans thus could continue to train other Germans as apprentices, thus strengthening the middle-class element of the group. British immigrants dominated certain skilled occupations, particularly brass and copper workers, tool and cutlery makers, and potters.

The Migrating Canal- and Railroad-Builders

When employment was tight in the port cities, immigrants with no other options were often recruited by labor brokers as they got off the immigrant ships. Labor brokers were the source of many of the canal workers who built a network across the eastern United States in the period from 1817 to 1850. Common laborers on the canals originally included English, Irish, and German laborers, and slave labor was sometimes used in the South, but as time went on the Irish tended to predominate as the pick-and-shovel workforce.

When the Erie Canal commenced construction after 1817, many of the workers were native-born local farmers who tended to leave the work and go home during planting and harvesting season. The canal managers then turned to immigrant workers from whom they could expect steadier labor.

Canal workers recruited at the ports of immigration were usually brought at the employer's expense to the places just being opened up by new construction. These were often remote locations, and workers were housed in makeshift shanty housing, sometimes even in caves dug into the nearby hills. The construction camps were mostly male, although some wives and children might be found among them. Single men might live communally in bunkhouses of fifteen or twenty men, others with their families in smaller shanties. Either way, the accommodations were usually rudimentary.

Canal construction was by all accounts the most grueling work that immigrants encountered. Workers toiled from sunup to sundown and were exposed to the elements. Their usual tools were basic ones like axes, picks, and shovels. There was little heavy equipment, and the earth which was excavated was shoveled into carts or wheelbarrows for removal. Workers on the Erie Canal were expected to remove about three cubic yards of earth a day. The lucky workers were teamsters who drove the wagons or carts. Otherwise, it was unremitting and backbreaking work. Men often worked in wet, swampy areas, sometimes in waist-high water. Mosquitoes were constant nuisances, and many workers succumbed to malaria or other diseases. Irish workers were in demand to dig canals and drain swamps in the South, partly because it was considered too risky to the health of slaves to use them. There were other hazards in places where solid stone underlay the surface. Blasting had to be used, with considerable risk to the workmen. There was work on the canal for skilled laborers, too, such as building locks, doing masonry work on canal walls, cutting stone, and constructing aqueducts. These jobs were typically the province of native-born, English, Scottish, and German workers.

The shanty camps along the canals generally were transient communities which moved from place to place as the work progressed. Turnover in the canal workforce was always high, and new workers were constantly being recruited in the major port cities. As new towns developed along the canal route and were made accessible by the canal, some canal workers would remain behind, abandoning the demanding construction work for jobs on canal boats, on the locks, or on public works in the town. This was the source of many Irish immigrant communities in the developing West, and the first Catholic church in many towns was often one established by an Irish priest to minister to canal workers.

The hardships of the canal, and the sometimes arbitrary behavior of the employers, made the canals the source of some of the first labor activism among immigrant workers. Protest outbreaks and rioting might stem from a number of causes: sometimes rivalry for jobs among ethnic factions, sometimes sudden layoffs or cuts in wage rates, sometimes simply non-payment of wages earned. Incidents increased during the depression years of the late 1830s and early 1840s, but generally were not successful in improving the working conditions or maintaining adequate wages.

The building of new canals flourished in the late 1820s and 1830s, but then there began a decline that brought a virtual end to new canal-building by 1850. The enthusiasm of state governments, eager to duplicate the success of the Erie Canal, led to their eventual downfall as sponsors of ambitious canal projects. Financial hardships in the Western states after 1837 forced the suspension of many canal projects because states could not pay off the bonds they had issued and were unable to float new bonds. When work stopped before the canals were functional, no tolls could be collected. Other canals might operate, but with far less revenue than had been anticipated.

In the process of this decline, jobs for canal workers diminished. Some might be retained to maintain and improve the existing canals—the Erie Canal, for example, had widening and branch-construction projects going on from 1836 to 1862. Other immigrants, including new arrivals, might begin to find railroad-building a better source of employment. The railroads had begun to come into their own in the 1840s, while the state-financed canals were still struggling in the aftermath of the depression of 1837. Once seen as useful only in providing links between waterways, the railroads were now developing long-distance routes which were faster and more efficient than the canals and were not shut down in wintertime. The states, many of which had defaulted on their previous canal bonds, could now do little directly to support railroad construction; instead, projects were being planned by private corporations, which sought funds from investors and from towns which lay alongside the prospective right-of-way. The states did what they could to facilitate railroad expansion by issuing charters to new companies and maintaining a business climate friendly to what were collectively called "internal improvements."

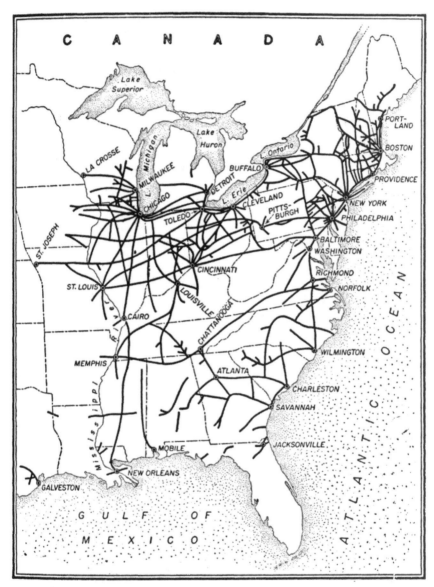

The railroad system of the United States in 1860. Railroads increasingly replaced water transportation after 1845, employing many immigrant workers and opening up new areas to settlement. From George R. Taylor, *The Transportation Revolution 1815–1860* (vol. IV of the *Economic History of the United States*), 1st ed. (New York: Holt, Rinehart and Winston, 1951). Reprinted with permission of Wadsworth, a division of Thompson Learning: www.thomsonrights.com.

By the 1840s, recruiters could be found on the docks of New York City and other ports, offering employment on railroad-building projects in places like Ohio, Michigan, and Indiana. In the late 1840s railroad-building went into a boom that lasted until 1854 and provided many employment opportunities for the immigrants of the famine immigration. Like the canals, the railroads used both skilled and unskilled workers, but the basic unskilled tasks of grading and laying rails were usually left to the Irish.

In Illinois, the building of the Illinois and Michigan Canal, envisioned as a critical link between the Great Lakes and the Mississippi Valley, had begun in 1836 and continued in fits and starts into the 1840s. It was beset by financial problems in the wake of the depression, and was the scene of many instances of labor unrest. In the mid-1840s the Chicago business community pushed for the completion of the long-awaited canal, which would prove to be the last of the major American canal projects. The work was finally completed in April 1848, thereby opening an agricultural hinterland to Chicago and Lake Michigan. Although the canal was a success, that success was soon eclipsed by the development of a railroad network leading out of Chicago, which would ultimately become the railroad center of the nation. The modest beginnings of that network took place in March 1848, just as the canal was being completed, when the first railroad from Chicago began construction to the west. Thus Irish canal workers just laid off from the Illinois and Michigan project and remaining in the Bridgeport community along the banks of the canal found new opportunities in railroad construction. In the railroad boom of the next five years, other immigrants found employment, and immigrants became the principal source of labor for railroad construction.

Labor in the Mills, Mines, and Factories

Recruiters of labor on the docks of the ports were also providing labor for the growing enterprises of America's industrial revolution. The rise of mass-production industry was most famously seen in the textile mills of New England, but there were similar industrial developments in places like northern New Jersey and the Philadelphia region. In New England the mill towns developing beside waterfalls had originally sought the work of factory girls from the nearby countryside. These were unmarried women who customarily returned after a year or two to their homes and, hopefully, marriage and a family. Acceding to the cultural norms of rural New England, employers housed the factory girls in company lodgings, where they were given room and board and, of course, careful supervision.

In time, however, the factory girls dwindled in number in the mills, and the numbers of immigrants increased. The change was noticeable after the depression of 1837, when factory owners, worrying about costs and efficiency, began to cut the wages of the operatives. They also tired of the constant turnover, with workers returning to their nearby homes more or less at whim. By this time, there were already Irish immigrants in many of the towns; they had come there in the process of building canals, mill-races, and dams, and were often housed in the shanties that usually developed near the construction sites. There were other immigrants, mostly English and Scottish, who had come bearing skills learned in the textile industries of Britain, where the Industrial Revolution was now fully developed.

In the 1840s, the employment of new immigrants in the mills began to rise along with the increase in immigration. Immigrants could provide the least-skilled workers needed, and did not need the care and housing once accorded to the country girls whom they replaced. The immigrant workforce contained both men and women. Like the canal workers, they joined the shantytowns, and the factory-owned dormitories were eventually closed down by the owners. Native and immigrant skilled workers meanwhile filled the more technical and supervisory jobs.

Industrial employment in New England and elsewhere made increasing use of the Irish immigrants as the tide of immigration rose into the 1850s. The continuing conversion over many years from water power, which required locations near waterfalls, to steam power allowed for the location of new industries in larger cities, where the supply of labor was more predictable. Labor drawn from the city's unskilled working classes drew many Irish and some Germans and English into the factories. Some who had previously been skilled artisans found their skills devalued as factory manufactures replaced small shops. Shoemakers, for example, who once crafted the entire shoe found themselves assigned one small task in the process.

The increasing use of steam power by industry, as well as the development of steamboats and steam-powered railroad locomotives, gave rise to an increased demand for fuel. As areas near the industrial centers were increasingly deprived of forests, industry turned to the coal resources nearby, particularly in the upper reaches of the Schuylkill and Susquehanna valleys in Pennsylvania.

The immigrants who played a role in the opening of the anthracite mines in that region were often from Cornwall in England and from Wales; there were many miners from Ireland as well. Most of these had had previous experience in the mines in their homelands. Earlier, Cornish and Welsh miners had been among the pioneers who opened up the lead mines in the upper Mississippi Valley; later, they were among those taking their experience to the hard-rock gold mines of California and the copper and silver mines of the northern Rockies. Their previous experience in the mines often led to their acquiring supervisory and engineering jobs in the United States, bringing them some upward mobility in the social scale.

Generally, unskilled labor in the industrial context was unstable labor. A given worker could be easily replaced, wages could be reduced arbitrarily, layoffs could swiftly occur at downturns in the economic cycles. One person's wages were insufficient for a family to live on, and some sort of work by women and even children was necessary for survival. Prospects for upward mobility in the hierarchy of work were slim for the industrial workers at the very bottom of the economic and social ladder.

IMMIGRANTS AND AGRICULTURAL LIFE

Immigrants who came from rural origins in Europe to the shops and factories of America's industrial revolution had to make a sharp adjustment. In the modern cities, time was measured by the clock, with starting and stopping times monitored by an often demanding employer. In agricultural life, however, time was measured by the seasons, alternating from periods of intense activity at planting and harvesting times to more leisurely times of the year. Immigrants who hoped to continue traditional ways of life found that goal to be more easily achievable in the countryside, but they nevertheless found that they, too, had to make some adjustments to American ways. In some respects, they were able to continue familiar practices and preserve ethnic identity. Rural life could enable settlers of common origin to stay together, to maintain some isolation from the rest of American society, to pursue traditional religious ways, to organize ethnic societies, and even to educate their children in school in the language of the mother country. Even differences and conflicts within an ethnic group were sometimes reduced by the great homogeneity that prevailed in some rural communities. Compared with those who ended up in the cities, immigrants probably did manage to cling to much of their ethnicity for a longer period of time.

In other ways, however, taking up farming in America brought about some rather swift changes in immigrants' ways of life. The general conditions and practices of agriculture were different from what most knew in the old world, and making a living required that they become American farmers. A basic reality confronting immigrant farmers was that, as the nineteenth century developed, American farming was becoming geared toward a market economy, wherein what one raised was determined by what could be sold in the market—meaning the national market, not the local ones immigrants might have known in Europe. The expansion of the transportation network beginning in the 1820s had enabled farmers to ship their produce to more distant places and concentrate on what the markets there demanded. Thus in America there was a trend toward larger farms, more efficient production, and concentration on a few important crops. The larger farms were also made possible by the introduction of new and more efficient farm machinery, which was becoming especially important in the growing West. Mowing and reaping machines, first invented in the 1830s, were improved and coming into more common use by 1850. During the 1840s seed drills for sowing grain were replacing the old broadcast method. Corn planters were being rapidly introduced in the 1850s. Immigrants, no matter how much they may have been influenced by nostalgia, had to abandon old ways and adopt new ones.

Irish immigrants were probably most aware of the differences awaiting them, even before they came. Accustomed to the ways of farming in Ireland, where agriculture was carried on in very small plots and housing was concentrated in the small villages, the difficulty of adapting to American agriculture was apparent from the start. For one thing, few had the money to buy a farm, even at the government price of $1.25 an acre, and most lacked the capital to equip a modern farm. The Irish peasant farms of five acres or so were not economically viable in the United States. While some strong farmers from Ireland were able to transfer the value of their land and purchase a farm in America, this was not possible for most, and especially not for the penniless masses of the famine years. Thus the Irish, who came in most cases from rural homes in Ireland, became mostly an urban people in America.

The British brought valuable farming skills with them as they began to establish farms in the Middle West. Most were experienced in the English methods of scientific farming that had revolutionized English agriculture in the eighteenth century. These methods, including crop rotation and the use of soil-conserving grasses and manure to restore the soil, would be continued by many in America. But there were also pressures upon farmers to adjust to American ways. Most notably, the American practice of clearing new land by removing all the trees, while foreign to the English, seemed necessary in the pioneer days in the heavily forested areas of Ohio and Indiana. And the English had to adapt to the basic economic reality of American farming: here land was cheap and labor was scarce— the opposite of the conditions they were used to in the old country. Thus many yielded to the American practice of mining the soil, rather than practicing conservation.

The English could influence changing American ways of life even as they adapted to them. They came to regions in the Midwest where hog-raising was already an essential part of agriculture, brought into the region by the early migrants from the upland South. The future agricultural economy, based on the pairing of corn and hogs, was beginning to take shape. The British adopted the raising of Indian corn, which they had not known in their homeland. They were experienced in scientific breeding practices, and began to improve the breeding of hogs, bringing in, around 1830, types like Yorkshires and Berkshires from England. After 1840 Midwestern farmers generally gave more attention to breeding hogs, striving for more meat production than could be afforded by the common, rangy "razorback" types that had been introduced by the migrants from the upland South.

The English and Scottish excelled in the raising of sheep, and also improved their breeding by importing new types from the British Isles. But the primary use of sheep in America was as a source of wool. Mutton did not do well in the American market, because it could not be preserved and shipped to other markets in the same way as pork. The English had to adapt to the American conditions, in which sheep raising declined, and eventually would be practiced more in the plains and plateaus of the West. The English were also experienced in dairying, and had been breeding cattle since the mid-eighteenth century. They introduced breeds such as the Ayrshire in the 1820s, as New England grain raising began to decline and dairying took hold on the rough and hilly lands. The use of improved breeds spread subsequently to the Midwest as it passed out of the pioneer period.

As for the Germans, and also the fewer numbers of Dutch and Scandinavians, a greater number could come with the wherewithal to purchase a farm, and it was axiomatic that selling a good farm in the old country would make possible the purchase of a much larger and better farm in places like Missouri, Ohio, Michigan, or Wisconsin. Although there were some early experiments with group settlements, in which a society would buy a larger tract and then parcel it out among the emigrants, the great majority of the Germans bent upon farming emigrated as individuals, usually with their families. Where they went was often dictated by chain migration, and advice from relatives and fellow townsmen usually made them aware of what life would be like.

This afforded many Germans opportunities to pursue their traditional culture, but like other groups they faced irresistible pressures to conform to the practices and ways of American farming. Like the English, they were accustomed to hog-raising, and adopted it widely in the Midwest, but also adopted the unfamiliar practice of raising Indian corn and feeding it to the hogs. The earlier German migrants in the 1820s and 1830s were among those who drove their hogs each fall to Cincinnati and other towns near the Ohio River for slaughter, curing, and export in barrels. Corn culture replaced much of the small-grain raising they knew in Germany. Where small-grain raising could still be practiced, as in the more northern states, it had to be carried on with the new machinery that efficient production demanded. By the middle of the century, agricultural life was in the West a far cry from what it had been in the small farms of Europe.

The Germans brought with them a tradition of gardening and pursued it somewhat more steadily than American farmers. Although some migrated to places like Missouri and Kentucky where tobacco-raising was common, they did not pursue tobacco-raising as much as did their American-born neighbors. While draft animals in Germany were still likely to be oxen, in America the Germans followed the American practice of using horses and mules. German farmers in the South—primarily in East Texas—opened farms on the western edges of the westward-moving Cotton Belt, and in many ways adopted the agricultural style of the Southerners. These included the essential crops of the South, corn and cotton, with which the Germans had no previous experience. The German farms were not large-plantation holdings, however, and they did not generally turn to slaveholding. German farm owners frequently obtained labor by hiring recent immigrants who would learn American farming methods and eventually obtain a farm of their own.

There were two slave states, Missouri and Texas, in which German farmers settled in appreciable numbers. In Missouri, only a very few German farmers owned slaves, and if so, usually only one or two. In 1850 in two counties just northwest of St. Louis, there were 3,000 slaves, but only 17 German slave-owners, who held about 75 slaves. The largest holding by a German was 7 slaves.[2] In East Texas, where Germans came as early as the 1830s, when it was still part of Mexico, about 10 percent of the German landowners in 1850 held slaves; the largest number held by a single owner was 27. Further west in Texas, where Germans settled later and cotton-growing was less common, slavery was completely absent.[3] Few Germans condemned slavery on moral grounds; they simply did not find it very compatible with their general style of farming.

THE LIFE AND WORK OF IMMIGRANT WOMEN

Immigrant women from Europe came from cultures which held to a traditional role for women; whatever power women held was exercised within the family. Politics in the European states in the early nineteenth century was reserved for a male elite. There was little room for women to exert direct or public influence upon the ways of the community, and their legal status marked them as clearly subordinate to men. Moving to America did not bring them to a society that was much more advanced than their home countries in defining the status of women. Women in America had little independence of action. Ironically, it was often widows who had some legal and economic independence; however, they might be so overwhelmed with family obligations that they could not do much with their freedom. While immigrant males often came in hopes of a greater degree of personal liberty, women could not entertain such hopes.

In the rural settlements, especially, immigrant women's lives continued in traditional ways. This was clearly the case among the Germans and the Scandinavians. While they were accustomed to hard labor as peasants in the old country, the burdens they had to assume were even greater on the frontier of America. Besides the traditional farm-woman's chores of tending a garden, cooking and baking, sewing, caring for children, caring for the sick, and maintaining a home, they could also be called upon to help clear new land and to help in the fields at harvest time. Most of the financial decisions were made by their husbands, while the women might make some pin-money by raising chickens and selling the eggs. Women often suffered from just plain loneliness. Men more frequently went to town to trade in the markets or buy supplies; women's sole contact with the outside world for long periods of time was at church. Some women found contact with other women in the organizations provided within the churches, and were active in carrying on charitable activities through the churches; but males ran the churches, made financial decisions, and hired the pastor (still at that time always a male). The roles of women in Germany were traditionally summed up as *"Kirche, Küche und Kinder"* (church, kitchen and children), and those German traditions changed only very slowly in American rural life.

In the cities and towns German women had more contact with society at large, but nevertheless their primary role remained in the family. The larger middle-class component of German-American society generally adopted the prevalent American standards of domesticity as the proper sphere of women. The great variety of German *Vereine* offered some opportunity for work in the larger community, but in most of them women were not allowed full membership, and instead were relegated to an auxiliary group. Even most of the societies founded by the free-thinking forty-eighters offered memberships only to men. One exception was the small movement of the secular German-American Free Congregations, which, following the precedent of similar societies in Germany, allowed women to become full members.[4] The Turner societies continued to have an all-male membership until the end of the century, although women took part in many of their activities.

German immigrant women in the cities also found some outlet in the church, through Ladies Aid and other charitable societies. But again they played no role in major church decisions. The Catholic religious orders for women did play a stronger role in charitable affairs, hospitals, and schools, but the number of German women in religious orders was exceeded greatly by the Irish. Later in the century some German women worked in science and the health professions, but this was largely a development among second-generation immigrants. German schools in the mid-nineteenth century clung to the tradition that the only proper teachers were male.

Irish women differed from the women of other immigrant groups in the nineteenth century in that they formed a majority of immigrants in their ethnic group. While they numbered only about 35 percent of the Irish immigrants in the 1830s, during the famine migration the number of women began to exceed that of men. Over the course of the century, women made up about 53 percent of the Irish immigrants, while women were only 41 percent of the migrants from Germany. A majority of the Irish immigrant women were single when they arrived (as was the case with Irish men).[5] Large numbers of both men and women had to look for employment as soon as they were off the ship. The demand for women workers was usually greater than it was for the males. Women were often sought after as household servants, and many began their lives in America as domestics, considering that work to be more desirable than factory jobs. Although the work might be demanding, and servants might be obliged to accept whatever duties an exacting housewife required, it did have its attractions for a new immigrant female. The wages were small—usually one to two dollars a week—but if the servants lived in the employer's house and received board, that sum could be used for discretionary spending, to assist relatives in the community, or, very often, to send back to Ireland to support a family there or pay for the passage of another emigrant. Domestic service also offered a degree of safety and security; even if one lost a job, another was usually readily available. And working in an American household generally gave the Irish servants a taste of middle-class life to which they could aspire, thus serving as a form of Americanization.

Other Irish women found their way to the factories and mill towns, where there were fewer openings for domestic servants; they also sought employment in the textile mills, garment factories, laundries, and other places that employed women. The pay was usually very poor, and the hours were long. In addition, women had to find their own places to live and provide their own food. Married women and single women living with their families worked in the factories as a way to bring a necessary addition to the family income. Otherwise, married women with children had to earn extra money by taking in boarders, sewing, or doing laundry.

As with other immigrant women, a principal outlet for the Irish woman was the church, and they provided much of the support for church activities, while men were mainly occupied with making a living. But the Irish women also could find a place in the rising numbers of Catholic sisterhoods that did valuable social work within the community, teaching in the parochial schools, running hospitals and orphanages, and providing refuges for "abandoned" Irish women. The religious orders for women provided important routes of upward mobility by training lay teachers and nurses. The second generation of Irish women in particular were often the beneficiaries of the work of these orders.

FAMILY LIFE AND CHILDREN

The stresses and strains of immigration and the instability and hardships of urban and industrial life took their toll on immigrant families. Working-class families needed the help of all members to survive, and child labor often was a necessity. Immigrants continued to raise very large families, partly because infant and childhood mortality was so common that families had to insure their future. The family was seen not only as a social unit requiring mutual obligations, but also as an economic unit. Children who were employable were expected to contribute to the family income until they were married.

Irish families were often a majority of the urban poor, and were afflicted by the adversities of famine, migration, and poverty. In the 1850s, the Irish were the largest ethnic element in the jails, poorhouses, and mental institutions of the larger cities. There was a high occurrence among Irish families of mother-dominated families. Fathers might be absent to work in remote places. Widows of men killed by workplace accidents or disease would be left to provide for families by themselves. Moreover, desertion of families by fathers was all too frequent. Even when the fathers were present, alcoholism, disability, and disease might weaken their role in family matters. Mothers left to fend for the family by themselves had great responsibilities, but also some crushing burdens. Those who could earn some living by taking in boarders, doing laundry, or working as seamstresses at home were among the fortunate. But the need to realize all possible sources of income could send mothers and children into the workplaces, and send those children not employed into the streets, where they might beg, sell newspapers, or simply wander the streets along with the homeless. The phrase "street Arabs" was commonly used for the nomadic gangs of young boys, mostly immigrants, that were found in all the major cities. And the stereotype of the young Irish woman prostitute was all too often a reality.

Families of the middle class had a better chance of maintaining stability, although there was always the fear that a depression or the loss of the breadwinner might plunge a family into the lower class. The Germans were in the middle class in greater proportion than the Irish. They could better follow traditional middle-class ways, including pursuing an education for their children. In urban areas, both public and religious schools were often available. But there were generally no requirements that children attend school (the first state compulsory education law, a rather weak one, was passed in Massachusetts in 1852). While Catholic bishops and religious orders were struggling to establish parochial schools, many poor Irish could not spare the labor of their children and the income it might produce. At best, children might spend a few years in school and learn to read, but by their early teens they were likely to be at work in the textile mills, garment factories, and day-labor jobs.

Immigrant farms were indeed family farms, with every member of the household typically playing a role in the farm's activities. Even rather small children could be found herding cows or helping in the garden. The family farm was an economic unit that tied family members together. For the young males, it often embodied their hopes for a future farm—either one they might inherit from the father, or another that might be purchased with family assistance. In the era of an expanding frontier and cheap government land, it was still possible for young males to anticipate a farm for themselves. Owning a farm established the farmer securely in the middle class. Even during economic depressions and collapses of the agricultural markets, the competent farmer usually could manage to survive. In some cases, specific contracts were made in which one son (not necessarily the eldest) would take over the farm, with an obligation to care for his parents in their old age. Other males could also be helped to purchase a new farm, either in the immediate area, or, as the land filled up, in some newer area in the West. Thus the chain migration of a family might continue into new locations. The farm daughters also learned the skills that would make them future farm wives themselves. The culture of the German, Scandinavian, and British immigrant family farm, at least in the North, conformed closely to that of the American family farm of the same place and time, helping to embed the immigrants in the prevailing American rural culture.

IMMIGRANT FOODWAYS

The process of cultural change by adapting old traditions to new surroundings is perhaps best exemplified by the foodways of immigrant people. While newcomers might attempt to continue their traditional culinary habits, immigrants often found new and different sources of food, the lack of customary commodities, and different means for preparing and cooking them. Nevertheless, traditional immigrant foodways did enter into the general American culture, even as they were affected by that culture.

The Irish were the people least able to continue their former diet—and perhaps they lacked the desire to replicate the ways of the old country. Since many had subsisted primarily on the potato before their migration to America, the availability of cheaper and more varied food in America could in itself change their ways. But they also had the opportunity to learn American food customs, especially those of the American middle class. The large number of Irish domestic servant women, obliged to cater to American tastes, learned American food styles and transmitted them to their families. Although poor working-class Irish might still be required to subsist on potatoes, soups, and a little salt-pork, those who were upwardly mobile might readily abandon such food for the more protein-rich American diet when the opportunity arose.

The Irish thus made few contributions to the mainstream American food culture. Americans were already familiar with potatoes and had a wide variety of vegetables available. The linking of corned beef and cabbage with traditional ethnic celebrations in Ireland probably stretches the historical facts. While the dish was known in Ireland, beef was expensive there and therefore restricted to the wealthy. The more common meat for festive occasions was bacon or ham. The more prevalent use of corned (i.e., salt-cured) beef seems to have arisen among the Irish in America because beef was less expensive in America, and people began to cure it as they ordinarily cured ham. This demonstrates again the way in which immigrant traditions changed in the American environment.

The Germans made larger contributions to American dietary habits, especially because the foods they were accustomed to—pork, vegetables, and the potato—were readily available in America. As gardeners, they cultivated a wide variety of vegetables, and as sellers of produce they made them available in the American local market. Germans entered the food processing industry in the days when mass-production bottling, canning, and preserving were in their infancy. In 1852, at age eight, the second-generation immigrant H. J. Heinz began to sell vegetables from his family's garden in Sharpsburg, Pennsylvania. By 1861 he was delivering produce regularly to grocers in Pittsburgh, packing horseradish in glass bottles, and beginning a pioneering career in food processing. German sauerkraut was marketed widely, and became a desired item in American kitchens generally.

By the middle of the century, Germans and Scandinavians had also come to dominate the baking industry, and their small shops marketing pastries and other baked goods were increasingly sought out by other Americans. Likewise, a majority of the butcher shops in the United States by the 1850s were run by Germans. In the times before refrigeration, when meat could only be preserved by curing, the wide variety of sausages marketed by German shops and street vendors became staples of American life. "Frankfurters" and "wieners," so called because of their German origins, would eventually lead to the American "hot dog." The Germans' most celebrated contribution to American foodways, however, was their lager beer. Americans came to expect beer from local breweries run by Germans, many of whom had brought the brewer's art to America with them.

Both Italians and Chinese had brought their own foodways with them by the 1850s, and they managed to continue many of their culinary customs, even importing many of the traditional ingredients. But they would have relatively little influence upon American food culture until the turn of the twentieth century. While the Chinese in California often had restaurants that fed both American and Chinese in the mining camps, in San Francisco their restaurants were not often patronized by outsiders, especially as anti-Chinese prejudices grew in the 1850s and 1860s. By the end of the 1800s, Chinese restaurants were familiar throughout the West, and other Americans began to patronize them. It was around the turn of the twentieth century that the melange known as chop suey (meaning "little pieces") and fortune cookies were invented in America, mostly for the non-Chinese customers.

Americans were already familiar with macaroni when Italian immigrants began arriving in the early nineteenth century, and recipes for it were found in many cookbooks of the time. They were not much influenced by other Italian culinary customs until late in the century. It was then that they began to take up the eating of spaghetti, the thinner strands of pasta which had begun to be made by modern machinery earlier in the century. This led to changes in both the Italian and American eating habits. Italian immigrants had made their own pizza during the nineteenth century, but the first pizzeria in America is thought to have opened in New York in 1905. Italian influences upon American cuisine are thus much more evident after the growing wave of Italian migration in the 1890s.

The setting of standards for high-style restaurant eating in America was due to the efforts of an Italian-speaking Swiss family, the Delmonicos. Two brothers, Giovanni and Pietro Delmonico, founded a small café in New York City in 1828. Originally it served a mainly European clientele. But an ambitious nephew, Lorenzo Delmonico, arrived in 1831 from Switzerland and began to revise the menu and expand the restaurant. Despite his Swiss-Italian background, he made French cuisine the specialty of the restaurant. He offered an immense list of special dishes and caught the fancy of the elite classes of New York. French and German chefs were imported to prepare the menu. Those who planned elegant restaurants in other cities fashioned them after Delmonico's, and French cuisine thus became the standard upper-class fare for the rest of the nineteenth century.

With the arrival of various ethnic groups in the mid-nineteenth century, one can see the beginning of the merging of food cultures which would eventually be seen as a single American food culture based upon many different origins. This slow but very evident development of one multiethnic cultural characteristic, foodways, reflected as well the slow emergence of a general American culture based on many sources.

THE CULTURE OF LEISURE

It was in their leisure habits that immigrants were most likely to preserve their traditional ways and their sense of ethnicity. These activities were pursued within their ethnic communities, which provided a relaxed environment free from outside intrusions. In the German beer taverns and the Irish saloons, traditional music could be heard, and traditional food and drink would be served. The Germans had a wide array of theaters, singing societies, gymnastic clubs, and social clubs, all attuned to the leisure customs of a predominantly middle-class group. The Irish, often having fewer occasions to enjoy any leisure time, found their opportunities in their church organizations and saloons.

At mid-century each group had its own style of sports. Americans and English favored horse-racing and the game of baseball, which was just forming at the time, having evolved from earlier English country games. The Germans practiced gymnastics and held target-shooting competitions. The Irish had prize-fighting, a sport looked down upon with considerable contempt by polite American society.

Only a relatively few leisure activities were held in common by all social groups, most notably civic celebrations like the Fourth of July. The emergence of spectator sports which appealed to all classes, along with the development of professional sports, brought different Americans together in a common experience, but this development was more prevalent in the last quarter of the century.

The political parties sought to draw all together for common action in political rallies and election campaigns. In the 1850s, when political controversies heated up, the turbulent world of politics became a major force pulling the immigrant communities more fully into American life.

INVENTING A NEW POLITICAL CULTURE

The coming of the immigrants to America in the 1820s and 1830s coincided with a great transformation in American political life, in which the old-fashioned politics of elitism gave way to the new methods of democracy and popular appeal. This was occasioned in many ways by the opening up of the franchise and the abolition of wealth and tax qualifications, a process that was occurring in many states in the 1820s. The wider participation of the masses in the political process has sometimes been considered the essence of Jacksonian Democracy, but Andrew Jackson himself probably did little to bring it about. When politicians had to appeal to the immigrant Americans as a major basis of their support, the age of democracy paid off for them, too. And in the next decades they would learn the techniques of the new democratic politics and make them their own.

In the 1820s, after foreigners once again had begun to arrive in America, they generally followed the path of the new Jacksonian Democratic party. That party first took shape between 1825 and 1828, as various political leaders emerged from the ruins of the previous party system and began to rally around the banner of Andrew Jackson in his campaign for the presidency in 1828. They sought support from the working-class elements of the eastern cities, and especially from the Irish and Germans who were beginning to be a significant part of that group. Immigrants responded particularly well to the message that Jackson represented the people, and the name "democracy," often contrasted with "aristocracy," reflected the reasons why many had left the old world for the new. The Democratic party rhetoric was particularly directed against the "aristocracy" that had allegedly stolen the 1824 election from Jackson by a "corrupt bargain," giving the presidency to John Quincy Adams when the election had to be resolved in the House of Representatives. That bargain, it was argued, had denied Jackson the presidency, even though he had more popular votes than any other candidate. Thus the true democratic will of the people had been frustrated.

There were other issues that served to tie the immigrants to the Democratic party. As Jackson's presidency developed, he took up the advocacy of what were called "hard money" policies, attacking in particular the Bank of the United States and the established currency system, which rested upon bank notes. Members of the working class who were forced to accept depreciated bank notes as payment for their labors naturally responded to this issue. But the most compelling issue tying immigrants to the Democracy— as the party was commonly called—was their perception that the nativists were beginning to gather in the opposition party. That party adopted the name "Whig" because it sought to attack the supposed abuses of power by the man they called "King Andrew the First," just as the Whigs in England had opposed the power of the monarchy there. The Whig party complained frequently of abuses of the political system by immigrants and the supposedly corrupt politicians who led them. With the immigrants easily recognizing the forces in the opposing party that were aligned against them, their attraction to the Democratic party became solidified.

Immigrant Politics at the Grassroots Level

However, the strongest ties of immigrants to the party were forged at the grassroots level. The Jacksonian Democratic party can be regarded as implementing a new style of politics, geared to the broadening of the franchise that was developing at the time. Votes were to be sought where they existed in abundance, at the lowest level in the urban wards and country precincts. Immigrant leaders were enlisted at that level, offered some access to patronage, and encouraged to find immigrant followers. They could enroll the newly arrived in the party organization, help them find jobs, and get them other favors. They stirred up popular enthusiasms with political rallies and torchlight parades. To the immigrants, the Democratic party was an active and visible presence that took up their cause; the opposition party was a distant power run by "aristocrats" who complained of the immigrants' presence.

The most striking example of the new style of politics was the role of Tammany Hall, which became the central organization of the Jacksonian party in New York City. Originally a fraternal and social organization, it was adopted by U.S. Senator Martin Van Buren in the 1820s as a useful tool in his effort to build the new Democratic party in New York State. It became the dominant force in New York City politics, based on its command of the immigrant, and particularly Irish, vote. It advocated such policies as universal manhood suffrage (adopted in New York in 1827), the abolition of imprisonment for debt, and, especially, opposition to nativism. The growing numbers of immigrants among the city's population in the booming years of the 1830s aroused nativist opposition, which in turn drew more immigrants into the Democratic fold. Tammany Hall solidified its ties with the immigrant communities through its grassroots connections in the saloons and volunteer fire companies. Within the community, Tammany Hall representatives doled out charitable contributions, dispensed jobs, and enlisted followers to march to the polls on election day. Opponents complained of widespread election frauds, such as the use of unnaturalized voters, repeat voting, and the buying of votes.

The severe political polarization developing in the 1830s was reflected particularly in the hard-fought New York City municipal election of April 1834, when the city in general was still controlled by the Whigs. As the Irish population grew in the Sixth Ward, the Whigs decided to contend with the Irish in that election for the control of the ward. Attempts by the Whigs to intimidate voters at the polling place on election day led to pushing, shoving, and the retreat of the Whigs. The next day, they returned in a parade down Duane Street through the middle of the ward. The Irish read this as a further attempt at intimidation, and soon organized an attack on the nearby Whig party headquarters. The Whigs started to obtain arms from an arsenal, when the mayor intervened and managed to put an end to the brawling. Tammany Hall was able to turn the affair to its political benefit by arguing that it was attempting to defend the Irish community against the attacks of the Whigs. Later that year, in December, German Democratic supporters in the city organized a newspaper to further their cause against the nativist administration. This was the *New Yorker Staats-Zeitung*, which would grow into a strong Democratic voice and the most powerful German newspaper in the country.

As long as their party appeared to stand for nativism, the Whigs had little chance of breaking into the solid immigrant Democratic vote. Many of the English immigrants and a few German immigrants were drawn to the Whig party, partly because it seemed to be the party of the supposedly "better" classes, but mostly because of their own dislike of the Irish Catholics. The most significant effort by the Whigs to win Irish support came to naught. This occurred in New York when, in the early 1840s, Governor William Henry Seward, a Whig, took the side of Bishop John Hughes in his effort to provide for Catholic immigrants an alternative to the Protestant-dominated schools in New York City. This move immediately aroused an outcry from the nativists against the use of public monies for parochial schools, but did little to win support from Democrats, who denounced Seward's proposal as an empty political ploy. Seward's concern for immigrant education was probably sincere, and reflected his desire that all the masses be uplifted by equal access to education. The eventual outcome was a compromise that prohibited any expenditure of public funds for religious schools, and put the New York City public schools in the hands of elected commissioners—and out of the hands of the Protestant-controlled Public School Society. As for New York's Catholic immigrants in general, they would cling steadily to the Democratic party.

The Southern Connection and Slavery

The close ties of the immigrants with the Democratic party made them a part of the traditional alliance of two critical elements of the national party: the urban working classes of the North, and the slave-owning planters of the South. Since the alternative for the immigrants was the abolitionism, nativism, and temperance fanaticism they perceived within the Whig party, there was not much chance that they would abandon the Democratic alliance. The immigrants' attitude toward slavery was based mostly on grassroots, everyday considerations. They had little reason to oppose the Southerners' "peculiar institution," and many harbored some fear of the consequences of its abolition, especially the competition of freed blacks who might fill the ranks of the unskilled workers. Although a few prosperous Irish and Germans in the South were slaveowners, the rank-and-file immigrants simply viewed slaves as persons who were naturally below them in the social scale, and who should remain there. In that sense, the immigrants were about as racist as was the rest of the country at that time. Abolitionism, on the other hand, was to be opposed because of its threat to the social order. Immigrants were not likely to espouse revolutionary measures in their adopted country.

In the early 1840s, the Irish nationalist Daniel O'Connell, pursuing a campaign for repeal of the Act of Union that subjected Ireland to the British Parliament, began to speak out in favor of joining the cause of slavery abolition with the cause of Irish freedom. He made common cause with American abolitionists, including William Lloyd Garrison. At a widely-publicized mass meeting at Faneuil Hall in Boston in February 1842, Garrison and other abolitionists read an "Address" that had been sent by O'Connell and signed by nearly 70,000 people in Ireland. The Address urged Irish-American supporters of the repeal movement to join in working for the freedom of American blacks: "We call upon you to *unite with the abolitionists,* and never to cease your efforts until perfect liberty be granted to every one of its inhabitants, the black man as well as the white man."[6]

The Irish Americans' reaction after the meeting was loudly negative. The Catholic press denounced the Garrisonians as fanatics and disturbers of the social order. Since the Irish repeal movement had its supporters among the elite classes of the South, the Address was seen as an attempt to divide the supporters of the repeal movement on the issue of slavery. And indeed, the repeated campaign of the abolitionists to convert the Irish population had the effect of seriously weakening the Irish nationalist movement in America.

The views on slavery held by many immigrant Catholics were generally given ideological support by official spokesmen of the church at that time. Catholics often agreed with Southern advocates of slavery who pointed to biblical precedents and long traditions in the Christian world. Slavery was said to be a natural institution brought on by original sin. Slave-owners were obliged to treat slaves humanely, but they could not be deprived of their right to property. Spokesmen like Bishop John Hughes of New York, who often expressed ambivalent views on the subject, seemed to believe that slavery would eventually be abolished by some gradual evolutionary process. He saw a model for this process in the transition in European societies from slavery to serfdom and eventually to freedom. Slavery was an evil, but a necessary one. Similar views were held by the bishop of Charleston, John England, who was considered the Church's leading theologian in America at that time. Arguing for the biblical justification of slavery, he stated that "the Savior did not repeal the permission to hold slaves; but he promulgated principles calculated to improve their condition, and perhaps, in time, to extinguish slavery."[7] Asked at another time about whether he was in favor of the continuation of slavery, England responded pragmatically: "I am not—but I also see the impossibility of now abolishing it here. When it can and ought to be abolished is a question for the legislature and not for me."[8]

Pragmatic views such as this were held not only by Catholic immigrants but by many others as well. Conservative German Lutherans also feared to disturb the existing social order. Many others felt that they should not agitate an issue about which nothing could be done, since the Constitution left the matter to the states, and the slave states seemed unlikely to abandon the institution. Norwegians, mostly having settled in the North and without many relations with Southern slaveholders, generally looked upon slavery with distaste. Some English-born immigrants also associated themselves with the New England abolitionists. But many Irish disdained abolitionist doctrine as just another hypocritical product of British moral-reform thought. And, they argued, was it not Britain which had ended the slave trade while at the same time holding the Irish people in bondage? Only the more radical German refugees of 1848 were likely to embrace abolitionism, and then only when the issue of slavery presented itself in a somewhat different light in the 1850s.

Immigrant Political Leadership

Political leaders developed rapidly in the local politics of the Democratic party. Their activities were vital in the effort to encourage grassroots participation in politics. In the cities, saloon-keepers, having the most accessible meeting places and a steady base of customers, became ward leaders. Those who organized fire companies and militia groups also gained access to power by finding jobs and benefits for their followers. The Germans had professional men, business men, and journalists who could exercise leadership over their middle-class constituents.

While there were many lower-level political leaders, it was another matter to rise above the level of ward leader, alderman, or councilman serving an immigrant neighborhood. Before 1850 the American-born leaders, usually of the elite class, continued to maintain control in the upper reaches of the party. In some places such as Pennsylvania, there were German communities that had been established since colonial times, and in the nineteenth century, members of the second or third generation might become legislators, acquire state offices, and even be elected to Congress. But the more recent immigrants arriving in places just becoming centers of immigrant communities had to wait before finding a place in the higher political leadership. Mike Walsh, a longstanding Irish-born journalist and activist in New York City, pressed for years to give the Irish workingmen more places in the Democratic leadership. In 1846 he was finally successful in getting elected, with the aid of Tammany Hall, to the state assembly, and in 1850 he was elected to the U.S. House of Representatives. Aspiring immigrants in other cities often had to wait longer for such electoral success.

Two examples from the developing Midwest, where the newness of the country made it easier to rise in the ranks of politics, show some of the variations of the immigrants' climb to higher political leadership. Two men who were born in the same decade, who came from middle-class backgrounds, who arrived in America about the same time, who resided in the same state, and who lived in communities close to each other pursued rather different courses, although both began like most immigrants within the Jacksonian Democratic party.

James Shields, born in 1806 in Tyrone County in Ulster, but of Catholic parentage, came to the United States in 1827, at a time of economic depression in Ireland. He migrated to Illinois and settled in Kaskaskia, not far from St. Louis and near the Mississippi River. Having had some formal education, he became a schoolteacher, then studied law with a prominent Democratic political leader. By 1832 he was admitted to the bar and in 1836 won election to the lower house of the Illinois legislature. Also elected to that same body in 1836 was the young lawyer Stephen A. Douglas, another Democrat. The Whig opposition was led by Abraham Lincoln, then in his third legislative term. After finishing one term, Shields sought appointive office (the state government being largely Democratic) and served on the Board of Public Works, then as state auditor. In 1843 he unsuccessfully ran for Congress, but was then appointed to the Illinois Supreme Court. In 1845 he was appointed to a federal office, Commissioner of the Public Lands, by President James K. Polk.

At the outbreak of the Mexican War, Shields, who saw military ambition as another route to political prominence, gave up his federal post in Washington and returned to Illinois, where he recruited a regiment to fight in Mexico; he was commissioned a brigadier general. He fought in several major battles, was wounded, and returned home to be greeted with great public approval. He then ran for U.S. Senator; the Illinois legislature finally elected him to that post in October 1840, after much controversy over whether he had been a citizen the requisite nine years. He served in the Senate with fellow Democrat Stephen Douglas, and generally supported Douglas on major issues. His loyalty to Douglas proved to be his downfall in Illinois when Douglas sponsored the Kansas-Nebraska Act, which allowed those territories to be organized and left the status of slavery in them to determination by popular sovereignty. The potential opening of the territories to slavery in places where it had previously been excluded aroused great opposition in Illinois.

The "anti-Nebraska" forces won control of the state legislature, and when Shields's senatorial term was up in 1855, he was replaced by an anti-Nebraska candidate, Lyman Trumbull.

A few months later Shields moved to Minnesota, taking part in land speculation there. When Minnesota became a state in 1857, he was elected a U.S. Senator by the legislature, but lost that seat in 1859 when the new Republican party took control. Shields thereupon removed to San Francisco, and in the presidential election of 1860 he campaigned for Douglas. After the Civil War began, Shields again was commissioned a brigadier general in 1862 and was assigned to a division in the Shenandoah Valley. After suffering a defeat at the hands of the Confederate general Thomas "Stonewall" Jackson and failing to be appointed a major general, Shields resigned his commission and returned to California in 1863. At the end of the war Shields moved again, this time to Missouri. He was again active in Democratic politics, ran unsuccessfully for the U.S. House, served in the Missouri legislature, and, in one final move, was elected by that legislature in January 1879 to fill a vacant seat in the U.S. Senate. His term was brief, however, ending in March 1879, and three months later he died at the age of 73. He is today remembered as the only person ever to serve in the U.S. Senate from three different states.

In 1833 the 23-year-old German-born lawyer Gustave Koerner arrived in St. Clair County, Illinois, just a few miles from where James Shields lived in Randolph County. He had just arrived from France, having fled there from Frankfurt in Germany after being involved in a failed revolutionary uprising known as the Frankfurt *Attentat*. He had been a student activist and a member of the liberal-nationalist *Burschenshaft* during his years in three different universities, but had nevertheless completed legal studies at the University of Heidelberg and had begun the practice of law in Frankfurt.

Although well-educated and of middle-class background (his father was a book dealer), Koerner had to ponder what he would do for a career in Belleville, the county seat of St. Clair County. The area was already known as a haven for German liberal intellectuals, called the Latin Farmers by many. Deciding he wished to remain a lawyer in America, he learned English, read on American law and politics, and pursued further legal studies at Transylvania University in Kentucky. In early 1835 he was admitted to the Illinois bar and began legal practice in Belleville.

Koerner was naturalized in 1838 after the requisite five years' residency. He had drawn attention by translating and editing a

German edition of the Illinois laws. Although somewhat aloof and formal in his demeanor, he won the respect of the German community and of the Democratic party leaders, who regarded him as a knowledgeable spokesman for the Germans. He was elected to the Illinois legislature for one term in 1842; in April 1845, he was appointed by the Democratic governor to be associate justice of the state Supreme Court, replacing James Shields in that position. In 1848 a new law made the Supreme Court positions elective; Koerner declined to stand for election and returned to his law practice in Belleville. In 1852 the party sought greater representation for the German element in the state administration, and nominated Koerner to be lieutenant governor. He was elected and served in that post from 1853 to 1857. He was the first of several German-American lieutenant governors elected in the Midwestern states during the pre-Civil War years, as the parties began to contend for the German vote.

Meanwhile, the turmoil over the Kansas-Nebraska Act had arisen, and this proved to be a turning point in Koerner's political career. The Democratic party leadership in the state was firmly tied to Stephen Douglas and supported him. But many Democrats, including some of the Germans, split with the party and declared themselves to be anti-Nebraska Democrats. A coalition of anti-Nebraska forces, including former Whigs and some nativists, took control of the state legislature in the 1854 election. As the Democratic lieutenant governor, Koerner still presided over the state Senate at the time, and hesitated to voice public opposition to Douglas's measure, although privately he tried to persuade other Democrats to oppose it. At the very end of his term, when the various anti-Nebraska forces had coalesced into the new Republican party and held a national convention in 1856, Koerner came out in support of the Republicans. He was able to persuade other Germans to follow, although many still showed concern over the influence of nativists and temperance activists who had also joined the party. The principal leaders of the Illinois party were also attempting to limit the nativist participation in the party. In 1858 Koerner was chosen to chair the state Republican convention, precisely to hold the nativists in check. In 1860 he attended the Republican National Convention in Chicago, and was among those trying to purge the party of nativist tendencies and to win the nomination for Lincoln. When the war began, Koerner was appointed a colonel and served with Union forces in Missouri. A year later he was appointed minister to Spain, but returned in 1864 to help campaign for Lincoln's reelection.

After the war, Koerner resumed his law practice in Belleville, and served on various state commissions and boards over the years. But his ties to the Republican party weakened as he began to disagree with the Republican Reconstruction policies in the South and was disillusioned by the corruption of the Ulysses Grant administration. In 1872 he joined the Liberal Republican faction of the party, which supported the Democratic presidential candidate; in 1876 he supported the Democratic candidate, and thereafter remained a Democrat until his death in 1896.

Both Shields and Koerner rose from immigrant origins to political leadership, but followed quite different paths. Shields rather quickly established himself as part of a larger community outside the immigrant community. There was no language barrier to mark him as separate from the general ranks of the Democratic party. Although he spoke out for Irish nationalism and for the defense of the immigrant, he could easily advocate for the party in all other respects. Koerner, however, was always seen as a representative of the German element and was accordingly granted power to use within that sector of the party. He was consulted on party matters when it was necessary to know the Germans' position.

Shields was the model of the loyal party member. He was always a Democrat, never straying from the policies set down by the leadership. When the party failed in Illinois, he took up its cause in other states. As with other Irish in the rank and file of the party, the ties to patronage and personal advantage were too strong ever to cut them. Koerner, on the other hand, while not without ambition, was moved by matters of principle. His disagreement with the Douglas leadership of the party took him into the ranks of the freesoilers; later, his unwillingness to support the policies of Grant and the Reconstruction Congress led him back to the Democratic party. In this way Koerner reflected the divisiveness that always plagued the Germans. Before the 1850s, the Germans had been bound together by a common opposition to nativism. After that point, they increasingly split on important political questions, and were seldom able to present a united front in the political arena. Thus the power of the Germans as a political bloc would be much reduced in comparison to the power of the Irish.

Opponents of the immigrants until mid-century had often accused them of being incapable of taking part in a democratic society, since that was a tradition not in the immigrants' experience. The accusation was particularly aimed at the Irish. Yet the Irish and the other immigrants quickly learned the techniques of a new

American politics as they were developing in the Jacksonian era. In doing so, immigrants contributed in their own way to the remaking of American political culture.

NOTES

1. Kathleen N. Conzen, *Immigrant Milwaukee, 1836–1860: Accommodation and Community in a Frontier City* (Cambridge, Mass.: Harvard University Press, 1976), 66.

2. Walter D. Kamphoefner, *The Westfalians: From Germany to Missouri* (Princeton, N.J.: Princeton University Press, 1987), 116.

3. Terry G. Jordan, *German Seed in Texas Soil: Immigrant Farmers in Nineteenth-Century Texas* (Austin: University of Texas Press, 1966), 109–10, 180.

4. Katja Rampelmann, "Infidels, Ethnicity and Womanhood: Women in the German-American Freethinker Movement," *Yearbook of German-American Studies* 39 (2004): 61–76.

5. Hasia Diner, *Erin's Daughters in America* (Baltimore: Johns Hopkins University Press, 1983), 30–31.

6. "An Address of the People of Ireland to Their Countrymen and Countrywomen in America," *Liberator*, September 10, 1841, quoted in Gilbert Osofsky, "Abolitionists, Irish Immigrants and the Dilemmas of Romantic Nationalism," *American Historical Review* 90 (1975): 898.

7. *Letters of the Late Bishop England to the Hon. John Forsyth, on the Subject of Domestic Slavery* (1844; reprint, New York: Negro Universities Press, 1969), 50, quoted in R. Frank Saunders, Jr. and George A. Rogers, "Bishop John England of Charleston: Catholic Spokesman and Southern Intellectual," *Journal of the Early Republic* 13 (1993): 320.

8. Ignatius A. Reynolds, ed., *The Works of the Right Rev. John England, First Bishop of Charleston*, 5 vols. (Baltimore: J. Murphy, 1849), 3:190–91, quoted in Saunders and Rogers, "Bishop John England of Charleston," 320.

7

Political Turmoil and War, 1850–1865

Before the middle of the nineteenth century, the political life of American immigrants was relatively predictable and untroubled by internal controversy, even though rough-and-tumble politics often characterized immigrants' battles with political opponents. In the early 1850s, however, a number of circumstances threatened to introduce divisions and doubts into the politics of immigrant communities. For one thing, the tide of immigration had recently brought many new potential voters into the picture, which made all political parties more aware of the weight the immigrants' numbers might bring into the political balance. This fear stimulated a new wave of nativism, as some politicians sought to restrict the political rights of the newcomers. At the same time, the Whig party, historically the home of nativists, was crumbling amidst controversy about the question of slavery and its extension, and anxiety was rising about what the new political party picture would look like. Immigrants were unable to resist the pressures introduced by the issues of nativism and slavery, and they became participants in the political battles that swept the country toward its greatest crisis.

NEW ISSUES, NEW DILEMMAS

The political crises of the 1850s would change the political lives of many immigrants and their leaders. Two different issues emerged to provide a political dilemma. One was the resurgence of nativism, this time on the level of national politics, in the form of the American or Know-Nothing party. Another was the re-emergence of the issue of the extension of slavery into the new territories of the West.

As the decade began, both major political parties were under strain as a result of the adoption of the Compromise of 1850. That legislation had attempted to resolve the difficult issue of the status of slavery in the western territories recently acquired from Mexico. The Missouri Compromise of 1820 had established a line west of Missouri at the latitude of 36 degrees 30 minutes, above which slavery would be forbidden. But that compromise did not apply to these newly acquired regions. Under pressure to resolve the matter because California was applying to become a free state, Congress agreed to admit California, but to allow New Mexico and Utah to be organized as territories without resolving the issue of slavery, leaving that to be settled when these territories applied to become states. To satisfy some abolitionists, the slave trade was to be abolished in the District of Columbia; to satisfy the Southern slave interest, slavery itself was to be continued there. The most controversial part of the compromise, however, was the Fugitive Slave Act, which required federal authorities and all citizens to assist in the capture and return of slaves who had escaped to the North. The provisions of this act were heavily weighted in favor of the Southern slave-owners, and aroused strong opposition from northern abolitionists.

The compromise, while in Congress, had been opposed by the Whig president Zachary Taylor, who threatened to veto the measure. But Taylor died in July 1850, and his successor, Millard Fillmore, was more open to the compromise and signed the measure. While in general the American public, fatigued from the controversy, accepted the compromise, divisions over the issue of slavery had been exposed within the Whig party. Over the next few years some dissident Whigs began to seek refuge in the developing American (Know-Nothing) party, and increasingly sought to have that party adopt clear antislavery policies.

The Democrats, anxious to preserve the traditional alliance of northern workers with Southern slave-owners, generally accepted the compromise. There were tensions, however, between northern and Southern Democrats about the rising power of the southerners in the traditional balance of the party. Western Democrats, among them Stephen A. Douglas of Illinois and Lewis Cass of Michigan, fearful of any splits within the party, took up a more moderate position. They tried to distract the party's disparate elements from slavery concerns by appealing to an interest in foreign affairs. The new movement, called "Young America," and based partly on the remaining enthusiasm over Manifest Destiny, repeated cries for an aggressive nationalism, further national expansion in the Caribbean, and support of the European revolutionary movements. In espousing these causes, Douglas was certainly aware that this activism about the European revolutions would appeal to some of the immigrants, especially the Germans.

Political Stirrings among the Germans

The German communities were particularly agitated in the early 1850s by the activities of the refugees from the 1848 revolutions. Although a relatively small element themselves, the forty-eighters were rapidly beginning to dominate German-language journalism and were organizing liberal or radical groups like the Turner societies within the cities. When they first arrived, they hoped to return to Europe and carry on new revolutionary movements; their organizational activities were reflected especially in "revolutionary societies," which supported the revival of revolutionary activities in Europe. Visits from European revolutionaries like Hungary's Louis Kossuth, urging support for renewed European crusades, were usually enthusiastically received, but efforts to collect significant new funds failed. Immigrants, like the rest of the American public, were too distracted by the booming economy of the gold-rush era to think of European adventures.

As the forty-eighters reluctantly gave up their revolutionary ambitions and resigned themselves to a more permanent life in America, they began to focus upon the issues of the time and on the traditional political ways of the Germans in America. With some disillusion they awakened to the fact that politics as actually practiced in America did not fit the ideal of democracy envisioned by the European republican intellectuals of the time. Conditioned to think of political parties as embodiments of great principles, they found the American system, with its mixture of local and national issues, its strong traditions of party loyalty and patronage, and its emotional campaign appeals, difficult to understand. This naturally led them to a critical attitude toward the ordinary German-American citizens' embrace of that system. Their attachment to the Democratic party, which condoned slavery, seemed to reflect mostly opportunism and very little idealism. Since the party system offered no viable alternative, some of the more radical forty-eighters, like Heinrich Boernstein, editor of the St. Louis *Anzeiger des Westens,* began to advocate a German separatist party that could act as a pressure group upon the major parties. Such a strategy would continue to be debated throughout the decade, and appealed mostly to German liberals in the eastern states, where they had little access to the leadership ranks of the Democratic party. In the West, however, where some German leaders like Gustave Koerner already were established in influential party positions, the idea of seceding from the party held little appeal.

German-Americans in general were not greatly swayed by these efforts, and continued in their traditional Democratic allegiance. The principal effect of the forty-eighters was to introduce division within the community by their harsh criticisms of previous German political leaders, in what became known as the conflict between the Grays—the earlier German leaders—and the Greens—those who came to America after 1848. In forty-eighter newspapers like Boernstein's *Anzeiger des Westens* and the New York *Deutsche Schnellpost,* which was now edited by the radical Karl Heinzen, the earlier German leaders were characterized as unprincipled opportunists enslaved by corrupt party leaders. Gustave Koerner, who undertook to respond for his generation through the pages of the *Belleviller Zeitung,* defended the Grays as the more pragmatic, experienced, and therefore more effective leaders of immigrants. The new critics of German-American politics, in contrast, were "slogan-makers, pretenders to culture, literary and political adventurers, a number of whom have unfortunately taken control of the press."[1] The debate would rage on during 1851–1852, but was already subsiding when a new controversy arose, stimulated by the fateful passage of the Kansas-Nebraska Act in 1854. This would excite the German community and the whole of American politics as well.

The Kansas-Nebraska Act and the Disintegration of Parties

In January 1854, the Democratic senator Stephen A. Douglas of Illinois introduced a bill to organize the new territories of Kansas and Nebraska. Douglas, who had served for years as the chair of the Senate's Committee on Territories, probably thought that his initiative would further his reputation as an advocate of Western development, solidify his support within the Democratic party, and prepare the way for the building of a transcontinental railroad along a proposed central route. Regarded as a rising star in the Democratic party, Douglas also had to pay attention to the Southerners who were an important element in the party. In order to gain support from some Southern senators, he agreed to divide the region west of the Missouri River into two territories, and to allow the issue of slavery to be decided by popular sovereignty—the vote of the actual inhabitants of each territory. This was in conflict with the existing provisions of the Missouri Compromise of 1820, which would have excluded Kansas from the territory open to slavery. Douglas was also persuaded to add a specific repeal of the Missouri Compromise to the legislation. Although Douglas probably believed that this change was only symbolic, and that slavery would never establish itself in the more arid areas of the West, the bill was seen by antislavery advocates as opening new areas to what they called an aggressive "slavocracy." After months of bitter debate, including strong opposition from some northern Democrats, the bill finally passed on May 30, 1854.

The protest against Douglas's bill erupted even before its passage. Antislavery Democrats, led by Ohio Senator Salmon P. Chase, issued shortly after the bill's introduction an "Appeal of the Independent Democrats," denouncing the measure as "as a criminal betrayal of precious rights; as part and parcel of an atrocious plot to exclude from a vast unoccupied region emigrants from the Old World and free laborers from our own States, and convert it into a dreary region of despotism, inhabited by masters and slaves."[2] This Appeal, though promulgated by more radical abolitionist spokesmen, also reached out to a wider field of public opinion, usually characterized as "free-soil" opinion. The wording of the Appeal reflected an effort especially to attract free-soil immigrants. The objective of free-soilers was not to abolish slavery, but to keep the vast new lands of the West available to free labor, and to exclude slavery. Efforts to open up the West to the possibility of slavery seemed to be a plot of the Southern slavocracy to deny those promising areas to the settlers of the free North and establish a slave empire instead.

The writers of the Appeal obviously sensed that potential support was available within the Democratic party from its immigrants, and especially from the Germans, who were more likely to perceive in the Kansas-Nebraska bill a move to restrict their opportunities in the West. As the *New Yorker Abendzeitung* put it, "if slavery should be introduced into the new territories, they will be lost to the European immigration, and especially to the Germans, since they are much more devoted to agriculture than the Irish, who prefer to work in the city."[3] Adding to the Germans' suspicions was the fact that Southerners had tried to add to the bill a "Clayton amendment," which provided that settlers who were not citizens would not be able to obtain land in the West. A similar provision was added to a proposed Homestead Act, which would have granted free lands to actual settlers in the West. Both the Clayton amendment and the Homestead bill failed to pass, but the Germans' suspicions were raised that strong nativist opponents in the South were trying to restrict immigrants' opportunities in the West.

Germans responded to the Kansas-Nebraska bill within a few days of its introduction. The protest was led by the more abolitionist-minded forty-eighters, but they were reaching out to the moderates with a free-soil appeal. In late January a group of Chicago German leaders had met and sent resolutions of protest to their congressmen. The *Illinois Staats-Zeitung* and the *New Yorker Demokrat* published strong attacks on Douglas's bill. During February, protest meetings of Germans were reported in Pittsburgh, Indianapolis, Cincinnati, New York, Cleveland, and Chicago. In March, there were definite signs that the leaders of the older Gray generation were joining the forty-eighters in their opposition. A March 16 meeting at the North Market Hall in the German district of Chicago included a fiery speech by Francis Hoffmann, formerly a country Lutheran minister from a rural area northwest of Chicago, and now a banker and alderman in Chicago. "I am for party organization," he proclaimed, "I have been a faithful adherent of the democratic party, for the last fourteen years. . . . but justice is paramount to party, and the dictates of conscience and humanity are superior to those of party leaders . . . we had better break the chains which fetter us to that party."[4] Other long-time German leaders also spoke out against the act, including Friedrich Münch of Missouri, who had first come to that state with members of the Giessen Emigration Society in 1834. Others were more hesitant, like Gustave Koerner, still the Democratic lieutenant governor of Illinois, who remained silent while hoping that the Independent Democrats would take control of the party leadership.

That was not to be, however, and as the year went on the splintering of all political parties raised questions about what the outcome might be. The congressional elections in November brought out a variety of anti-Nebraska candidates, including some running under that title, others as free-soil Democrats or free-soil Whigs, still others under the label "Fusion" or "People's party." A few chose the label "Republican," but there was not yet an organized party structure to gather together the dissident elements. Adding to the confusion was

the fact that the Know-Nothing party was achieving stronger organization nationally, and some Whigs were looking to it as a refuge
from their disintegrating party. While many of the state and local
elections were won by candidates opposing the Kansas-Nebraska
Act, the many differences among them seemed to militate against
the forming of an effective free-soil coalition.

Some began to speak of a new national free-soil party that would
incorporate all these various elements, but this raised the question as to what other issues that party might adopt to broaden its
political platform and its appeal. In some states, particularly in
the East, the Know-Nothings had been the biggest element in the
anti-Nebraska movement, a fact which immediately alienated the
Germans. In other states there was a strong movement toward
temperance and prohibition legislation that was supported by
many in the anti-Nebraska ranks. In Wisconsin, for example, the
anti-Nebraska movement was led by a "People's party," which
had taken shape the year before, primarily with the objective of
passing a prohibition law. In 1854, the party was among the first to
adopt the title "Republican," but the temperance forces still visibly
in the leadership discouraged nearly all immigrants from having
anything to do with it.

The Germans found themselves during 1854 "between two fires,"
as the radical intellectual Christian Essellen put it:

On one side threatens the slaveholders' party, with its caucuses, nomi-
nations, its corruption and undermining of our political honor and
independence; on the other side stands nativism, with its fanatical Puritanism, as dangerous today as it was in Cromwell's time, with its hatred
of the immigrant population, its Sunday and temperance laws, which
comprise only the beginning of a chain of attempts that will end with
the complete political and social subjection of the immigrant population.
Against both the German people must take a stand.[5]

Essellen's favored course was an independent German party, which
could incorporate a national network of German societies. Other
radical types across the country were taking a similar position,
especially in the eastern states where they could not influence any
of the contending factions or parties. More moderate German leaders, however, shied away from such proposals, feeling that such
an organization would lead to a platform including all possible
German reform goals, and the Germans would be left alone and
impotent in such an overly ambitious undertaking. The *Illinois
Staats-Zeitung* counseled great caution in the steps to be taken by
the Germans:

One is a politician only when he seeks to attain that which he can attain. . . . If . . . in the old parties necessity has so manifested itself as to abandon all platform-riding, and to apply oneself to the immediate political necessity, so those who belong to the party of the future and of progress will surely not fall back into the old errors and, by a detailed system and an artistically intricate platform, reduce a great general movement of the people to a sectional, private affair.[6]

Although the 1854 election showed many successes for the coalition forming against the Kansas-Nebraska Act, immigrants in general were not drawn to the movement. The Germans who had been particularly vocal against Douglas were faced with Know-Nothings and prohibitionists within the movement opposed to him. In Iowa, Dutch voters who previously had inclined toward the Whigs, whose party now represented the anti-Nebraska view, rejected the Whigs and turned overwhelmingly to the Democrats, largely because the Whigs had also proposed a new prohibition law. The only sizable successes in gaining the German vote were in Illinois and in Missouri, especially in the heavily German areas around St. Louis. Frustrated by the increasingly anti-immigrant nature of the free-soil movement, the more radical German leaders began again to promote the idea of a separate German party.

In 1855 the dilemma presented itself again in a very real way in Illinois. The new legislature, solidly anti-Nebraska, also produced a liquor prohibition bill, one which referred the question to a public referendum. And in the municipal election in Chicago in March, Dr. Levi Boone, the only anti-Nebraska candidate to come forward, defeated the incumbent mayor, Democrat Isaac Milliken. Boone, who was known as a nativist leader, supposedly had been recommended by the local Know-Nothing lodge. The election produced the largest turnout in Chicago history to that time, and it showed that the immigrants who had previously opposed the Kansas-Nebraska Act had returned to the Democratic camp. Nevertheless, the nativist Boone prevailed. In his inaugural address, Boone promised strict enforcement of the liquor and Sunday laws, and shortly thereafter the city enacted a new liquor license law raising the price of a license to $300 annually. This was a direct strike against the small Irish grog-shops and German beer saloons. The city administration moved swiftly to remove Irish and German policemen from the force. Within two weeks of Boone's inauguration, raids were conducted on the immigrant neighborhood saloons for violation of the Sunday laws. Some saloon keepers were arrested because they refused to take out the expensive licenses and were operating without them.

On Saturday, April 21, 1855, one of the saloon keepers was being brought to trial in the court house, and a crowd of immigrants, both Irish and German, began gathering outside in the square. A fife and drum, sounding continuously, drew others to the scene. The mayor became alarmed and told the police to clear the crowd. They did so with liberal use of their billy clubs and carried a number of immigrants off to jail. At about 3:00 that same afternoon a new crowd assembled on the North Side and again began marching down Clark Street toward the courthouse square. Some in the crowd were armed. They were met by police and militia that had been called out to restrain them. Chaos reigned, and shots rang out. One demonstrator was shot and later died. Others, both police and rioters, were wounded. The riot was dispersed with considerable bloodshed, and the whole city was in a state of siege for the next four days. Recriminations from both sides boiled the political pot for weeks afterward. The events of April 1855, remembered as the "beer riots," would become a part of Chicago lore for many decades.

About six weeks later, the state of Illinois voted on the prohibition referendum. The turnout was much larger than it had been in the anti-Nebraska legislative elections the year before. Immigrant participation was certainly greater, and newspapers reported that many foreign-born were rushing to take out their naturalization papers. The prohibition law was defeated, with about 54 percent of the electorate voting against it. The overwhelming immigrant turnout made the difference. In Chicago's Seventh Ward, largely Irish and German, the vote was 91 percent against the referendum. The number of voters there was almost twice as large as in 1854. In rural German areas across the state, votes of 80 to 90 percent against the prohibition law were common. It was apparent to political observers on both sides that the immigrant population was much more excited by the temperance issue than by the free-soil issue.

Around the same time in Ohio, Know-Nothingism was on the rise, and was broadening its appeal from anti-Catholicism to opposition to all foreigners. The nativists were becoming the dominant element in a loose free-soil coalition called "Fusion," and consequently some more radical Germans who had previously been in the coalition were breaking their ties and moving back to the Democratic party. The municipal elections in Cincinnati in April showed the growing polarization when the Germans and Irish once again united behind the Democratic candidate and against the nativist candidate. On election day, nativist mobs roamed the streets with the principal purpose of intimidating Germans from going to the polls. In two primarily German wards, ballot boxes were stolen and destroyed. The following day the German militia took up arms and barricaded the German district known as Over-the-Rhine against feared nativist incursions. That evening, nativist mobs responded and attempted to invade the German quarter. Before order was restored, two men were dead and several more wounded. A court ultimately decided that the Democratic ticket had won the election. The election proved a turning point in Know-Nothing fortunes, and support for the movement in Ohio declined rapidly in subsequent years.

The free-soil Germans faced similar frustrations in other states across the North. In Indiana, Michigan, and Iowa there was an alliance of Know-Nothings and prohibitionists intent upon achieving their agenda. In Pennsylvania, a particularly strong alliance formed among free-soil former Whigs, free-soil Democrats, and the Know-Nothings, leaving Germans who had potentially been supportive of the free-soil cause with nowhere to go.

As the country entered the presidential election year of 1856, the anti-Nebraska forces, at this point more generally calling themselves Republicans, faced the problem of how to achieve a unified national structure and calm the antagonisms between nativists and immigrants. Certain free-soil Republicans, hoping to win the votes of Germans to the party, looked for a strategy that would reassure the Germans that the party would not adopt nativist policies, yet still retain the nativists' support. Ohio's Salmon P. Chase pointed to his success, having won the governor's post on the Republican ticket in 1855 by adopting a platform that contained only free-soil planks and made no concessions to the nativist-temperance faction. At the same time, nativists were listed in other party positions. The ticket was successful, and some Germans did support it, even though in Cincinnati most Germans were put off by the names of all-too-familiar nativists.

In Illinois, the editors of the *Chicago Tribune*, previously a voice of anti-immigrant views, began to argue for efforts to quiet nativism and enlist the free-soil Germans in the Republican cause. The editor of the *Illinois Staats-Zeitung*, George Schneider, joined with them in these efforts. In New York, the former Whig William Henry Seward, who had been re-elected to the Senate in 1855 on a Republican ticket that gathered together anti-Nebraska forces but avoided nativist positions, counseled a similar position for the national party. Such a strategy now seemed more promising because the Know-Nothing party was falling apart, having split into Northern and Southern elements over the slavery issue in 1855. If the Germans were not accommodated, they would quickly return to the Democratic party; but if the nativists were ignored, they would not turn to the Democrats and would have nowhere else to go.

The nativist-German dilemma was prominent in the minds of Republican politicians when they held their first truly national meeting in Pittsburgh on February 22, 1856, a date sometimes marked as the beginning of a national Republican party. The meeting adopted policies which stuck to the free-soil issues and invited all elements to rally about that standard. Although nativists in the northern states were migrating from the collapsed Know-Nothing party to the Republicans, the party leaders privately reassured German representatives that the party would not allow any nativist policies.

On the same day in Decatur, Illinois, a group of anti-Nebraska editors (still avoiding the term "Republican") met to consider the direction of a new free-soil coalition. They purposely wished to avoid identification with the nativist coalition that had taken control of Chicago the year before, and which was about to go down to defeat within the next week and hand the city back to the Democrats. A committee was chosen to draft resolutions; it included the German editor George Schneider. The committee was also joined by the Whig lawyer Abraham Lincoln. He added his arguments to those who said that the new party must take an anti-nativist position. The result was resolutions disavowing religious intolerance and giving a pledge against any alteration of the existing naturalization laws. The Illinois meeting had gone a step further than the Pittsburgh meeting by explicitly rejecting nativist positions. In the wake of the Decatur meeting of editors, the official state Republican convention was organized with great attention to finding convention officials who would be favorable to the Germans while at the same time encouraging the nativist and temperance forces to stick with the party. The convention, held in Bloomington, produced a platform stating "We will proscribe no one, by legislation or otherwise, on account of religious opinions, or in consequence of place of birth."[7]

The next challenge, a more difficult one, was to influence the national Republican convention, scheduled to meet in June in Philadelphia, to follow a similar course. The delegates from the western states worked hard to find a presiding officer for the convention who would be friendly to the immigrants. The person found was Henry Lane of Indiana, a former Whig who had held temperance views but had no connection with the Know-Nothing party. He agreed to persuade the platform committee to concentrate on the free-soil issues, avoid abolitionist and nativist language, and reassure immigrants of a proper reception within the party. The platform presented to the convention included a statement designed to appeal to all: "*Resolved*, that we invite the affiliation and co-operation of all parties, however differing from us in other respects, in support of the principles herein declared; and believing that the spirit of our institutions, as well as the Constitution of our country, guarantees liberty of conscience and equality of rights among citizens, we oppose all legislation impairing their security."[8] The resolution received some strong opposition from eastern states where the Know-Nothings were an important source of support for the party. Amid considerable animated debate, Lane finally gaveled the opposition down and declared the plank accepted, although many felt that the majority of votes were against it. The convention nominated for the presidency John Charles Frémont, who was acceptable to the immigrants. On the final day Germans from Illinois addressed the assembly, emphasizing how important the Germans were to party success in the western states. When the convention broke up, the Germans had been welcomed into the party with favorable platform language, but the Know-Nothings had merely been passively accepted without any recognition of their views.

The subsequent campaign showed for the first time a genuine struggle between two parties for the immigrant vote, making 1856 a landmark in immigrant political life in America. The Irish of course remained solidly Democratic, but the Germans were now being sought by both Democrats and Republicans. The results in this presidential election did not show a majority of German votes for the Republican candidate Frémont. But in the western states at least there were signs of departure from the old Democratic ways. In Illinois, Germans could see within the Republican ranks a number of their former Democratic leaders, as well as other influential Democrats. Gustave Koerner, for instance, was now declaring that what he called the "true Democrats" were to be found within the Republican party. The extant election returns are not complete, but the numbers suggest that a slight majority of the Germans in Illinois voted Republican. In other western states, the German Republican votes were fewer, but there were the beginnings of movement away from the Democratic party. In some states temperance advocates were still active within the Republican party. It was more common to find German Catholics and conservative Lutherans continuing to shy away from the former nativists they could identify among the Republicans. Democratic campaigners, sensing this uneasiness, did not fail to point out some of the old nativist enemies now among the Republicans. In the eastern states, however, Republicans made little attempt to win the German vote, since the adherence of the nativists seemed the more important goal for party leaders.

During the next four years the western Republicans continued their efforts to win over Germans. Ominous developments in the West helped their cause, as a civil war broke out in Kansas over political control of the territorial government and as Southern efforts to establish slavery in the territory were denounced by free-soilers. A greater threat seemed to loom when the Southern-dominated Supreme Court handed down the Dred Scott decision, which seemed to argue that slaves could be brought into any state or territory without restriction. In the late 1850s there were also efforts to pass a Homestead bill that offered free lands to settlers, an idea much desired by Germans. The Germans were very much aware that the homestead proposals were defeated at the hands of the Southern Democrats, who regarded the measure as primarily promoting the Northern small farmer without any comparable benefit to the Southern slave system. With such developments, it was easy to present the immigrants with a picture of an aggressive slavocracy that was attempting to take over the entire Union to the detriment of free laborers and free farmers alike. The success of the Republicans in some state and municipal elections in the West made it possible for them to award offices and positions in the party leadership to the Germans, and thus to begin a process of tying them to the party with patronage just as they had once been tied to the Democratic party.

The Democrats in the northern states made every effort to counter the loss of German adherents, and played constantly on the theme that Know-Nothings still lurked within the ranks of the Republicans. The Democrats themselves by 1857 were split between the followers of Douglas and those of President James Buchanan, who had backed the Southerners' fraudulent Lecompton Constitution, which proposed to establish Kansas as a slave state. Douglas denounced the Lecompton measure as a travesty of his idea of popular sovereignty, and so began to present himself as a moderate free-soil advocate, thus appealing to the Germans who had once been his supporters. The Democrats also had to give greater attention to the patronage for immigrants, and not appear to take them for granted. There was an effort by many Democratic politicians to establish German news-papers that would bear the party's banner, and thereby replace the newspapers run by forty-eighters who had deserted to the Repub-licans. The important change in the status of the Germans was that their power and influence in both parties had been enhanced, now that both sides were competing for their votes.

There was still some reason for Germans to worry about their future in the Republican party. In Wisconsin in 1857, the Democrats continued in their traditional practice by making room for German candidates for office on their state ticket. The Republicans responded by naming Carl Schurz, who was living in Watertown at the time, as their candidate for lieutenant governor. The choice of this prominent German-American probably won many German Democrats to the Republican side; however, it proved also to alienate many native-born Republicans who refused to vote for Schurz. The Republican candidate for governor, Alexander Randall, was narrowly elected by less than five hundred votes; Schurz, on the other hand, was defeated by about a hundred votes. Many of the German Republi-cans in Wisconsin were beginning to talk of the need for Germans to form their own separatist party—an idea mostly found among Germans in the East.

The elections of 1858 seemed to show that the Republicans were continuing to hold those Germans in their ranks who had supported their ticket in 1856. The returns showed only minor differences from their voting record in 1856. Western German leaders were attempt-ing to build on this record in anticipation of the presidential election of 1860. But a major setback confronted them when in Massachu-setts the Republican-controlled legislature passed a new amend-ment to the state constitution that required foreign-born citizens to wait two years after naturalization before being able to exercise the franchise. The amendment was approved by the Massachusetts voters in a general election in May 1859. Those in Massachusetts probably saw the measure mostly as restricting the political power of the Irish, but German leaders generally read it as a repudiation of the party's promise of equal rights for all citizens, as expressed in the national party platform of 1856. Germans in the eastern states began again to complain of nativism in the Republican party, and eastern German journalists began to call for a separatist movement that would stand between the major parties.

The controversies between Germans and nativists thus loomed large as the Republican party looked forward to the presidential nominating convention of 1860. A group of German Republicans from New York put out a call for a convention of Germans to meet in Chicago at the time of the Republican convention to decide on strategies both to persuade the party to renounce the Massachusetts amendment and to prevent any nativist candidates from gaining the nomination.

When the German meeting convened in Chicago two days before the national convention, it was apparent that the eastern Germans had not won support from the westerners. Germans from Illinois, Iowa, Wisconsin, Ohio, Minnesota, and Indiana had been elected as delegates to the Republican convention, and they plotted their own strategy while studiously avoiding the separatist German conference. Four of those German delegates—including Carl Schurz and Gustave Koerner—were appointed to the platform committee. Their efforts were useful in getting a platform plank that supported equal rights for all citizens—thereby implicitly rejecting the Massachusetts "two-year amendment." The party platform also included support of a homestead act that would grant free lands to western settlers, another issue of great importance to the Germans. While that inclusion was primarily the work of other Republicans on the committee, the two planks together were widely referred to as the "Dutch planks." Meanwhile, the German separatist conference had come to nothing; it produced some modest resolutions which appeared after the platform committee met, and had little influence.

German party leaders within the national convention's halls also managed to upset the efforts of candidates with nativist attachments to gain the party's nomination. The principal candidates feared by the Germans were Edward Bates of Missouri and Nathaniel Banks, the governor of Massachusetts. The efforts of people like Schurz and Koerner to dissuade others from supporting the nativists were probably effective. The candidate most favored by Germans was William Henry Seward of New York, who was considered friendly to the immigrants. Although Seward was considered the front-runner coming into the convention, delegates began to fear that his more radical antislavery opinions would be detrimental, and the convention, moving in a more moderate direction, ultimately selected Abraham Lincoln. The Germans therefore contributed to the nomination of Lincoln by reducing the chances of the nativists Banks and Bates; others rejected the possibility of Seward, and Lincoln remained as a moderate compromise candidate.

German Republicans generally were not put off by Lincoln's nomination. While not a man of radical abolitionist views, he was a strong free-soil advocate. Although his background was as a Whig, he had not been connected to the party's nativist elements, and in fact had argued on several occasions for the civil rights of immigrants. Since the Kansas-Nebraska Act he had solicited the cooperation of the Germans, and in 1859 he had purchased the press and type to start a German-language newspaper in Springfield, Illinois, in order to further his views and those of the Republican party. After his nomination the Illinois German leaders worked hard to persuade the Germans of other states of Lincoln's freedom from nativist views and of his commitment to free soil and free labor in the West.

The campaign that followed in 1860 featured the greatest attention given thus far in a presidential election to the interests of an immigrant group. Carl Schurz persuaded Lincoln of the importance of reaching the Germans, and he and other German politicians made frequent visits to German communities thought to be divided between the parties. The Democrats suffered from a considerable handicap because of the breakup of their own party; two different candidates were in the field, Stephen Douglas, representing largely northern Democrats, and John Breckenridge, representing the Southerners. Douglas worked to retain immigrant support by pointing to the alleged nativism and temperance advocacy within the Republicans; he also tried to represent his own position as favoring free soil. A Democratic problem, however, was the party's position on homestead land in the West. Douglas favored it, as did most of the Germans in either party. But homestead bills had failed several times in the 1850s because of opposition from Southern Democrats, and in 1860, just a month after the Republican convention, the Democratic President Buchanan had vetoed the latest effort at homestead legislation. The inadequacy of the divided Democrats in achieving anything on this issue probably swayed many free-soil Germans toward the Republicans.

In the final result, Lincoln and the Republican party prevailed, having gained a majority of electoral votes entirely in the states of the North. The role played by immigrant groups, particularly the Germans, in achieving this victory has been much debated. The Republicans did maintain the German votes they had received in 1856, and increased the percentage of the German vote in many places by a few points. They had succeeded in recovering support from the wavering Germans concerned about the Massachusetts two-year amendment. Overall, there still were probably a majority of Germans voting Democratic in the election, but in a few states,

Illinois in particular, the Germans were in the majority Republican. Republicans ran stronger among Germans in the western states, in urban areas, and among those who had immigrated since 1850. It was in these areas that Germans had been welcomed more freely into the party and its councils, while the nativists had been isolated. Older German communities, especially those with more Catholics and Lutherans, showed their traditional fear of nativism and remained more closely tied to the Democrats. The real success for the Germans, however, was in shaping the Republican party to their needs by ridding it of nativist tendencies and committing it to equal rights for the foreign-born. In that sense, the struggle for the party that had been taking place since 1854 paid off.

As for the Irish, during the entire 1850s, they remained tied closely to the Democratic party. They still tended to detect anti-Catholicism within the Republicans, and continued to be moved by the local political ties that gave them power and patronage on that level.

Many English voters, especially those of the middle class, made their transfer from the Whig to the Republican party without controversy. They had often brought antislavery reform views with them from England, and also tended to be moved by free-soil sentiments. The Norwegians, having less fear of the nativists and holding to a strong antislavery position, were largely converted to the Republican cause by 1860. The Dutch remained on the Democratic side, largely in response to fears about temperance reformers and nativists. Those in Michigan mostly remained Democrats during the 1850s despite the influence of the Dutch leader and minister Augustus C. Van Raalte, who had argued for the Republican cause.

THE OUTBREAK OF CIVIL WAR

After the election of Lincoln (and before his inauguration in March 1861), the states of the lower South, anticipating federal government attacks on the slave system, began to secede from the Union, beginning with South Carolina in late December 1860. President Buchanan made no move to restrict the movement of states to secession, arguing that he had no constitutional power to do so. While Lincoln felt otherwise, he stated after his inauguration that he had no intention of disturbing the domestic institution of slavery in the states of the South, but that he was pledged to preserve the Union. He made no overt move to raise military forces until April 12, when the South Carolina artillery forces in Charleston fired on Fort Sumter, the principal Union military post that was still occupied in the lower South. With the fall of Fort Sumter, Lincoln called upon the public to answer this aggressive act, and sent out a call for volunteers to defend the Union and put down what he called a "rebellion."

The Immigrant Response

Like many others in the North, few immigrants had really expected that the long controversy would lead to war, let alone a war that would cost so many casualties and last four years. At the beginning, it seemed like an easy task for the greater numbers of Union soldiers to advance out of Washington and throw back the smaller Confederate forces coming from Richmond. That optimism was rudely shattered, however, when the Union forces were defeated in July 1861 at the first battle of Bull Run, southwest of Washington, and the Union troops' retreat turned into confusion and panic. Lincoln and the general public had to resign themselves to a longer war, and more calls went out to recruit soldiers.

Feelings of support for the war varied greatly among different immigrant groups and different elements within each group. Those who had supported Lincoln and the Republicans before the war tended to give him support and to rally to the call for volunteers. The many who had attachments to the Democratic party ended up with divided opinions, just as the party itself had become divided between North and South. In the North, previous followers of Stephen Douglas, whose leadership would end with his death in June 1861, heeded his call to support the Union in the struggle with the South. But there were many Democrats in the North who were Southern sympathizers and called themselves "Peace Democrats."

After the war, many immigrant spokesmen celebrated the heroism and sacrifice of the ethnic troops for having proven the loyalty of the foreign-born and for validating their claim to be Americans as worthy as any native-born. But it is doubtful that many enlisted in the war simply for the purpose of disproving the accusations of nativists. The reasons varied widely, but many found they could willingly respond to the purpose of defending and preserving the Union. That was the purpose Lincoln had defined in 1861, and at that time he was not advocating a crusade to wipe out slavery. Archbishop Hughes, who had become the most widely acknowledged spokesman of the Irish Catholics, repeatedly denounced in debates and publications the idea of a war against slavery. The sole legitimate purpose of the war, he argued, was the preservation of the Union. The assault upon the Constitution posed by secession was the challenge that had to be met.

The rallying of many immigrants about the Union cause might be understood in the light of their sense of nationalism—both about the independence and unity of their homelands and about their sense of national identity in the United States. The Irish who fought for the Union were acknowledging that the nation had given them a new identity as well as opportunities they had not had in the old country. They could visualize themselves as worse off if the Union were to be dissolved. They also could see parallels to the struggle for freedom and independence in Ireland. In fact, some saw themselves as preparing for a future military effort to free Ireland from British rule. Peter Welsh, an Irish sergeant from Massachusetts serving in Virginia with the Irish Brigade wrote to his father-in-law in Ireland in 1863:

I have felt from my childhood that i might one day have an oppertunity when the right man to lead should be found and the proper time should arive to strike a blow for the rights and liberty of Irland. For such an oppertunity this war is a school of instruction for Irishmen and if the day should arive within ten years after this war is ended an army can be raised in this country that will strike terror to the saxons heart.[9]

When during the war there were suspicions that Britain might recognize and aid the Confederacy, that strengthened even more the will of the Irish against the South.

As for the Germans, some of course did rally to the leadership of the forty-eighters and other radicals who saw the war as a cleansing of the Republic and the extinction of the slave power. That mission would achieve the ultimate goal of the free-soilers. But many Germans, like the Irish, saw mainly the values of preserving the Union. While most Germans probably did not hold to the vision of the ideal Republic that motivated some intellectuals, Germans could thank the Union for the grassroots, pragmatic democracy they enjoyed and for the freedom that had helped many of them to get ahead. The South was still seen as being in the hands of an aristocracy that offered less opportunity to the immigrant, an aristocracy that had denied the promise of land in the West to the foreign-born. Most immigrants could recognize that, whatever their current status in the United States, they were better off than they would have been in the old country, and so defending the Union was for them a worthy cause.

The motive drawing many of the recruits to military service, and perhaps a majority of them, was that they were in need of a job, and, as in the decades previous, the army could offer them that. The years of the late 1850s were years of an economy in recession, and the rate of immigration fell to about one-third of what it had been in the early 1850s. In the first years of the war it fell even further. Railroad-building had fallen off as well, and construction work in the West was less plentiful. The cutoff of the North from trade with the South had affected the economies of many cities that were links in that trade, and unemployment was rising in those places. Many new arrivals in the eastern ports found military recruiters waiting for them, while there were fewer labor contractors looking for wage-laborers. There were very often promises of bonuses and future benefits for enlistment, which seemed to the new arrivals to offer better possibilities than any others to be found.

A 34-year-old immigrant, Private Wilhelm Hoffmann, wrote a letter home to his mother in Silesia in November 1862. He complained of the hardships and dangers of the army (he had recently survived the second battle of Bull Run), but also explained why he had joined the 54th New York Infantry Volunteers, a largely German regiment:

I don't advise anyone from Germany to come over here, at least not if he values his life, because every immigrant, after he's been here in this country for a few weeks, finds he can't get by unless he becomes a soldier. Business is so bad no one can earn his daily bread, no matter how hard one works. . . . Normally, after an immigrant has been in the country for 3 to 4 months, no matter if he's rich or poor, he shows up in rags, poor as a church mouse, at the recruitment office, ready to sacrifice the last thing he has, namely his life, for this country.[10]

There were, of course, many who saw no interest in the war and found a way to avoid it. Some could move to Canada without any interference. There were new mining frontiers in the West, particularly in Nevada, Idaho, and Montana. The flush times in those frontiers peaked during 1863, when the most furious battles of the war were occurring in the East. Immigrants, like others, could head to the mines with the same hopes that others had, and there would be little effort to recruit them there. And when issues of state or federal conscription arose, immigrants who had not taken out naturalization papers were normally excused from the draft. There were those who refused to take out their first papers for that reason.

Whatever enthusiasms brought immigrants to support the war in 1861 and 1862 were inevitably going to decline in the subsequent years. As the war went on with no end in view, and the casualties mounted, recruitment became more difficult, and immigrants as well as others began to question the purpose of the war. When after the issuance of the Emancipation Proclamation in 1863 the goal of abolishing slavery across the entire Union came to the fore, many began to protest. The first federal call for a military draft in 1863 led to even more resistance.

The Response of Immigrants in the Confederate States

Immigrants in the seceded southern states were presented with the same questions as those in the north, and for many the motivation to enlist was a simple issue of protecting their new homeland against foreign invasion. The Irish could sense the analogy between the imposition of British power over Ireland and the imposition of the power of the Union over the Confederacy. The South had its own nationalism, too, with which many immigrants could identify. That nationalism had been carefully cultivated by some politicians and journalists during the preceding decade. The necessity of the slave system to the vitality of the South was a part of that nationalism, and something that many immigrants could appreciate. Their place in the society of the South, while often lowly, was always superior to that of the slave class.

An Irish entertainer, Harry McCarthy, penned the first verses to *The Bonnie Blue Flag*, which became one of the favorite marching songs of the Confederate army. It was set to a traditional Irish melody called *The Irish Jaunting Car*:

We are a band of brothers, natives of the soil,
Fighting for our property we gained by honest toil;
But when our rights were threatened the cry rose near and far,
Hurrah for the Bonnie Blue Flag that bears a single star.
Hurrah! Hurrah! for Southern Rights hurrah;
Hurrah for the Bonnie Blue Flag that bears a single star.[11]

Germans in the South presented a much more complex picture as to their support for the Confederate cause. In cities like Charleston, Richmond, and New Orleans, where they were embedded in the bourgeois society and economy, the Germans tended to accept the existing social system and support the effort to establish a Southern nation. The few German radical forty-eighters who had migrated to those cities had little influence on other Germans. In some of the more rural areas, there was evidence of the disapproval of secession and of the war. In Texas, many German communities voted against secession, which was approved by the state's voters generally in a referendum of February 1861. In places where they constituted a smaller minority, the Germans seemed to have been more intimidated by the larger society around them and did not show as much resistance. Nevertheless, suspicions about the loyalty of the Germans, who were thought to still secretly support abolitionism, were common among Southerners.

In one of the more notorious cases of German resistance to the Confederacy, in 1862 in the Hill Country west of Austin, a group of 68 Texas Germans who were being subjected to conscription in the Confederate army decided to escape the Confederacy and volunteer for the Union army instead. Their exit route took them southward toward Mexico. At the Nueces River they encountered a large band of Confederate troops, and a massacre occurred at what became known as the Battle of the Nueces. Nineteen were killed in the battle, nine others were killed after being taken prisoner, and eight were killed while attempting to cross the Rio Grande into Mexico. There were doubtless others who did not support the Confederacy but remained quietly in their place. In January 1863, five Texas counties were placed under martial law because of resistance to the draft, coming primarily from Germans.

THE ETHNIC MILITARY UNITS

When President Lincoln sent out the call for volunteers in April 1861, the regular army numbered about 16,000 officers and enlisted men, some of whom had already gone over to the side of the Confederacy. The regular army had a large contingent of foreign-born enlisted men—probably a greater proportion of the ranks than had existed at the time of the Mexican War. To add to the meager army of 1861, the most available volunteer forces were the existing militia units of the states. As at the time of the Mexican War, the militia forces were loosely organized associations often identified with urban neighborhoods, social groups, labor organizations, or ethnic groups, and usually led by some prominent citizen from among them. They still were known primarily for marching in public parades and celebrations, often dressed in colorful but impractical dress uniforms. However, they responded quickly, confident that the three months' service requested by Lincoln would be more than sufficient to quell the insurrection in the South.

When the nation resigned itself to a longer war, the existing ethnic militia units were augmented from 1861 onward by new ones organized specifically to answer the call for service to the Union. These units were often led by ethnic leaders who claimed some military experience and were eager to put it to use in promoting the participation of their own group. Thus, former Irish nationalists and revolutionaries, as well as refugees from the European revolutions of 1848, came forth to play a role in rallying immigrants to the call of the Union.

The Germans in a Crucial Role

Among the earliest militia units to be mustered were those from the German neighborhoods in St. Louis, where, even before the firing on Fort Sumter, there had been concern that the state of Missouri might join the movement of other slave states to secession. The pro-slavery governor, Claiborne Jackson, who favored secession, hoped to gain arms from the federal arsenal at St. Louis in order to equip the Missouri militia units supporting him. Pro-Southern militia units from rural Missouri were assembled at what they called "Camp Jackson" in the city. The Germans constituted the principal Unionist and Republican element in St. Louis, and the federal army officers who had been sent to secure the arsenal and prevent the taking of the arms by secessionists called upon the local German units for aid. In mid-March 1861, four German regiments occupied the federal arsenal, and its commander, a Southern sympathizer, was removed. After the firing on Fort Sumter, when Confederate military action in Missouri seemed even more likely, the arms from the arsenal were spirited away to Illinois under cover of night. The German regiments then surrounded the pro-Southern militia groups at Fort Jackson; they surrendered without a shot, and over a thousand were taken prisoner. A riot ensued as the prisoners were marched through the streets of St. Louis, resulting in numerous deaths. Thus began a conflict of several years which amounted to a civil war within the state of Missouri, and which to some extent became an ethnic conflict as well. The Germans continued to be the mainstays in holding the city of St. Louis for the Union, and were credited with preventing the state government from seceding and joining the Confederacy.

German Troops and Their Leaders

The weeks after the firing on Fort Sumter saw the raising of many German militia units, and in the end there would be more of these than of any other ethnicity. The complex organizational structure

A German militia force, having secured the federal arsenal at St. Louis for the Union, is attacked by a mob of Confederate sympathizers as it marches prisoners through the streets. The Germans claimed proudly to have saved Missouri for the Union. From *Harper's Weekly*, June 1, 1861. Courtesy Bryn Mawr College Special Collections.

of the German communities in general was mirrored in the variety of German militia groups. In New York City, for example, the 20th New York Regiment was put together from the various Turner societies within the city, and soon became known as the United Turner Rifles. The Cincinnati Turners provided the original base for the 9th Ohio Regiment, one of the most celebrated ethnic units at the time. It was led for most of the duration of the war by a prominent American lawyer, Colonel Robert McCook, who although not of German background was nevertheless well-liked by the German troops. McCook, who was well-connected politically, saw to the state's support of the unit; the actual training of the Ohio 9th was undertaken by his adjutant, a radical forty-eighter and former Prussian military officer, August Willich, who would eventually go on to command other German units.

Other German units drew recruits from the numerous active *Schützenvereine* (shooting clubs). In Chicago, various German companies were organized under names such as "Black Sharpshooters,"

"Chicago Hunters," and "Pioniers." They were incorporated into the 24th Illinois Infantry, which included other companies from outlying towns in the state. The command of this regiment was accepted by Friedrich Hecker, the legendary forty-eighter from southern Illinois, who had once led an army of rebels in Baden. Hecker would eventually resign from his post when intramural conflicts arose within the regiment, primarily among the officer corps. The 7th New York, known as the Steuben Rifles, included many—both officers and enlisted men—who had former military experience in Europe.

For many of the German units, the power that drew recruits was that of the personality of their well-known German leaders. Hecker's name lent more prominence to the Illinois 24th over other units being organized at the time. Willich was known for his ability to inspire troops while still imposing discipline. From his original post in the Ohio 9th, he went on to organize the Indiana 32nd Infantry; beginning as a colonel, he was appointed a brigadier general after his unusually brave behavior in rallying his troops amidst withering enemy fire at the Battle of Shiloh.

The New York 8th Regiment was organized by Ludwig Blenker, a forty-eighter who had had previous experience in the Bavarian army. Blenker, a dashing and colorful commander, rose from colonel to brigadier general when his regiment was incorporated into a brigade and he was made its commander. He became one of the more controversial German commanders; there were suspicions of his extravagant life-style and of his cultivation of a seemingly excessive number of aides drawn from former aristocratic elements of the Prussian officer corps. Blenker became the object of criticism by other prominent forty-eighters, including Karl Heinzen, who accused him of squandering regimental funds to support his high style of living. None of the charges were ever proven, and Blenker did become a general, but not long afterwards retired to his farm in upstate New York. The controversy was another one which showed that the long-standing conflicts and divisions within German America were not lessened during the war.

There were more Union generals of German background than of any other ethnicity, not only because they had had some military experience in the revolutions of 1848, but also because the Lincoln administration believed that the Germans had given the Republicans important support in the 1860 election and that the adherence of Germans to the party should be encouraged. The best known of these to the general American public was Carl Schurz, who had traveled widely among the German communities seeking support for Lincoln in the 1860 election. He was originally appointed minister to Spain, but his desire for a military appointment was granted in 1862, when Lincoln appointed him a brigadier general. He later became a major general, serving first in Virginia, and after Gettysburg transferring to the West, where he served with General William T. Sherman's forces at Chattanooga. In 1864 he withdrew from service to work on Lincoln's 1864 campaign, and in 1865 served as chief of staff to General H. W. Slocum during Sherman's march through Georgia.

Another German major general was Peter Osterhaus, a former Prussian officer and forty-eighter who at the beginning of the war had been working in a hardware business in St. Louis. He participated with the German regiments that saved the federal arsenal from attack, then served with various of the Missouri German regiments. In 1862 he was commanding a division as a colonel in the Army of the Southwest, and after the battle of Pea Ridge he was made a brigadier general. In 1863 he served with General Ulysses Grant's army in the siege of Vicksburg. After the fall of Vicksburg, he joined in the march on Chattanooga and fought at Lookout Mountain, making his greatest fame in that battle, in which his unit captured thousands of Confederate soldiers. He then joined in Sherman's march on Atlanta, in the midst of which he was promoted to major general. After the fall of Atlanta, he commanded a division in Sherman's march to the sea, and by the end of the war was reducing Confederate resistance along the Gulf coast.

The most popular of the generals among Germans by far was Franz Sigel. The revolutionary leader from Baden had become by 1860 a prominent German leader in St. Louis, where he was a professor in the German Institute, a member of the Turner society, a district superintendent in the school system, and an active supporter of the Republican party. Sigel rallied Germans to the defense of the St. Louis arsenal when pro-Confederate forces attempted to take it in March, 1861. He was a colonel in the 3rd Missouri Infantry when the Union militias captured the secessionist forces in St. Louis. Subsequently he served in various actions in Missouri, but did not compile a very distinguished record. Nevertheless, popular acclaim for his efforts in preserving Missouri for the Union brought him a promotion to brigadier general in August 1861. He had anticipated taking command of the forces in the District of Southwestern Missouri, but when that post was assigned to another general, Sigel, his pride offended, resigned.

Outcries from the public and support from the Republican party caused his superiors to reconsider, and Sigel took part in March 1862 in the battle of Pea Ridge, Arkansas, which was a victory for the Union forces. He was appointed a major general after that battle, and transferred to Virginia. His career, however, went sharply down-hill after that. He took part in the second battle of Bull Run, which was another Union defeat. His superiors sent him to less significant posts, but intense lobbying by Sigel and his supporters brought him the command of the Department of West Virginia. In that command he suffered defeat in May 1864 at the battle of New Market, where Confederate forces overwhelmed his army and precipitated a humiliating Union retreat two months later northward down the Shenandoah Valley and all the way to Harper's Ferry. Sigel was relieved of his command and in May 1865 resigned from the army. He had maintained his places in the army largely because he was of symbolic importance to the German immigrants, who came to his defense when he was criticized for his poor military record; he nevertheless helped to tie these immigrants to the Union cause. Sigel's detractors called that a very costly political appointment.

The Irish Units

Perhaps the most famous Civil War ethnic unit was the Irish Brigade, formed from several previously existing Irish regiments. The core regiment was the 69th New York State Militia, which, at the beginning of the war, was already well-known and closely connected to Tammany Hall. In 1859 its commander was Colonel Michael Corcoran, who had worked his way up through the enlisted ranks in the previous decade. In October 1859, when the young Prince of Wales arrived and was celebrated in New York, Corcoran refused to allow the 69th to join in the parade in his honor. State militia officials moved to bring him to a court martial, but then, recognizing his ability to recruit new members of the regiment, they cancelled the trial, allowing him to take command once more as the regiment was being mobilized. The 69th thus departed for Washington just 11 days after the firing on Fort Sumter.

In the defeat of the Union troops at the first battle of Bull Run, Corcoran was captured by the Confederates and held for over a year; he would die soon after his release, when he was thrown from a horse. The 69th returned to New York, its three-month service having expired, but then many of its soldiers joined the new 69th New York Volunteers. The new 69th was combined with other regiments that were being organized as the "Irish Brigade" by the well-known Irish nationalist Thomas Francis Meagher, who had previously commanded a company of the 69th at Bull Run. Meagher as brigadier general raised a brigade composed of the 69th, 63rd and 88th New York Regiments, all predominantly Irish. Later, in 1862, the 28th Massachusetts and 116th Pennsylvania regiments were added to the brigade.

The brigade returned to Washington in December 1861, then in 1862 served in the Peninsular campaign. It suffered heavily in the battle of Antietam (September 1862), losing 540 men in the bloodiest battle of the war, when the brigade failed in an effort to penetrate the center of the Confederate line. Two months later, at Fredericksburg, the brigade suffered casualties of half its forces in a valiant attempt to charge up a hill occupied by the forces of Robert E. Lee. It was during this battle that Lee was supposedly the first to call the brigade, admiringly, the "Fighting 69th." In May 1863, Meagher asked permission to seek new recruits for his brigade, but resigned after the request was denied.

Members of the Irish Brigade resting at Harrison's Landing, Virginia, during the Peninsular campaign, summer 1862. In September, the brigade would suffer heavy losses at the battle of Antietam. Library of Congress, Prints and Photographs Division.

A considerably reduced Irish Brigade, now under Colonel Patrick Kelly, fought at the battle of Gettysburg in July 1863, and suffered casualties of about 40 percent of its strength. The brigade was reorganized under new leadership with new recruits during the winter of 1863–1864, and fought in the battles of the Wilderness, Spotsylvania, and Cold Harbor. After the heavy losses of those battles and the death of the new commander, Richard Byrnes, at Cold Harbor, Colonel Kelly once again took command, but he was killed at Petersburg in July 1864. The brigade was broken up after that, its regiments going to other units, but the three New York regiments and the Massachusetts regiment were once again united in a new brigade that fought in Virginia until the Confederate surrender at Appomattox. When the Irish Brigade marched through the streets of Washington in a victory parade in May 1865, it was already one of the most celebrated units in the Union army. It also had suffered some of the heaviest losses of any unit.

Although the New York Irish units were the best known, other Irish communities provided their own regiments. Boston provided two, one of which, the 28th Massachusetts Infantry, was later incorporated into Meagher's Irish Brigade. Three other regiments came from other parts of New England. Pennsylvania provided two. The 23rd Illinois Infantry, recruited by James Mulligan, actually drew some of its units from Michigan, Missouri, and Wisconsin. Missouri and Wisconsin, though largely identified with German militia groups, each rallied an Irish regiment.

There were three Irish-born generals who became identified with Irish participation in the war. Two were the leaders of the Irish Brigade, Michael Corcoran and Thomas Francis Meagher. The third was James Shields, who was reviving his military ambition of Mexican War days. He came from California to be recommissioned in the Union Army, and again was made a brigadier general. He commanded units which were not specifically Irish, and his record with troops in the Shenandoah Valley was not outstanding. After the Senate refused to appoint him a major general (as Lincoln had recommended), he resigned his commission and returned to California.

Other Ethnic Units

The French immigrants in New York City organized a regiment based on the long-standing militia regiment, the 55th New York Volunteers, known as the Gardes Lafayette. When new recruits were added in early 1861, the unit also contained many Germans as well as French-born volunteers. One company was exclusively German. The regiment suffered heavy losses in severe fighting in 1861 and 1862; after the battle of Fredericksburg it was greatly reduced in numbers and was consolidated into another regiment. The 79th New York regiment, also a previously existing militia group composed mainly of Scotsmen, was known as "Cameron's Highlanders," its commander being Colonel James Cameron, brother of Secretary of War Simon Cameron. The unit was sent to Washington and suffered the loss of Colonel Cameron and other officers in the first battle of Bull Run. It gained notoriety when after that battle it was ordered again to join the brigade of General Daniel Sickles in Virginia and mutinied. Other Union forces had to be sent to compel the troops to move, and the regiment was deprived of its colors for a month. The troops redeemed their reputation later in the war.

Various Norwegian and Swedish companies were raised early in the war in Wisconsin, Illinois, and Minnesota. In September 1861, a meeting of Scandinavian leaders in Wisconsin concluded with a decision to recruit a regiment, the 15th Wisconsin. Appeals went out to both Norwegians and Swedes, and some members were recruited from Iowa and Illinois.

Perhaps most remarkable was the 39th New York, known as the Garibaldi Guard. It had few Italians and was commanded by a Hungarian, George D'Utassy. It enrolled soldiers of nearly every ethnicity, including Latin Americans, Spanish, Swiss, Portuguese, and Germans. The regiment showed the problems of multiethnic organizations: there were internal conflicts about what language to use, and constant tensions between the officers of various backgrounds. D'Utassy himself, whose actual background was never very clear, was accused of misusing the regiment's resources and was eventually court-martialed in 1863 for various frauds involving the supply of his unit. He was cashiered and sentenced to a year at hard labor in Sing Sing prison.

Although there were many units considered exclusively of one ethnic background or another, most of them tended to lose that distinctiveness as the war progressed. As terms of enlistment ran out and mounting casualties required replacement troops, new recruits were often not of the original ethnicity. Finding new replacements became more of a problem as disillusion grew with the war, especially among the immigrants. The imposition of the draft brought conscripts of all sorts into the units, individuals who were not always from the originating state and were seldom from the particular ethnic group.

OTHER IMMIGRANTS WHO SERVED

An estimated 500,000 immigrants served in the Union army in the Civil War, about one quarter of the roughly two million total Union soldiers. The Germans were the largest group, perhaps numbering 185,000; the Irish numbered approximately 144,000. An estimated 54,000 English-born immigrants were in the Union Army. Among the native-born were roughly 189,000 blacks. To the numbers of foreign-born should probably be added an unknown number of second generation, American-born members of the immigrant communities.

The majority of the 500,000 immigrants were not in the ethnic units, but served along with the native-born soldiers and other immigrants in the regular regiments of volunteers. About one in every six Union soldiers died during the conflict; there is no reason to believe that the proportion of immigrant soldiers was lower, and given the immigrant participation in some of the bloodiest battles, it may have been more. About one out of every ten Union soldiers deserted, with perhaps 40 percent of those returning to duty. There is no reason to believe that the proportion of immigrant soldiers who deserted was lower.[12]

The heavy casualties of the war brought tragedy to many immigrant families and communities. One example among thousands was that of two Norwegian-born brothers, Lars and Knud Olsen Dokken, who left the family farm in Dane County, Wisconsin, and joined the largely Scandinavian 15th Wisconsin Volunteer Regiment when it was organized in Madison in late 1861. The community from which they came, like other Norwegian communities, had readily supported the Republican party and was now responding to Lincoln's call for volunteers. Lars was twenty-two, Knud just eighteen. They had come to the United States with their family in 1857, full of hope for the opportunities of America. The regiment, numbering about 3,500, was ordered to Tennessee, where it first saw action in March 1862. It was part of the forces which opened up the Mississippi Valley and denied the Confederates access to it. The 15th Wisconsin first occupied Union City, Tennessee, then New Madrid, Missouri, and then took part in the takeover of the strategic Island No. 10 in the middle of the Mississippi River, which gave the Union control of the middle Mississippi Valley.

The letters the brothers wrote home told of the usual concerns of soldiers—the impenetrable designs of the superior officers, the poor rations, the long and apparently purposeless marches through Tennessee and Kentucky, the slowness of their pay, their worry over conditions back home and the well-being of their parents, and, occasionally, their actual encounters with rebel forces. But in May 1862, Lars had to report that his brother Knud was ill with typhus, along with many others in the regiment. Knud died a few days later. As with so many others, it was disease, not enemy fire, that caused his end. Lars wrote to his parents: "He was in a clear state of mind until he drew his last breath. But it was sad for me to be parted from him in this enemy land, but the Lord does all for the best." Lars went on with the regiment in numerous campaigns across Tennessee during 1862, but at the end of the year, he was wounded in a battle near Murfreesboro. As he reported in January 1863 from the general hospital in Nashville: "On the morning of December 31, I was wounded in both buttocks. The bullet was removed from the right side, close to the surface; so it passed almost clear through. The pain has been hard to bear sometimes. I cannot stand on my feet at all, and so I am bedridden."

Lars continued to express hope for his recovery for the next three months, but he developed an infection and died in the hospital on April 1, 1863.[13] Those who served in an ethnic unit may have had some source of comfort in the familiarity of their comrades, the common language, and perhaps the similarity of religion. Those not in immigrant-dominated units suffered the same woes as the immigrants who had served in the regular army in the 1840s and 1850s. Nativism, especially anti-Catholicism, was rife among the officer ranks. Some immigrants were given demeaning duties because of their foreign origin; insults and stereotypes were common, just as they pervaded the popular press and the comedy stage at the time.

For all, of course, there was the constant terror of the potential battles that lay ahead, and the risks they posed. And amidst the everyday routines there was the constant boredom, frustration, and bewilderment at the confusing and uncertain orders that came from above. The New York *Irish American* in 1863 printed weekly dispatches from a writer identifying himself as "Fenian" who was apparently in the ranks of the Irish Brigade, then in Virginia. Fenian recounted apparently aimless marches outward eight miles from a base, then eight miles back again. He described (with some sympathy) the motives of soldiers who raided local farmers' hen-houses for chickens. He told of assaults on a fortress already aban-doned by the enemy. And he expressed wonderment at conflicting orders from various superiors. These were of course the complaints and effusions common to rank-and-file soldiers at all times. And in them we can see some evidence of the assimilation of the immigrant soldier into American society.

IMMIGRANTS FOR THE CONFEDERACY

While the Confederate military officers often spoke contemptu-ously of the alien hordes of immigrants that confronted them in the northern army, and prided themselves on the supposedly pure American character of the South's army, the fact was that many immigrants served in the Confederate gray uniform as well as in the Union blue. The South's total enlistments were only a little over a million—about half the number who took part at one time or another in the Union army. Given the incomplete Confederate records and the sketchy information contained in them, historians have come up with only vague estimates—usually running from about 5 percent to 10 percent of Confederate soldiers who were foreign-born. By all accounts, the Irish were the most numerous, and the Germans second. The state enrolling the most immigrants was Louisiana, with its multi-ethnic port of New Orleans. The state with the fewest immigrant recruits was probably North Carolina. Irish sailors and riverboat men also were found in the Confederate navy. The Confederate army also had one Irish Protestant immi-grant, Patrick Cleburne, who attained the rank of major general. A lawyer from Arkansas who had once been a soldier in the British army, he rose in the ranks from being the captain of a local mili-tia before the war to being the commander of a division. He was among several generals who died in November 1864 at the disas-trous Battle of Franklin in Tennessee.

Some of the immigrants who rallied to the Confederate cause were willing volunteers, since they identified the South as their home, to be defended against invasion by hostile Northern forces. For the Irish, this could be likened to the defense of Ireland against the hostile British, and prominent Irish spokesmen, including some of the Catholic bishops, called for recruits to defend the Southern homeland. The Confederacy, with its smaller pool of military-age men, resorted to a draft at an earlier time than did the North, and many of the immigrants were brought into the army by the draft.

As the war went on, morale worsened, recruits of all types were less willing to enter the army, and desertions increased.

The Confederate army also had its ethnic units, more often companies in contrast to the regiments of the North. At the outset of the war the existing militia units were called into service for the South, and these included some longstanding militias such as Charleston's Irish Volunteers, Savannah's Jasper Greens, and Mobile's German Fusiliers. Additional ethnic units were organized during the war. Among the more colorful was the Louisiana Zouaves, a regiment recruited by the French Major Gustave de Coppens in New Orleans and consisting largely of French and Italians, many of whom had served previously in the Crimean War and in recent wars in Italy against Austria. The larger towns of Texas provided German companies. The port cities of the South recruited many Irish from the docks and levees to serve in ethnic companies, but many others served in the multi-ethnic units. However, when New Orleans fell to Union forces in April 1862, immigrants there were no longer available for recruitment by the Confederacy.

The best known of the Irish Confederate units was the 6th Louisiana Infantry, recruited from the levees of New Orleans, and known as the "Irish Tigers." These troops were famous for their rowdiness, and were put under the command of General Richard Taylor, a former Know-Nothing, who characterized them as "stout, hardy fellows, turbulent in camp and requiring a strong hand." The rough-and-ready Tigers, however, distinguished themselves in grueling actions in the Shenandoah Valley of Virginia. Following a trying day in June 1862, when the Tigers provided rear guard action during a retreat, and then insisted on remaining on guard duty through a stormy night, the old Know-Nothing Taylor admitted that "my heart has warmed to an Irishman since that night."[14] Notwithstanding their reputation for courage under fire, the Irish Tigers also had one of the highest desertion rates; studies of the regiment's records have yielded a desertion rate of 27 percent, although many of the deserters may have returned to serve in other units.

IMMIGRANTS ON THE HOME FRONT

The war had mixed effects on immigrants at home in the North. The American economy, although shocked by the disruptions following secession, nonetheless recovered and showed continued growth through the end of the war. In the face of great demand for military supplies and provisions added to everyday home consumption, productivity increased, and business in general was booming. But for the unskilled immigrant workers in particular, the benefits of the boom were not always apparent. Inflation raised the cost of many ordinary consumer items, a cost which nearly doubled over the course of the war. While wages rose somewhat, the increases were not as great for unskilled workers as for skilled ones.

Some industries became more mechanized and more concentrated during the war, responding to the war demand. The manufacturers of boots and shoes, for example, increased their use of sewing machinery, and hastened the transfer of shoemaking from small shops to large factories. A similar phenomenon was seen in clothing manufacture, where ready-to-wear clothing was increasingly produced in factories rather than in small shops. The huge demand for military uniforms was largely met by such production. Changes like these meant that lower-wage unskilled labor was more likely to be used than the higher-wage labor of skilled craftsmen. Because many male workers were sent off to the war, some of the labor shortage was now being met by women, who were customarily paid only about half as much as the men for the same work. The employment of child labor also increased during the war. There were many instances of significant war profits by large businesses who could respond to the great demands of the war, but little of this was to be felt by the workers; their wages did not rise as much as did the cost of living.

Agriculture also prospered during the war years, and the increase in production managed to meet military demands, satisfy domestic needs (at higher prices), and even export about 4 percent of agricultural produce to Europe. Producing more horses and mules for the insatiable demands of the army was an especially profitable enterprise (the Union army lost an estimated five hundred horses every day toward the end of the war). There was of course a demand for farm labor, in view of the absence of many younger farm laborers and farmers' sons; in some rural areas of the Northwest, nearly half the adult males aged 18 to 45 were gone from the farms and off to the war. The lack of labor meant that many farm women had to take on greater amounts of work in the fields, and it also increased the tendency toward mechanization of the farms, which in turn raised the cost of establishing a farm. Thus many new immigrants during the war who hoped for a farm of their own found themselves working as farm laborers instead.

One of the long-desired goals of immigrants, a Homestead Act to provide free grants of land for those who would settle and live on

160 acres for five years, was realized in 1862 when the Republican Congress passed such an act. It was in part a special gesture toward the immigrants, particularly the Germans and the English. It fulfilled the Republicans' promise in the platform of 1860 to reward immigrant free-soil constituents. Little land was opened up for settlement by the Homestead Act, however, until after the war had ended.

A slow economy in Europe and the increasing availability of nonmilitary employment in America tended to raise the rate of immigration during the last two years of the war. The numbers nearly doubled from what they had been in 1861 and 1862. In 1864 Congress passed the Emigrant Aid Act, which allowed businesses to recruit workers abroad. It was especially aimed at finding skilled workers. Labor leaders saw it as a further depressing influence on wages, and it roused once again stirrings of nativism among the working class. The Lincoln administration denied accusations that it was recruiting military personnel abroad, as that would have violated the neutrality of the German states and Britain. However, military recruiters were on hand to greet new immigrants as they landed in the ports, offering them bonuses and benefits for their service.

And there were examples of state officials who sought out foreigners abroad to fill the quotas placed upon them by the draft. In early 1864, about seven hundred Germans arrived in Boston and were immediately sworn into the Union army. They had apparently been recruited in Antwerp as contract laborers under the Emigrant Aid Act, not knowing that they were destined for army service. The promoters of the scheme were said to have pocketed half a million dollars by taking some of the bonuses and substitute payments owing to the German recruits. The Prussian minister in Washington protested vigorously, but to no avail. In June 1864, the foreign minister of Sweden warned the U.S. minister in Stockholm against any recruitment of soldiers by American consuls. He was apparently particularly concerned about assistance given by William Widgery Thomas, Jr., the consul at Gothenburg, to Swedish emigrants who expressed a desire to take service in the Union forces. Thomas himself admitted in a dispatch to Washington that he was pushing the limits, but not crossing them. "We have forwarded over thirty this week. . . . I am well aware that as Consul I have nothing to do with soldiers, but no international law can prevent me from paying a soldier's passage from here to Hamburg out of my own pocket."[15]

Immigrant families, like others, could be profoundly affected by the war. The heavy casualties left many widows and orphans to fend for themselves. Although local charities tried to offer assistance, government benefits and pensions for bereaved families were only slowly adopted after the war. Meanwhile, women and children had to fill in for the males gone from the family for the war. This often brought German wives into the small family businesses that many of those immigrants ran.

In some of the major cities, tensions between immigrant groups, especially between Irish and Germans, were heightened. Such tensions were not new, but before the war a common allegiance to the Democratic party and a common opposition to nativist and temperance reformers usually kept the two groups in an uneasy alliance. As some Germans began to leave the Democratic party for the Republican, and as more Germans remained Unionist while some Irish became Peace Democrats, frictions between the groups began to mount. In Chicago, where a majority of Germans adhered to the Republican party, several outbreaks of violence occurred; the most notable incident occurred when a picnic being held by a German labor union was attacked by an Irish mob in July 1862. In St. Louis as well, where all Germans were marked as Unionists and where the Irish frequently harbored Southern sympathies, there were violent encounters between the two elements. Ethnic conflict was less common in areas where a majority of immigrants still adhered to the Democratic party.

Conflicts between immigrants and free blacks, however, escalated during the war. It was the Irish who were most responsible for attacks upon the blacks, since they were often in competition for the unskilled jobs. In Chicago, the Irish workingmen on the city's docks attacked and beat up African-Americans who sought jobs unloading lumber ships, and employers were intimidated from using black labor by delegations of white workers. In many northern cities these conflicts increased in frequency as the Union seemed more and more to turn toward the goal of emancipation of the black slaves, thus signaling the possibility of even greater competition in the workplace. Eventually the call for a draft in 1863 would set off anti-black riots in many cities.

Immigrants and the Politics of War

The voting records of immigrant communities during the war generally followed the patterns that had been set in 1860: Germans were divided between Republican and Democratic allegiances, and the Irish continued to be almost exclusively Democratic. But this conceals the fact that within the two parties and their immigrant constituents there were some severe disputes that threatened to disrupt both parties.

Within the Democratic party, there were serious factional splits between those who supported the war and those who opposed it—some of whom held outright Confederate sympathies. The opponents of the war generally called themselves "Peace Democrats," but Republicans generally dubbed them "Copperheads." Copperheads were frequently accused of treasonable activities, although many of them confined their opposition to voting against the Republicans, calling for an end to the war, and resisting enlistment in the Union army.

Both Irish and German immigrants were among the Copperheads. More of the Irish came from the big cities; more of the Germans, often Catholics and conservative Lutherans, were from rural areas of the Midwest. For many, the reason for their opposition to Lincoln's war policies was connected with their perception of the nativist and abolitionist reformers in the Republican party. This perception was heightened when some abolitionists began to demand that the purpose of the war be changed from simply the preservation of the Union to a more radical attempt to extinguish the system of slavery. Lincoln himself by 1862 was looking for ways to abolish slavery constitutionally, as when he tried unsuccessfully to persuade those slave states that were still within the Union to act to terminate the institution there, perhaps with compensation to slave-owners, perhaps in very gradual ways. The reaction of the Peace Democrats to efforts to couple the war's purpose with emancipation usually involved the fear that the emancipation of the slaves in the South would send the freed blacks swarming northward, and thus the immigrant laborers would have to deal with their competition in the northern cities.

New York City's mayor at the outbreak of the war was the veteran politician Fernando Wood, a longtime denizen of Tammany Hall, who had in the late 1850s organized his own rival Mozart Hall in the midst of divisions within the Democratic party. Although he supported the war at its outset, he became a leader of the Peace Democrats, a faction that included many of the working-class Irish. Mozart Hall would remain a center of the Peace Democrats in the city, and would marshal enough political power to elect Wood to the U.S. House of Representatives in 1862. Disillusion with the war by 1863 began to increase the numbers of the Peace Democrats. The Irish were among their principal adherents. Many were disturbed by the heavy losses of the Irish Brigade in bloody battles such as

Antietam, Fredericksburg and Gettysburg, and felt that the New York Irish were being sacrificed to the designs of the abolitionists.

On January 1, 1863, Lincoln used his executive powers as commander-in-chief to issue the Emancipation Proclamation, which freed all slaves behind the Confederate lines. This seemed to confirm immigrants' fears that they were being sacrificed to the aims of the abolitionists. The willingness of immigrants and others to volunteer for the army diminished, and opposition to Lincoln's war policies grew.

Divisions among the German Republicans

Among the Republicans, the same issues over the purposes of the war generated division, but there was, for a while at least, a three-way split. Some supported Lincoln's administration steadily, others questioned the movement toward a policy of slavery abolition, and a third element claimed that Lincoln was not moving toward abolition fast enough. These last, called Radical Republicans, included many Germans, especially those who had been the strongest supporters of the Republican party in 1860.

Discontent among the radical Germans first became evident in Missouri, where Germans had been the strongest element of the state's Republican party and had played a role in 1861 in keeping the state from falling into the hands of the secessionists. When Major General John C. Frémont arrived in St. Louis in July 1861 to take charge of the Department of the West (which had many German units) and to engage the secessionist forces throughout the state, the Germans welcomed him enthusiastically. Frémont also stirred controversy when he took up the issue of slave emancipation by declaring martial law in late August 1861 and declaring all slaves held by rebels within Missouri to be free. When Lincoln, who was still trying to conciliate those slave states that remained in the Union, failed to persuade Frémont to rescind that order, and himself countermanded it, the line between the administration and the radicals was drawn. In November 1861, Frémont was removed from command in Missouri, and later transferred to Virginia. His replacement in Missouri was Major General Henry Halleck, who further outraged the Germans by passing over General Franz Sigel for an important command. This led to a great outburst from German Republicans around the country, and Sigel, after some further campaigns in Missouri, ultimately received a promotion to major general and a command in Virginia.

The German radicals thus played a special role in mounting a protest within the Republican party against the Lincoln administration as the election year 1864 drew nearer. Republicans who were discontented with Lincoln's moderation began to rally around the name of Frémont. By the year 1863 it was evident that the Lincoln supporters controlled most of the state party organizations, and that the administration had quelled the protest somewhat by issuing the Emancipation Proclamation. The radical movement began to wane, and the Germans were left as the mainstay of the movement to elect Frémont. In June 1863, some of the Germans, mostly from the East, began to call once more for a separatist German movement that could possibly throw the weight of the Germans toward radical reform. A call for a convention in Cleveland in October 1863 produced a mixed reaction among Germans. Many Germans had been favored with patronage positions from the Lincoln administration, which was anxious to keep German support. Established German leaders in the West ignored the call for the convention, pointing out that it had by now been clearly demonstrated that it was too much to expect all the fractious Germans to unite on anything. About seventy delegates, mostly from the East, showed up in Cleveland and immediately began quarreling over how broad a platform for reform the convention should draw up. The convention did come out in favor of immediate emancipation and of the confiscation of all slaveholders' property. The meeting had little effect, but there was a wider group of Germans still agitating for the nomination of Frémont.

By early 1864, the supporters of Frémont were beginning to talk of a (mostly German) third-party movement, and they held another convention at Cleveland on May 31. The German-language press reported that the party would be called the "Radical Democrats." About four hundred people showed up, and the German radicals presented a platform of radical social reforms. The nomination of Frémont was achieved without much difficulty, and he accepted the nomination, but also disappointed the German radicals by disavowing the platform plank that called for confiscating all rebel property.

Frémont may have believed that the support of the Cleveland convention would assist him in a bid for the Republican nomination in the regular party convention, which was to be held in Baltimore one week after the Cleveland convention. But Lincoln was quickly seen to be in control of affairs there. He supported the seating of the Missouri German radicals in a dispute over credentials from that state; more importantly, he accepted a Republican platform that called for the complete abolition of slavery. Frémont withdrew his candidacy, and Lincoln was easily nominated. The radical Germans were unwilling to desert the party in favor of the Democratic candidate, General George B. McClellan, who had to run on a platform written by Peace Democrats, one which called for an immediate stop to the war. By the time of election day in November, Union armies had penetrated deeply into Georgia and captured Atlanta, and the Democrats' platform seemed irrelevant. McClellan was defeated by a landslide.

Although the national Republican majority in 1864 was greater than in 1860, the support of Germans for the party was ebbing somewhat. This was not attributable so much to the disaffected radicals, but rather to the many who had become disillusioned with the war and the heavy demands it had made upon the immigrants. The Democratic appeals were directed at this war-weariness, and they also raised again the fear of nativism within the Republican party. The 1864 election showed the Germans' political leanings to be about the same as they had been in 1860, but with some erosion of their Republican votes.

1863: The High Point of Immigrant Dissent

In the early months of 1863, a number of events concurred to bring resistance to the war effort to a peak. First was the Emancipation Proclamation, which intensified the feeling that the war's objective had become the freeing of the slaves. In the minds of many immigrants, particularly those of the working class, that prospect portended a rush of freed slaves to the northern cities, where they would compete with the immigrants for the unskilled jobs. The Union army was suffering heavy casualties in battles such as the defeats at Fredericksburg and Chancellorsville and in Ulysses Grant's campaign on the Mississippi against Vicksburg. Efforts to recruit more volunteers to supply the depleted ranks were met with increasing resistance from those groups who had volunteered previously.

In March 1863, Congress passed and Lincoln signed the first U.S. attempt at federal conscription. The Conscription Act subjected all men between the ages of 20 and 45 to military service, and made them liable to a draft. However, it also allowed those conscripted to avoid military service by a payment of $300, or by hiring a substitute. That $300 amounted to about half the annual wages of an unskilled worker. The $300 exemption was eventually canceled, but the provision for hiring a substitute remained. The cost of such a substitute frequently exceeded $1,000. The available substitutes were very often immigrants. All of this made it, as many immigrants said in the widely-heard slogan, "a rich man's war, but a poor man's fight."

There were immediate protests to the Conscription Act in many cities. Condemnation of the draft came particularly from the working classes, and many were of course Irish. They protested that the workers had already provided disproportionate volunteers to the Union army, and that these had borne the brunt of exceptional casualties in battles such as Fredericksburg. The provision of recruits was still assigned by the act to the states, but if their governors failed to provide the numbers specified in certain quotas, then the federal draft was to be used to make up for the deficiency. The Peace Democrats pointed to the fact that this was another abuse of states' rights and an aggrandizement of federal power. Protests were particularly strong in the regions where the Copperheads were most active.

The New York Draft Riots

The most notorious protest occurred in July in New York City. The governor, the Democrat Horatio Seymour, had delayed implementing the draft in his state, but began to do so in early July. News was just arriving of Union victories at Gettysburg and Vicksburg, but they were victories at the cost of considerable casualties, especially at Gettysburg. New York's Irish Brigade (now reduced to a smaller battalion) had suffered some of those casualties at Gettysburg. When the lots began to be drawn for the draft, there erupted the most violent urban riot in the country's history to that date.

What started as an organized protest on July 13 soon got out of hand, and many who were neither liable for the draft nor affected by it joined in. The draft officials and the policemen enforcing the draft were attacked, and the draft offices burned. Newspapers which advocated abolition, like Horace Greeley's *New York Tribune,* were attacked and burned. The conspicuously rich, the policemen, the abolitionists, and the people involved with carrying out the draft were targeted by the mob.

But the most furious assaults were upon the black people of the city. In random fashion, any black person who happened to meet with one of the mobs was set upon and beaten, and a number were killed, some by being lynched from a lamppost. Pillaging and burning raged through the black neighborhoods, and the inhabitants ran for their lives, many of them fleeing the city entirely. In the most egregious act of the riots, mobs set upon the Colored Orphan Asylum, ultimately burning the facility to the ground. The children narrowly escaped through a back entrance, even as the building was being torched by the mob. As the riots increased over three days, they became in effect a race riot.

In the end, martial law was declared. The police forces and local militia were overwhelmed, and federal troops had to be brought in, many of them just returning from the battle of Gettysburg. Reckoning with the damage and death precipitated by the riots was nearly impossible; estimates of the deaths range as high as 100. At least 50,000 people are estimated to have taken part in the riots at some point. The number arrested was 443, but only 19 were ever convicted. The property damage was estimated at over $1.5 million, but some historians have argued for a much higher figure.

Rioters in the New York draft riots of July 1863 exchange shots with military forces called in to suppress the disorder. From *Illustrated London News*, August 8, 1863. Courtesy Swarthmore College Library, via Bryn Mawr College Library Special Collections.

While some native-born artisans and German workers were said to have been among the early protesters, there was no escaping the fact that the majority of the rioters were Irish. The *Irish American*, which had bitterly denounced the draft and its New York administrators, could not condone the actions taken to protest it: "Violence has left a stigma on the fame of our city, which years of good order will hardly efface. The assaults on unfortunate negroes and the burning of their houses and the Orphan Asylum cannot be condemned in language too severe. These poor people were innocent of bringing about our present troubles."[16]

The Irish would indeed bear the burden of the riots and their damaged reputation. In the years after the war, the radical Republicans would adopt in nearly every election the strategy called "waving the bloody shirt"—assailing as treasonous all those who had opposed the war or aided the Confederates. Their favorite examples were the Southern slaveholders, the Ku Klux Klan, the Copperheads generally, and the northern Irish Democrats, who were frequently pictured by cartoonists as rioting and attacking the black freedmen. These political assaults on the Irish were part of the reason that the German spokesmen, ignoring the records of many of their own group as Copperheads, emphasized instead the German support of the Lincoln administration and their considerable military efforts for the Union.

THE IMMIGRANTS' LEGACY OF THE WAR

No matter what the immigrants' individual roles in the war and its turbulent politics, the Civil War and the years preceding it were the most momentous period thus far in defining American immigrant life. At the time of the greatest influx of immigrants yet experienced in American history, the newcomers were forced into confrontation with a turbulent political situation that they could not avoid. Their presence became a central issue of national politics, and struggles ensued for their political loyalty. A war not of their own making, one which few immigrants desired, demanded their support, took the lives of many, and left the lives of others drastically changed. Probably more than they wanted, they were drawn out of their communities and into the fabric of American life during the most critical period of the Republic. To call that assimilation probably understates the ways in which the whole world of the immigrants changed.

NOTES

1. *Belleviller Zeitung* (Belleville, Illinois), August 8, 1850 (my translation). (Files in the Illinois State Historical Library, Springfield).

2. "Slavery Extension. The Nebraska Bill in Congress," *New York Times,* January 24, 1854.

3. Quoted in *Anzeiger des Westens* (St. Louis), March 11, 1854 (my translation). (Files in the St. Louis [Mo.] Public Library).

4. As translated in Chicago *Journal*, March 17, 1854, quoted in Frank I. Herriott, "The Germans of Chicago and Stephen A. Douglas in 1854," *Deutsch-Amerikanischen Geschichtsblätter: Jahrbuch der deutsch-Amerikanischen historischen Gesellschaft von Illinois* 12 (1912): 394–95.

5. Christian Essellen, "Die Thätigkeit der deutschen Vereine," *Atlantis,* n.s. 1 (1854): 231 (my translation).

6. *Illinois Staats-Zeitung,* as quoted in *Belleviller Zeitung,* August 3, 1854 (my translation). (Files in the Illinois State Historical Library, Springfield).

7. *Illinois State Journal,* May 30, 1856, quoted in McLean County Historical Society *Transactions* 3 (1900): 160–61.

8. *Proceedings of the First Three Republican National Conventions of 1856, 1860 and 1864* (Minneapolis, 1893), 44–45.

9. Lawrence F. Kohl and Margaret C. Richard, eds., *Irish Green and Union Blue: The Civil War Letters of Peter Welsh, Color Sergeant, 28th Regiment, Massachusetts Volunteers* (New York: Fordham University Press, 1986), 103.

10. Walter D. Kamphoefner and Wolfgang Helbich, eds., *Germans in the Civil War: The Letters They Wrote Home,* trans. Susan Carter Vogel (Chapel Hill: University of North Carolina Press, 2006), 131–32.

11. The 1861 Song Sheet was published by A.E. Blackmar & Bro. of New Orleans and is available from http://history.sandiego.edu/gen/snd/bonnieblueflag.html, accessed April 5, 2007.

12. Statistics from Maris Vinovskis, "Have Social Historians Lost the Civil War? Some Preliminary Demographic Speculations," *Journal of American History* 76 (1989): 36–41.

13. Lars Olsen Dokken and Knud Olsen Dokken, "Two Immigrants for the Union: Their Civil War Letters," trans. Della Kittelson Catuna, *Norwegian-American Studies* 28 (1979): 109–37.

14. As quoted in David T. Gleeson, *The Irish in the South, 1815–1877* (Chapel Hill: University of North Carolina Press, 2001), 144–45.

15. Nels Hokanson, *Swedish Immigrants in Lincoln's Time* (New York: Harper and Brothers, 1942), 69–70, as quoted in H. Arnold Barton, *The Old Country and the New: Essays on Swedes in America* (Carbondale: Southern Illinois University Press, 2007), 149–50.

16. *New York Irish American,* July 25, 1863 (files in Balch Institute Collections, Historical Society of Pennsylvania).

8

Into a New Era,
1865–1870

After four years of war, returning soldiers in the summer of 1865 found an America much changed. The veterans returning to immigrant communities found differences equally profound. After a war which resulted in over 600,000 deaths, there were few communities which had not experienced the loss of young men and the bereavement of families. The absence of many of that generation would be felt for years afterward. Many returned wounded and disabled, others disillusioned and regretful that they had ever set sail for America. Some did not return to the communities where they had enlisted, perhaps because they did not have long-established ties to any community. Some sought new opportunities in the newly expanding West, or even in the cities of the South. Some continued with life in the army, once again committed to fighting the Indians on the western plains.

The number of newly arriving immigrants turned sharply upward in the years immediately following the war. Immigration had been below 200,000 annually in the latter years of the war, but rose steadily to just under 400,000 in 1870 and to 460,000 in 1873, surpassing the pre-war high of 428,000 set in 1854.[1] That upsurge was followed by decreased immigration during the middle of the 1870s, as the country was gripped by depression and the postwar economic boom came to an end. When immigration rose sharply again in the early 1880s, the migration streams would include not only the traditional Germans, Irish, and Scandinavians, but also newcomers from eastern Europe, Poland, and Italy. Thus the two greatest waves of migration in the nineteenth century (the 1850s and the 1880s) would differ greatly in character.

NEW FRONTIERS FOR IMMIGRANTS

For newcomers and returning soldiers alike, opportunities were abundant in the rapidly expanding West. New land was being opened and new cities were being established beyond the Mississippi. The railroads were the driving force in both developments. And it was immigrants who would build the new rail lines and who would settle alongside them as the rails were laid outward across the Great Plains and toward the Pacific.

During the decade and a half before the Civil War, there had been aspirations among the proponents of Western development to build a transcontinental railroad for easier communication with the Pacific Coast, and thus to fulfill dreams of creating a trade route to Asia that would avoid the water route around South America. Although the project was frequently discussed in Congress, sectional rivalries prevented the dreams from becoming reality until the South seceded and the North was free to plan its own route. That proved to be a line westward from the Missouri River through Nebraska and across the Rockies, the Great Basin, and the Sierras toward the Pacific. In 1862 Congress authorized the building of a railroad along that route, provided it with a large land grant along its right-of-way, and committed the work to two corporations—the Union Pacific, which would build westward from the Missouri River, and the Central Pacific, which would build eastward from Sacramento. Actual construction began in 1863, but proceeded very slowly until the war ended. Then activity picked up, ending in a race between the two corporations. They finally settled upon a meeting place near the Great Salt Lake in Utah, where the final spike joining East and West was driven in 1869.

The Union Pacific found a steady supply of labor for its construction in the rising wave of immigrants once again arriving in East Coast ports. The majority of the newcomers were Irish. Other Irish men who had been building railroads in the 1850s, as well as some who had served in the Civil War, also found renewed employment as the construction work went westward from Omaha. As the pace of construction picked up in 1865 and 1866, crews were laying rail across the plains of Nebraska at the rate of a mile a day. As they had in the previous days of canal- and railroad-building, many would find permanent employment on the railroad; they also would be among the first settlers in new towns like North Platte and Cheyenne, now being created along the line. Irish, along with Germans and English, were also to find jobs as operating personnel on the transcontinental line.

As the Central Pacific moved eastward from Sacramento, the original construction labor was provided by white laborers, most of them Irish, who were hired in the cities and mining towns of California. But this proved to be an insufficient supply of labor, and the workers tended to be unreliable, leaving as soon as more desirable jobs became available—especially when new mining discoveries lured them to other places like Nevada and Idaho. The construction was proceeding slowly from 1863 to 1865, and the problem was confronted by the principal owners of the railroad, a group of Sacramento businessmen including Leland Stanford, president of the Central Pacific, and Charles Crocker, who was in charge of the construction work. It was Charles Crocker's brother, E. B. Crocker, who suggested the use of Chinese labor. Charles Crocker disliked the idea; the Chinese were too frail and weak, he felt, to undertake heavy construction work, especially through the High Sierras. Stanford intervened, however, and started gathering up Chinese laborers from the mining camps and the Chinatowns of the cities. They quickly proved their usefulness, and also proved cheaper to hire than the previous white laborers—they were paid a dollar a day, out of which they supplied their own food and lodging. Soon Stanford was sending to China for the importation of more laborers, and recruits from China proved to be the main source of labor for the railroad during the rest of its construction. At the peak of the construction work, 11,000 of the 14,000 employees of the railroad were Chinese. Observers marveled at the ability of the Chinese to dangle on ropes over cliffs in the Sierras and bore holes in the rock to blast away a ledge for the roadbed.

On the day in 1869 that the golden spike was driven to join the two railroads together at Promontory, Utah, E. B. Clocker rose at a celebration in the California Assembly to propose a toast to the Chinese: "The early completion of this railroad we have built has been in large measure due to that poor, despised class of laborers called Chinese—to the fidelity and industry they have shown."[2] Others in California were not as appreciative, and the Chinese immigrants were in fact entering into an era of increasing nativist

European and Asian laborers mingle together as they work on the last mile of the transcontinental railroad before its completion in May 1869. The Chinese were particularly valued for their work in blasting. Library of Congress, Prints and Photographs Division.

opposition, much of it coming from the white working class (both immigrant and native-born), who feared further competition from the Chinese. The opposition intensified during the depression years of the 1870s and eventually led to federal laws excluding new immigrants from China.

THE RAILROADS AND NEW LANDS IN THE WEST

The railroads being built into the new areas of the West also had to dispose of generous land grants from the federal government, which led them to foster colonization projects, many of them directed toward settling immigrants in the new regions. The first major federal grant to aid in the construction of railroads was made to the state of Illinois in 1850; the next year the state chartered the Illinois Central Railroad to build a major line from the Mississippi near Dubuque to Cairo at the southern tip of the state, with a branch line leading south from Chicago. The pattern of the grant was the same as that followed by later railroads: alternate sections (square miles) of land were given to the railroad for 20 miles back from the line of construction on each side. If the land was already taken up, compensation was made with land further afield. The grant was intended to aid construction of the railroad, which generally had to float bonds to be paid off eventually from the sale of the land. Before the Civil War, other grants were being made west of the Mississippi: they included 600,000 acres in Missouri to support the Hannibal and Saint Joseph line, the only road to reach the western border of that state before the war; and 359,000 acres to support the Burlington and Missouri as it was built across southern Iowa. Eventually that line would be extended into Nebraska with another grant of 2,734,000 acres.

Generally, the railroads were not able to begin sale of the land until it had been surveyed and apportioned to the railroad. Thus the process of selling it really began during the Civil War, and sales increased after the war's end. The Illinois Central advertised its land widely, but gave special attention to attracting immigrants (mostly German) to its tracts in eastern Illinois. In 1862 the railroad hired Francis A. Hoffmann, the German Republican immigrant leader who was the lieutenant governor of Illinois at the time, to be its German land agent. He oversaw the sale of 80,000 acres of railroad land and settled over 1,500 families on the prairies of Illinois. German villages with names like St. Peter and Sigel sprang up along the railroad.

The same colonization model was followed by other railroads that had started building beyond the Mississippi. Agents were sent to Europe to attract settlers, who sometimes came in colonies sent out by one town, thus renewing under railroad auspices the earlier process of chain migration. Railroads sometimes donated town sites and church lots to provide centers for the surrounding immigrant community. The Union Pacific received extra grants from Congress for its construction through unoccupied and difficult terrain. The Union Pacific and other railroads building across Nebraska, Kansas, and the Dakotas also created homogeneous immigrant communities throughout the Great Plains.

Although Congress had passed the much-desired Homestead Act in 1862, and the act allowed new immigrants to claim land under its provisions, most immigrants who came to take up land after 1862 did not use the provisions of the act to obtain it. There were many other ways to acquire land. There were, for example, the railroads, which were eager to sell their grants and thereby develop new customers along the right-of-way. The Illinois Central in about 1868 was offering lands in Illinois for $6–12 per acre, and giving buyers up to three years to pay. In Kansas around 1870, the Kansas Pacific had five million acres for sale at $1–6 per acre, and the Atchison, Topeka, and Santa Fe in 1871 was selling its land for an average of $5.91 per acre. It was also still possible to buy land for cash directly from the federal government; it still cost $1.25 per acre, but the price doubled to $2.50 per acre if the land lay among the so-called "alternate sections" adjacent to the railroad. In addition, the states had lands granted to them which they often promoted for sale to immigrants, and some states, like the railroads, set up bureaus to market their land in Europe. A potential buyer could also deal with speculators, who may have acquired the most desirable land from the government. These various sources of land provided an element of competition that restrained price gouging.

Immigrants who chose to settle on homestead claims were of course tied up for the five years they had to wait before taking title to the land. And the land was very often more remote, since one could not acquire a homestead of 160 acres within the areas of the railroad grants. In an era when farmers were increasingly dependent on access to transportation for their supplies and for marketing their produce, immigrants were hesitant to take up a homestead far from the railroad. And those who sought a congenial ethnic community could very often find it near the railroad towns. A new settler had to weigh the uncertainties of the homestead method against the certainties of a cash purchase with a clear title. Certainly a great majority of immigrant farmers, Germans and Scandinavians mostly, opted for the latter course.

THE BURGEONING CITIES AND THEIR WORKING CLASSES

After a calm period following the war, the economic cycle turned upward beginning in 1867. This coincided with the rising wave of immigration, and newcomers could find employment in the cities and factory towns where the Industrial Revolution in America was now in full swing. The key industries of iron and steel, along with the developing railroad network, were critical elements in this rapid development. New immigration from England, Ireland, and Germany brought many of the working classes to the growing industrial centers and to the coal-mining regions. Many of the English and Germans had previous experience in the industrial cities of their homelands. The German immigrant flow was increasingly coming from regions in the east of Germany, and included many who came from the industrial and mining centers there. There were even cases of industries from Europe that were transplanted to American soil, in an effort to circumvent the new protective tariffs passed by Congress during the Civil War on imported manufactured goods. In 1865, for example, the owners of a textile mill in the kingdom of Saxony transferred their production to Holyoke, Massachusetts, bringing with them many of their workers—and providing yet another example of chain migration. The workers in the Germania Mill comprised the principal German community in Holyoke, a city otherwise dominated by French-Canadian and Irish immigrant workers.

As before, many newcomers found employment in the industrial cities of the east, which were developing rapidly. New York grew in population by 26 percent during the 1860s, Boston by 41 percent, and Pittsburgh by 78 percent. But even more remarkable was the growth of the western cities which became centers of the new railroad network. Chicago grew by 66 percent during the decade, St. Louis by 93 percent, and Indianapolis by 53 percent. Cities such as these, already attracting immigrants before the war, now served as magnets for the postwar influx.

The United States began to see more labor unrest in the postwar years. There had been a growing labor movement in the years before 1857, when the depression and then the war had brought labor activism to a downfall. There had been two elements, seldom harmonious, in the pre-Civil War activism of immigrants. The Irish, along with many English and native-born workers, bred a pragmatic, power-oriented movement that set its goals upon immediate remedies of workers' complaints. The Germans more often organized skilled-workers' labor organizations of artisans and tradesmen. These were often led by more intellectual leaders who sought to realize certain radical ideologies which envisioned the transformation of societies. Some of these organizations were Marxist, but more prevalent were the ones inspired by the German-born immigrant tailor Wilhelm Weitling, who was influenced by the French Utopian socialist Charles Fourier and his theories of ideal industrial communities.

When labor activism began to revive in the late 1860s, the same two divergent ways were evident. The Irish began to organize for their pragmatic ends and for relief from the oppressive wages and working conditions of the growing large industries. Their Catholicism led them to shun socialist remedies and to try to tame capitalism rather than destroy it. The Germans and other recent arrivals were now coming with experience in the European industrial centers, and were more often schooled in Marxist ideas of class consciousness and revolutionary change. The two elements would continue to compete for the rest of the century, but in the long run the largely Irish labor union model would prevail as the American standard.

THE COURSE OF IMMIGRANT POLITICS

The basic pattern of partisan immigrant politics created in the 1850s continued during and after the Civil War. The Irish immigrants, driven by strong local connections in the cities, continued their adherence to the Democratic party. Their party loyalty was strengthened by their opposition to the Republican policies of slavery abolition and of citizenship rights for the freed blacks in the South during Reconstruction. Having lost the strength derived from Southern Democrats during the war, the party struggled to reconstitute itself under the leadership of its national chairman, the German-born financier August Belmont. He had generally tried to steer the party away from pro-Southern Copperhead views, and supported the faction called War Democrats, who sought a Union victory. Belmont exercised particular power in New York City, where the Democratic party and Tammany Hall had become the province of the prototypical urban boss William Marcy Tweed. Tweed's power rested in considerable part on his cultivation of the Irish with generous patronage, which many saw as a type of welfare system for the poor. Belmont and Tweed had a falling-out in 1869, when Tweed attempted (albeit unsuccessfully) to remove Belmont from the national Democratic party chairmanship. Belmont reacted by becoming part of a growing anti-Tweed coalition, joining forces with Oswald Ottendorfer, the editor of the powerful *New Yorker Staats-Zeitung*, which was a strong Democratic influence among Germans in New York politics. The coalition would play a vital part in the downfall of the Tweed ring in the early 1870s. Ottendorfer continued to play a role as a Reform Democrat for the rest of his career.

German support for the Republican party was probably at its strongest during the 1860 election; after that, the proportion of Germans voting Republican slowly declined. Among the various factors eroding German support were disillusion with the war, disagreement with the policy of slavery abolition, criticism of Republican

Reconstruction policies in the South, and the apparent resurrection of nativist and temperance forces within the party. Some were put off in particular by renewed efforts after the war by Republicans in some states to pass new liquor-restriction and temperance laws. There were still elements of German Republican strength, as in Missouri, where Germans constituted the majority of the Republican party, and in Chicago, where Anton Hesing, the publisher after 1867 of the *Illinois Staats-Zeitung*, operated as a sort of Republican boss with a strong following of German voters. Generally, most German Catholics and conservative Lutherans maintained their allegiance to the Democrats. Many German Civil War soldiers, influenced by the veterans' organization, the Grand Army of the Republic, stayed loyal to the Republicans.

The English immigrants tended to adhere to the Republican party, with the exception of some working-class elements in the cities. Dutch immigrants were split in their political allegiances, resembling in some ways the Germans. Dutch Catholic communities usually remained fearful of nativism among Republicans and voted Democratic. While there were Republican majorities in some Dutch areas, they were not overwhelming majorities. Other areas retained Democratic majorities. Some Dutch deserted the Democratic party because it was so strongly dominated in their locality by Irish Catholics. Scandinavians tended toward the Republicans in their political inclinations.

ISSUES OF IDENTITY AND NATIONALISM

The turbulent years of the Civil War brought many immigrants into new and unexpected environments. Soldiers who had entered the war with an ethnic unit found themselves eventually in a unit with a great cross-section of American society. Those who had come from a largely ethnic rural community found themselves afterwards in a much more heterogeneous one. Immigrant women left in charge of a family enterprise were drawn further into a diverse community. The second generation of immigrants after the war would set out for a wide variety of destinations, in which the close culture of their parents might not be easily maintained. Evolving immigrant communities in a developing network of transportation and communication would increasingly have to see themselves as a part of a larger and more complex American society.

Terms like "Irish-American" and "German-American" had been heard since the 1820s and 1830s at least, but usually as a term applied to those groups by outsiders. By the 1850s, however, immigrants were beginning to describe themselves in that way, partly as a response to nativists who claimed that the foreign-born could never really become Americans. In 1849 the aspiring journalist Patrick Lynch named his newly established newspaper in New York City the *Irish American,* convinced that it could lead the Irish population into greater involvement with American life. By 1870 the German-born Alexander J. Schem, a former journalist for the New York *Tribune,* would begin the compilation of what he labeled a "German-American Encyclopedia,"[3] which would record the various contributions of Germans to American life in eleven volumes. The assertion by immigrants that they were also Americans was becoming much more common in the post-Civil War era and represented an acknowledgment of the cultural changes many immigrants were undergoing.

Irish Nationalism and the Fenian Adventures

Nationalistic pride among Irish Americans had been on the rise in the 1850s. Much of it was defensive, as nativist attacks centered on the illiterate and rowdy new immigrants coming in the famine flood and accused them of unsuitability for life in a democracy. Much of Irish pride in response to the nativists was content with extolling the virtues of the Irish and their contributions to civilization and to American life. However, Irish expressions of nationalism frequently contained hostility to British rule of the Irish homeland, as well as hopes for the freedom of Ireland. American politicians, usually Democrats, even sometimes encouraged this Anglophobia, as for example in the Young America movement of the 1850s, which seemed to argue for American support of republican governments abroad. Some events of the Civil War made Anglophobia in America more popular, since Union supporters suspected that Britain was giving support to the Confederacy by such actions as allowing naval ships to be built in British shipyards.

It was out of this more general nationalistic spirit that the organization of the Fenians took shape. The failed attempt at a rebellion in Ireland in 1848, which was harshly put down by British authorities, only stimulated more extreme nationalists both in Ireland and in the United States to pursue the goal of Irish freedom and the establishment of an independent Irish Republic. These nationalists now rejected as insufficient the earlier calls for the repeal of the act of 1801, which had led to the merging of Ireland and England under one parliament. According to them, only complete Irish independence from England, as the United States had declared in 1776, would be acceptable, and armed rebellion against English power was the only possible course by which to achieve it.

Various organizations in America took up the cause of Irish nationalism in the 1850s. Among them was the Emmet Monument Association, organized by two refugees of the 1848 rebellion, John O'Mahony and Michael Doheny. In late 1857 the two contacted James Stephens, a participant in the failed 1848 rebellion who had recently returned to Ireland, and proposed a new organization on both sides of the ocean to undertake the overthrow of British rule in Ireland. Stephens undertook to establish such an organization in Ireland, and in 1858 inaugurated the Irish Revolutionary Brotherhood. Later that year Stephens came to New York and installed O'Mahony as the head of the I.R.B. in America. During the next year O'Mahony renamed the American organization the Fenian Brotherhood. The name came from ancient Irish history: the legendary warrior Finn McCumhail was said to have gathered together the fighting forces known as the Fianna (or Fenians), which won many battles in third-century pre-Christian Ireland.

The Fenian Brotherhood gathered many nationalist supporters, but sworn members always represented a tiny minority of the Irish population either in Ireland or in America. The organization was generally condemned by the Irish Catholic hierarchy on both sides of the ocean, partly because its oath-taking, committing members to secrecy, made it a "secret society," which the Church proscribed. Nevertheless, Fenianism won the sympathy of followers in Ireland and of many Irish immigrants in America as well. The numbers of circles in which the membership gathered grew, and in 1860 O'Mahony made a trip to Ireland, consulted with Stephens, resolved some of their differences, and planned an ambitious strategy for an insurrection in Ireland.

Shortly after the return of O'Mahony, the Civil War broke out. Although Fenian plans in America had to be suspended, the organization continued to gain members. Many were enlisted in the Union army, and a number of officers in the Irish Brigade were Fenians. Fenian leaders began to regard the war experience as training recruits for an eventual rebellion in Ireland. Some Union military recruiters even held out vague promises of American aid for such a rebellion after the war. Many Fenians assumed that deteriorating relationships between the United States and Britain would promote such aid, although the Lincoln administration was careful not to allow a complete breakup between the two powers.

The Fenians in America continued to grow in number during the war, often enlisting additional members from the army's ranks. By the end of the war the Brotherhood claimed 10,000 members. There also began to develop an increasing factionalism, much of it based on opposition to the autocratic leadership of O'Mahony. In 1863 a convention of the Brotherhood had established a Council of Five in order to impose some limitation on O'Mahony's authority. In a reorganization of this group in 1865 this was supplanted by a "Senate," the president of which was William R. Roberts, a New York dry goods merchant and ardent Irish nationalist. The substantive issue that came to divide the two Fenian leaders was a strategic one. Roberts, aware that the many Fenians recently discharged from the army were craving some action, argued that the Fenians should immediately invade Canada, the closest and supposedly most vulnerable British possession. O'Mahony opposed the idea, believing that it was better to concentrate on preparing for a rebellion in Ireland itself.

Roberts found a brigadier general recently mustered out of the Union Army, Thomas W. Sweeny, who was persuaded to join the Fenians and was named the organization's "secretary of war." Sweeny proceeded to gather arms and men to pursue Roberts's plan of an attack on Canada. The Canadian government was well aware of these preparations, and sought out volunteers to assist the British regular troops in guarding the border against possible invasion. The opposition of O'Mahony to Sweeny's military preparations led to the complete breakup of the Fenians into two rival organizations. In early 1866 Sweeny was proceeding with plans to invade Canada from several points along the U.S. border.

On the night of May 31, 1866, a band of Fenian troops, about 600 in number, crossed the Niagara River near Buffalo, New York, and occupied the Canadian town of Fort Erie. The Canadian government sent 800 British soldiers and volunteers to counter the invasion, and the two forces met on June 2 at the small village of Ridgeway. The Canadian forces were initially driven back, but when the Canadian reinforcements arrived, the Fenians were forced to withdraw back toward the Niagara River. The boats they had used to carry themselves across the river were apprehended on their return in mid-stream by American authorities in a naval ship. The Fenians were put under arrest, and President Andrew Johnson issued a proclamation of American neutrality, calling for

The "Fenian Banner," issued by the Fenians in America in 1866. The illustration celebrates various famous Irish nationalists and revolutionaries. Library of Congress, Prints and Photographs Division.

the arrest of any Fenians found to be involved in the invasion. The fiasco had cost the lives of 8 Fenians and 10 Canadians. The overconfident Fenians had hoped that the American government would tolerate their adventure, but that was a false hope. They also hoped to be joined by Irish sympathizers in Canada, but resistance from the more numerous Protestant Irish and the Orange Order in Canada was too great. Under pressure from Roberts and other leaders to take some action, they had entered Canada with insufficient supplies, no artillery, and very few cavalry horses. The American government thereafter kept a close eye on the activities of Fenians, and the movement began slowly to wither. There would be other minor attempts to invade Canada in the next few years, but they would be easily put down by the Canadian authorities.

The Fenian Brotherhood was eventually replaced by another organization, the Clan na Gael, which had been organized in New York City in 1867. The Clan concentrated more directly on fomenting revolution in Ireland itself. In Canada, concern about the country's weak defenses against the Fenians hastened the movement for confederation that had been developing for a number of years. This consolidation of the various parts of British North America was finally achieved in the same year, 1867, by the passage in the British Parliament of the British North America Act.

Provincialism, Nationalism, and German Immigrants

In the era before the American Civil War, German Americans had very often clung to identities based on the various states from which they had come. Nationalism in Germany and the unification of its diverse states, goals tied closely with liberal republicanism in the efforts of the refugees of 1848, had failed in the collapse of that revolution. The future of that sort of nationalism seemed dim when Otto von Bismarck, known as an arch-conservative and an enemy of all parliamentary government, became the minister-president of Prussia in 1862. Bismarck pursued a strategy of achieving the unification of the many German states under Prussian leadership (and without the involvement of the Austrian empire). In a complicated series of wars in the 1860s, many changes occurred: Austria was defeated by Prussia; a new North German Confederation (without Austria) was formed (1867); and Prussia pursued a victorious war against France, which led to the defeat of the Emperor Napoleon III in the decisive battle of Sedan (1870). Napoleon was subsequently deposed by the new French Third Republic and sent into exile. In the course of the war, Bismarck had formed alliances with all the German states, who were fearful of French dominance by a new Napoleon and who therefore supported Prussia. In early 1871 the German Confederation was transformed into the new German Empire, and King William I of Prussia became Emperor William I of Germany.

The successful unification of Germany under conservative Prussian rule posed problems for German Americans. Many were torn in various directions between their dislike of authoritarian Prussian government on the one hand and, on the other, their pride in Germany's emergence as a unified great power and the achievement of a German nationalism that could override previous provincial loyalties. Many German leaders rallied to the theme of nationalism—even many of the men of 1848 who had always regarded the Prussian crown with suspicion and hostility. In 1868, even before the Franco-Prussian War, Carl Schurz visited Germany and, through the intervention of George Bancroft, the American ambassador to Prussia, had an interview with Bismarck. In answer to Bismarck's question about his reaction to the present condition of Germany, Schurz recounted later that he said, "I had become sensible of a general atmosphere of newly inspired national ambition and a confident hope for the development of more liberal political institutions."[4] This hope that national unification under authoritarian rule would somehow make way for liberal republican institutions was also expressed by other forty-eighters. Those who once had regarded national unity and liberty as goals that were to be reached simultaneously now began to argue that German national unity was a necessary precondition for liberty; the former having been achieved with Bismarck's efforts, the latter would soon follow in a new era of republicanism. Old-time liberals such as Cincinnati's Frederick Hassaurek, Illinois's Gustave Koerner, and Milwaukee's Fritz Anneke reconciled themselves to Bismarck's Germany in the same way. The important thing was that German courage and power had rescued Europe from another Bonaparte, and German-Americans could take pride in that. "Once we fought gladly for the German Republic," said Wilhelm Rapp, another of the men of 1848, at a rally in Baltimore in September 1870. "But if we cannot have it, let us at least have a powerful, constitutional German Empire, and grant a German crown to the Hohenzollern who flings the crown from the French usurper's head."[5]

Many German-Americans took part in the celebrations during 1870 and 1871 of the Prussian victory and of Germany's unification. Both achievements would provide a basis for the emergence of a common German-American identity. But the long-standing divisions among Germans in America were not so easily overcome. Provincial and regional loyalties still prevailed among many. Catholics and socialists (never themselves very compatible) pointed to Bismarck's well-known hostility to both of their groups, and shied away from any attempt to tie Prussian success to German-American pride. Only at the turn of the twentieth century, as more German immigrants arrived with established loyalties to the unified Germany and as the German Empire could claim many successes as a great power, did German-Americans begin to recognize a shared common culture.

BECOMING AMERICANS

In 1870 the United States had in its population over 5.5 million foreign-born residents—an increase of about 1.5 million since 1860. Immigrants numbered about 14.4 percent of the country's population, but their presence was much more significant in some of the large cities: 48.4 percent of Chicago's population was foreign-born, as was 44.5 percent of New York City's population, 49.3 percent of San Francisco's, and 39.5 percent of Buffalo's. The development of the immigrant population in the new areas of the West and in the cities along the pathways to the West was evident in the statistics. Wisconsin was 34.6 percent foreign-born; Minnesota was 36.5 percent. The new booming mining frontiers of the West were teeming with newly-arrived immigrants; they accounted for 52 percent of Idaho Territory's population, 44 percent of Nevada Territory's, and 39 percent of Montana Territory's. Heavy immigrant populations were also found in the industrial towns of New England and northern New Jersey.[6] The figures for foreign-born did not include the American-born children of immigrants, although that second generation was commonly perceived by other Americans as part of the immigrant community.

Immigrants and Cultural Change

The older and more heavily populated immigrant communities had a well-developed institutional framework, which other Americans saw as evidence of the immigrants' solidarity and their adherence to their traditional ways. But, as we have seen, immigrant communities were very often divided and faction-ridden, and their institutions often served to emphasize their divisions, rather than to bring them together. The Irish relied heavily on the Catholic Church, now in a process of revival and commanding the devotions of the Irish immigrants more strongly, and the bishops and clergy served as their leaders and spokesmen. But other leaders were provided from the political realm as the Democratic party in many of the cities came to serve as a stronghold of the Irish. As for the Germans, the churches, clubs, Turner societies, and cultural organizations competed for their loyalty, and the political parties learned to compete for the allegiance of the various groups of Germans.

While the institutional frameworks of the immigrants helped to preserve their culture and traditions, they also served the more important purposes of introducing the newcomers to American society and helping them with their adjustment. For many immigrants, the time would come when they would loosen their ties to the immigrant community and begin to transfer their loyalties to newer institutions more identified with the society in general. This might happen only partially for the first-generation immigrants, but the process might continue with the second generation, and the third generation might be considerably distanced from the organizational structures that had welcomed their forebears. So the appearance of social and cultural cohesiveness that many outsiders saw actually disguised a process of gradual adaptation, accompanied by a gradual cultural change. The institutional structures, while appearing stable and unchanging, in practice became a channel through which individuals passed in the process of cultural change.

Daily Life and New Cultures

It is in the mundane activities of daily life that we can see the immigrants' gradual cultural change that would make them into Americans. "Culture" in this sense means the collectively shared habits, customs and traditions of a group. Cultures might be based on ethnicity, class, geographic origin, religion, and other sources. Those between two cultures, as immigrants almost always were, might be seen as taking part in overlapping cultures, behaving sometimes as immigrants from a certain place, sometimes as Americans, sometimes as working class, sometimes as adherents of a certain religion, and so on. The important thing was that they were offered choices, and certain factors could encourage their abandonment of old ways for newer and more promising ones.

That cultural change for most immigrants had begun while still in the old country, when they made the decision to emigrate. Whether under duress or with high hopes, the decision declared an openness to new environments, a willingness to adopt different habits, and an acceptance of new ways. The long ocean voyage, especially in the days of sailing ships, brought home the realization that these decisions would be very difficult to reverse. Once landed in a new environment, they would have no choice but to conform to the practices of American life—its economic system, its money, its work routines, its technology—or else fail in America. In the most important of their activities, those of the workplace, they would work by the clock, as the new country demanded, and would abandon the comprehensive skills of the artisan for the more particular tasks demanded by the Industrial Revolution and its mass-production methods. Immigrant farmers would by necessity abandon the ways

Illustration drawn by Thomas Nast for the Thanksgiving issue of *Harper's Weekly*, November 20, 1869. Uncle Sam is seen carving the turkey for members of a wide variety of races and ethnicities. Nast, himself German-born, was famous for his stereotypical representations of ethnic groups. Library of Congress, Prints and Photographs Division.

of the European peasantry and its near-subsistence economies for the national market economy and its demands for the specialized production of staple crops.

In all of these steps toward cultural change, immigrants were becoming part of a much larger social network than they had known in their European origins. Within their own ethnic group, they were moving away from narrow provincial outlooks toward more cosmopolitan outlooks. Upward mobility in the social scale often led them beyond ethnic boundaries into a larger American society. This might invite further adaptations, as for example when immigrant children married outside the immigrant community.

Rural communities might offer some refuge from drastic changes. In such places language could be preserved, small-town societies could be organized around churches and traditional ways, and family relationships could be preserved longer, at least by those staying within the community. But even then, the pressures of inevitable change came into play. The language of the new country was necessary to deal with the outside world. Demands were made by politicians to deal with the problems of the larger society. Agriculture changed to meet the need for more efficient production and the demands of the national market.

For many of the Irish, ethnicity became merged into the religious culture, allowing the persistence of many folkways for a longer time. The leadership of the clergy and the revival of Irish Catholic devotional practice during the century provided the Irish with a protected culture in some ways. Yet that culture itself was a different one from what they had known in the old country, and was partly geared to the transition to American life and always in communication with the political side of Irish life, a more potent source of their cultural transformation.

The challenge of nativism invited immigrants to stay in their ethnic enclaves and away from the general American society. Yet the immigrants responded by arguing that they belonged within American society, had a right to participate in its political life, and could willingly conform to the cultural norms of a democracy. That was the burden of the most famous expression of the immigrants' willingness to change: Carl Schurz's speech against Republican nativists, delivered in Faneuil Hall, Boston, in 1859, and entitled "True Americanism." In his speech, arguing against the Massachusetts legislature's two-year amendment restricting the rights of newly naturalized citizens, Schurz argued that the immigrants sought equal rights, which were the essence of American liberty, and that they would willingly abandon old ways to achieve that goal. With arguments such as these, the immigrants embraced change, even to the abandonment of old ways of life.

For some, particularly the Chinese, the pressure against their admittance to American society virtually denied them any opportunity to change. The Chinese fell back on their protective cultural enclaves, and the possibilities of their partaking in American life would be withheld for nearly a century. But for others, the attractions and advantages of American culture drew them slowly toward the general society, and there was the slow withering of native cultural habits. These changes must be seen across generations. Those of the first generation, the foreign-born, would never completely abandon their nostalgia, their traditions, or their family ties to the old country. The second generation, however, had never known the old country, and had only a memory derived from that of their parents. The third generation would generally accept that their future depended on their willing adaptation to American life and culture; they retained only a vague knowledge of their roots being in some other place. That shadowy sense of their origin and heritage would be shared by virtually all Americans who were not themselves immigrants.

American culture changed, too; it could not resist the many influences coming with the hordes of new immigrants, who could sometimes dominate the society and economy of certain cities and states. These changes were never as great as those experienced by the immigrants, but they were perceptible and significant nonetheless. The lager beer introduced by Germans became the common drink of the America working class, and middle class too. Other items of food culture became standard American cultural possessions. The old American standard of the somber Puritan Sunday disappeared, especially in urban places, while the European Sunday became the day not only for worship but also for common recreation and celebration. Americans slowly, if with some difficulty, accepted the proposition that all religions deserved an equal place in the marketplace of American life. Immigrants, slowly and sometimes painfully, taught Americans a new standard of tolerance, and reminded them that they were all descended from immigrants.

In the last quarter of the nineteenth century, American culture began to offer great common experiences that drew Americans together and brought ethnic Americans out of their narrower cultures. Most of these common experiences—for example, department-store consumerism, professional sports, the popular music-hall entertainments, amusement parks, and great world fairs—still lay ahead in 1870. But nearly all Americans had one recent shared experience that drew them into a national community. That experience was the Civil War, which had cost many dearly in blood and sacrifice, but which immigrants as well as others could point to as their claim to be a part of American life.

In 1870 some newcomers were just beginning their introduction to American life. Others, those who had come in the 1830s, had become firmly planted in the web of American society. Those from the 1850s had undergone a more difficult trial to find their place in a turbulent America. And the tide of immigration would roll on, with its cycles of ebb and flow, and new waves would bring newcomers from still different lands, and the process of becoming Americans would continue.

NOTES

1. "U.S. Immigrants and Emigrants: 1820–1998," Table Ad1–2 in *Historical Statistics of the United States, Earliest Times to the Present: Millennial*

Edition, ed. Susan B. Carter et al. (New York: Cambridge University Press, 2006), available from http://dx.doi.org/10.1017/ISBN-9780511132971. Ad1–89, accessed May 6, 2007.

2. *Sacramento Union*, May 8, 1869, quoted in Alexander Saxton, "The Army of Canton in the High Sierra," *Pacific Historical Review* 35 (1966): 141–52.

3. *Deutsch-amerikanisches Conversations-Lexicon*, 11 vols. (New York: E. Steiger, 1869–1874).

4. *Reminiscences of Carl Schurz*, 3 vols. (New York: McClure, 1907–1908), 3:266–67.

5. As translated in Dieter Cunz, *The Maryland Germans: A History* (Princeton, N.J.: Princeton University Press, 1948), 376.

6. Statistics from Campbell Gibson and Kay Kung, *Historical Census Statistics on the Foreign-Born Population of the United States: 1850 to 2000*. U.S. Census Bureau, Population Division, working paper no. 81, Washington, DC, 2006, passim.

Glossary

abolitionism—Advocacy of the elimination of the institution of slavery.

acculturation—A type of assimilation, in which one ethnic group acquires the cultural characteristics of another ethnic group.

Act of Union—British law passed in 1798, eliminating the separate Irish Parliament and placing Ireland under the governance of the British Parliament.

Age of Reason—See *Enlightenment.*

ague—Illness involving fever and shivering, generally caused by malaria.

Ancient Order of Hibernians—Fraternal order of Irish Catholics, developed in the United States after 1820.

Anglicanism—Adherence to the established Protestant church of England.

Argonauts—Gold seekers who came to California during the gold rush of 1849.

artisan—A skilled worker, usually in a nonindustrial context.

assimilation—A process whereby people of one cultural background take on characteristics of another culture.

Battle of New Orleans—Last major battle of the War of 1812; in 1815, Andrew Jackson defeated British troops who had landed on the Gulf Coast and were advancing toward New Orleans.

Bear Flag Revolt—An uprising against the Mexican authorities in California, carried out by Americans in 1846.

B'nai B'rith—Fraternal society founded by German Jews in 1843.

Catholic Emancipation Act—Law passed by the British Parliament in 1829, freeing Irish Catholics from the restrictions of the Penal Laws.

census—Official counting of the population, usually under government auspices.

chain migration—Process by which new immigrants travel along a path originated by other immigrants, leading them to a previously settled destination.

charlatan—A person falsely claiming to have certain abilities.

Chartists—A workingmen's reform movement that sprang up in England during the 1830s in reaction to the Industrial Revolution; it advocated democracy and relief of the poor.

cholera—An infectious disease of the small intestine, typically contracted from infected water and causing severe vomiting and diarrhea.

clipper ship—A fast sailing ship, especially one of nineteenth-century design with concave bows and raked masts, used primarily in the trans-Pacific trade.

Compromise of 1850—Legislation admitting California to the Union as a free state, providing popular sovereignty for Utah and New Mexico territories, forbidding the slave trade in the District of Columbia, and requiring northerners to return runaway slaves by a Fugitive Slave Law.

Congress of Vienna—International meeting held from 1814 to 1815 after the defeat of Napoleon; resulted in widespread changes in the map of Europe.

Copperheads—Northern elements who opposed the Civil War; accused by others of treasonable actions.

Corn Laws—In Britain, tariffs imposed on imported agricultural goods, thereby protecting British farmers; repealed in 1846.

cottiers—Laborers without land and on the lowest level of Irish society, living in primitive cottages.

Cotton Belt—An area of cotton plantations that underwent settlement across the central parts of Georgia, Alabama, and Mississippi in the 1820s and 1830s.

Creole—A person of mixed European and African descent.

culture—The collectively held customs, institutions, and values of a particular nation, people, or group.

customs—In international trade, the taxes (duties) collected on goods being imported into a country; usually collected by government officers.

demography—The scientific study of human populations using statistical evidence.

displacement—The volume or weight of water displaced by a floating ship, used as a measure of the ship's size.

dysentery—Severe diarrhea caused by an intestinal infection.

Enlightenment—European intellectual movement of the eighteenth century emphasizing reason and individualism rather than tradition; sometimes called the Age of Reason.

entrepôt—A port offering facilities for transshipment or reshipment.

Erie Canal—Artificial waterway constructed across western New York 1817–25, connecting the Hudson Valley to the Great Lakes and opening up much inland trade.

established church—A church supported by a government or officially approved by a government.

Fenians—Members of an Irish nationalist group advocating rebellion in Ireland; originated in Ireland and spread to the United States in the 1850s.

Foreign Miners' Tax—Law enacted by California legislature in 1850 and subsequently amended several times; imposed a tax on foreign miners.

franchise—The right to vote.

free-soil—Political ideology arguing that the American West should be open to free labor and not to slavery.

French Revolution—Uprising in France beginning in 1789, leading to the overthrow of the monarchy, the establishment of a French republic, and a period of European wars.

Gold Mountain—In Chinese, *Gam Saan;* Chinese name for California.

Great Plains—The semi-arid region of the United States lying between approximately the 100th meridian and the Rocky Mountains.

Guadalupe Hidalgo, Treaty of—Treaty ending the Mexican War and transferring the American Southwest and California to United States sovereignty.

Hanseatic—Pertaining to towns associated with the medieval Hanseatic League, formed to promote shipping and trade in the North and Baltic seas.

Harugari—German-American fraternal order founded in 1847.

hui-kuan—Social organizations formed among Chinese in America, based on ties to regional origins in China.

indenture—A type of contract by which a person agreed to work for a set period of time for an employer in exchange for passage to America; more common in the colonial period.

Industrial Revolution—The process of economic and social change from small hand manufactures to manufacturing based on industry and technology; began in Britain in the late eighteenth century and spread to other western European countries and to the United States in the early nineteenth century.

Kansas-Nebraska Act—Law of 1854 providing for organization of Kansas and Nebraska Territories, and allowing slavery to be introduced into new territories of the West by popular sovereignty.

Know-Nothings—Adherents of an anti-immigrant political party that took shape in the 1850s; the term was also applied generally to nativists. See also *nativism*.

Kwangtung (Guangdong)—Province in southeastern China near Canton, whence many Chinese emigrated to California.

lager beer—Type of beer introduced to America by Germans; the beer was stored for a time after brewing.

lithography—Printing process using a flat metal or stone surface treated so as to repel the ink except where it is required for printing.

malaria—Disease characterized by recurrent attacks of fever, caused by a blood parasite transmitted by mosquitoes; common on the early American frontier.

Manifest Destiny—Political ideology of the 1840s and 1850s holding that America had a special mission to extend democracy across the continent and to other parts of the world.

Missouri Compromise—Act adopted in 1820 admitting Missouri to the Union as a slave state, and providing that thereafter slavery would be forbidden above the line of 36° 30′ latitude.

National Road—The first federal road project in the United States, built in stages beginning 1811 from Cumberland, Maryland to the Ohio Valley, thence westward through Ohio, Indiana, and Illinois.

nativism—Opposition by the native-born to the presence of foreigners within the country.

Orangemen—Irish Protestants, especially Presbyterians.

orlop—The lower deck of a sailing ship, beneath the steerage and above the cargo hold.

packet ships—Ships carrying passengers and mail on a regular schedule between ports.

partible inheritance—Practice whereby the property of the father is divided among several or all of his heirs; contrasts with primogeniture.

Penal Laws—A series of laws passed between 1691 and 1759 to restrict the rights of Catholics in Ireland.

Pennsylvania Main Line—Officially the "Main Line of Internal Improvements of the State of Pennsylvania," it was a state-sponsored system of rails and canals built in the early 1830s, connecting Philadelphia with the Ohio River valley.

placer mining—Searching for gold in the gravel of stream beds by "panning."

Poor Law of 1838—British law passed by parliament, establishing workhouses throughout Great Britain and requiring the poor to labor on public works while staying in the workhouse.

popular sovereignty—Doctrine that slavery could be introduced into new territories if permitted by a popular vote of the territory's residents.

primogeniture—Practice of inheritance of the father's property only by the eldest child (usually a son).

Prohibition—Banning the sale or use of alcohol by law. See also *temperance.*

Reformed churches—Protestant churches adhering to the theological traditions of the sixteenth-century reformer John Calvin.

Repeal movement—Organized effort to repeal the Act of Union with Great Britain and reestablish a separate Parliament for Ireland.

Revolutions of 1848—Uprisings against monarchical rule, with attempts to establish republics; after beginning in France, Germany, and Austria, they spread to other countries, but ultimately failed.

rundale—In Ireland, a communal system of landholding in which specific tracts were assigned to each landowner.

runners—Individuals who met immigrants at the ports and tried to induce them to go to a particular lodging, transportation agent, or employment recruiter.

Sabbatarians—Advocates of measures to preserve the sanctity of Sunday.

Sängerfest—Festival of German singing societies.

Scandinavians—Inhabitants of Norway, Sweden, and Denmark, who shared related languages.

ship fever—See typhus.

ship lists—Reports on passengers on board ships as recorded by ship captains and submitted to federal government officials when the ship arrived in an American port.

Sierra Nevada—Mountain range along the eastern side of the central valleys of California.

sloop—A single-masted sailing ship.

social mobility—The ability to rise within the structure of a society, in social status or wealth.

sojourners—Temporary immigrants who intend to return to their homeland after a period of business, employment, or study.

Sons of Hermann—German-American fraternal order formed in 1849.

steerage—Space on a ship between the top deck and the hold, usable for either cargo or passengers.

suffrage—The right to vote.

tack—To maneuver a sailing ship by turning its head into and through the wind.

temperance—Belief in restraining or forbidding the consumption of alcohol, by law if necessary. See also *Prohibition*.

tongs—Secret societies formed by Chinese in California, based on predecessors in China; also known as Triads.

Turner societies—Gymnastic societies formed by Germans in America beginning 1848; they also served as cultural and social organizations in many communities.

typhus—Infectious bacterial disease characterized by a purple rash, headaches, fever, and usually delirium.

union—In the nineteenth-century British system of welfare, the area served by one workhouse.

Ursulines—A Catholic religious order for women.

Verein—German word for "union," applied to many different kinds of social organizations among Germans.

wake—A watch or vigil held beside the body of someone who has died; in Ireland, a party held before a funeral.

Whig party—In the United States, the major political party from the 1830s to the 1850s in opposition to the Jacksonian Democrats.

workhouses—In Britain, the principal form of welfare for the unemployed; institutions meant to house the poor while they were employed on the public works.

Young America—Political faction within the Democratic party in the 1850s, calling for an aggressive nationalism, further national expansion in the Caribbean, and support of the European revolutionary movements

Zollverein—German customs union, formed in 1834 by combining the customs systems of many German states, removing trade barriers among those states.

Bibliography

GENERAL STUDIES

Barkan, Elliott R., ed. *A Nation of Peoples: A Sourcebook on America's Multicultural Heritage.* Westport, Conn.: Greenwood Press, 1999.

Barton, H. Arnold. *The Old Country and the New: Essays on Swedes and America.* Carbondale: Southern Illinois University Press, 2007.

Bayor, Ronald H., ed. "The Irish in America." Special issue of *Journal of American Ethnic History* 10 (1990–91), nos. 1–2.

Benson, Adolph B., and Naboth Hedin, eds. *Swedes in America, 1638–1938.* New York: Haskell House, 1969.

Berthoff, Rowland. *British Immigrants in Industrial America, 1790–1950.* Cambridge, Mass.: Harvard University Press, 1953.

Blegen, Theodore C. *Norwegian Migration to America,* 2 vols. Northfield, Minn.: Norwegian-American Historical Association, 1931–1940.

Bodnar, John. *The Transplanted: A History of Immigrants in Urban America.* Bloomington: Indiana University Press, 1985.

Brinks, Herbert J. *Dutch American Voices: Letters from the United States, 1820–1930.* Ithaca, N.Y.: Cornell University Press, 1995.

Chang, Iris. *The Chinese in America: A Narrative History.* New York: Viking, 2003.

Daniels, Roger. *Asian America: Chinese and Japanese in the United States since 1850.* Seattle: University of Washington Press, 1988.

———. *Coming to America: A History of Immigration and Ethnicity in American Life,* 2nd ed. New York: HarperCollins, 2002.

Diner, Hasia. *A Time for Gathering: The Second Migration, 1820–1880.* Vol. 2 of *The Jewish People in America,* 5 vols., ed. Henry L. Feingold. Baltimore: Johns Hopkins University Press, 1992.

Dublin, Thomas. *Immigrant Voices: New Lives in America, 1773–1986.* Urbana: University of Illinois Press, 1993.

Erickson, Charlotte. *Invisible Immigrants: The Adaptation of English and Scottish Immigrants in Nineteenth-Century America.* Coral Gables, Fla.: University of Miami Press, 1972.

Ferenczi, Imre. *International Migrations,* vol. 1: *Statistics.* New York: National Bureau of Economic Research, 1929.

Gjerde, Jon. *From Peasants to Farmers: The Migration from Balestrand, Norway, to the Upper Middle West.* New York: Cambridge University Press, 1985.

Glazier, Michael, ed. *The Encyclopedia of the Irish in America.* Notre Dame, Ind.: University of Notre Dame Press, 1999.

Gurock, Jeffrey S., ed. *Central European Jews in America 1840–1880: Migration and Survival.* New York: Routledge, 1998.

Handlin, Oscar. *The Uprooted: The Epic Story of the Great Migrations That Made the American People,* 2nd ed. Boston: Little, Brown, 1990.

Hansen, Marcus Lee. *The Atlantic Migration, 1607–1860.* Cambridge, Mass.: Harvard University Press, 1940.

Hawgood, John. *The Tragedy of German America.* New York: Putnam, 1940.

Kamphoefner, Walter D., Wolfgang Helbich, and Ulrike Sommer, eds. *News from the Land of Freedom: German Immigrants Write Home,* trans. Susan Carter Vogel. Ithaca, N.Y.: Cornell University Press, 1991.

Kenny, Kevin. *The American Irish: A History.* Harlow, England: Pearson Education, 2000.

Lovoll, Odd. *The Promise of America: A History of the Norwegian-American People.* Minneapolis: University of Minnesota Press, 1984.

Miller, Kerby A. *Emigrants and Exiles: Ireland and the Irish Exodus to North America.* New York: Oxford University Press, 1985.

Miller, Randall M., ed. *Germans in America: Retrospect and Prospect.* Philadelphia: German Society of Pennsylvania, 1984.

O'Connor, Richard. *The German-Americans: An Informal History.* Boston: Little, Brown and Company, 1968.

Potter, George. *To the Golden Door: The Story of the Irish in Ireland and America.* Boston: Little, Brown and Co., 1960.

Qualey, Carlton C. *Norwegian Settlement in the United States.* Northfield, Minn.: Norwegian-American Historical Association, 1938.

Rippley, LaVern J. *The German Americans.* Boston: Twayne, 1976.

Swierenga, Robert P. *Faith and Family: Dutch Immigration and Settlement in the United States, 1820–1920.* New York: Holmes and Meier, 2000.

Takaki, Ronald. *Strangers from a Distant Shore: A History of Asian Americans,* rev. ed. Boston: Little Brown and Co., 1998.

Taylor, Philip. *The Distant Magnet: European Emigration to the U.S.A.* New York: Harper and Row, 1971.

Trommler, Frank, and Joseph McVeigh, eds. *America and the Germans: An Assessment of a Three-Hundred-Year History,* 2 vols. Philadelphia: University of Pennsylvania Press, 1985.

Tsai, Shih-shan Henry. *The Chinese Experience in America.* Bloomington: Indiana University Press, 1986.

Van Vugt, William E. *Britain to America: Mid-Nineteenth-Century Immigrants to the United States.* Urbana: University of Illinois Press, 1999.

Wittke, Carl F. *The Irish in America.* Baton Rouge: Louisiana State University Press, 1956.

———. *We Who Built America: The Saga of the Immigrant.* New York: Prentice-Hall, 1939.

EMIGRATION AND ITS CAUSES

Adams, William Forbes. *Ireland and Irish Emigration to the New World from 1815 to the Famine.* New Haven: Yale University Press, 1932.

Boyce, D. George, and Alan O'Day, eds. *The Making of Modern Irish History: Revisionism and the Revisionist Controversy.* New York: Routledge, 1996.

Crawford, E. Margaret, ed. *The Hungry Stream: Essays on Emigration and Famine.* Omagh, County Tyrone, Northern Ireland: Ulster American Folk Park; and Belfast: Institute of Irish Studies, Queen's University, 1997.

Duffy, Patrick J., ed. *To and from Ireland: Planned Migration Schemes c. 1600–2000.* Dublin: Geography Publications, 2004.

Erickson, Charlotte. *Leaving England: Essays on British Emigration in the Nineteenth Century.* Ithaca, N.Y.: Cornell University Press, 1994.

Fanning, Charles, ed. *New Perspectives on the Irish Diaspora.* Carbondale: Southern Illinois University Press, 2000.

Fleming, Donald, and Bernard Bailyn, eds. "Dislocation and Emigration: The Social Background of American Immigration." *Perspectives in American History* 7 (1973).

Galvin, Michael. *Black Blight: The Great Famine, 1845–1852: A Four Parish Study.* Middleton, County Cork, Ireland: Litho Press, n.d. [1995?].

Hvidt, Kristian. *Flight to America; The Social Background of 300,000 Danish Emigrants.* New York: Academic Press, 1975.

Larkin, Emmet. *The Making of the Roman Catholic Church in Ireland, 1850–1860.* Chapel Hill: University of North Carolina Press, 1980.

———. *The Pastoral Role of the Roman Catholic Church in Pre-Famine Ireland, 1750–1850.* Washington, DC: Catholic University of America Press, 2006.

Litton, Helen. *The Irish Famine: An Illustrated History.* Dublin: Wolfhound Press, 1994.

Moch, Leslie Page. *Moving Europeans: Migration in Western Europe since 1650,* 2nd ed. Bloomington: Indiana University Press, 2003.

Moller, Herbert, ed. *Population Movements in Modern European History.* New York: The Macmillan Company, 1964.

Ó Gráda, Cormac. *Black '47 and Beyond: The Great Irish Famine in History, Economy, and Memory.* Princeton: Princeton University Press, 1999.

———. *Ireland: A New Economic History, 1780–1939.* Oxford: Oxford University Press, 1994.

Richards, Eric. *Britannia's Children: Emigration from England, Scotland, Wales and Ireland since 1600.* London: Hambledon and London, 2004.

Schrier, Arnold. *Ireland and the American Emigration, 1850–1900.* Minneapolis: University of Minnesota Press, 1958.

Sperber, Jonathan. *The European Revolutions, 1848–1851,* 2d ed. New York: Cambridge University Press, 2005.

Swords, Liam, ed. *In Their Own Words: The Famine in North Connacht, 1845–1849.* Blackrock, Co., Dublin: Columba Press, 1999.

Walker, Mack. *Germany and the Emigration, 1816–1885.* Cambridge, Mass.: Harvard University Press, 1964.

THE TRANSATLANTIC VOYAGE

Albion, Robert G. *The Rise of New York Port, 1815–1860.* New York: Charles Scribner's Sons, 1939.

———. *Square Riggers on Schedule: The New York Sailing Packets to England, France, and the Cotton Ports.* Princeton, N.J.: Princeton University Press, 1938.

Bayor, Ronald H., ed. "Special Issue: European Ports of Emigration." *Journal of American Ethnic History* 13, no. 1 (1993).

Coleman, Terry. *Going to America.* New York: Pantheon, 1972.

Guillet, Edwin C. *The Great Migration: The Atlantic Crossing by Sailing-Ship since 1770.* New York: Thomas Nelson and Sons, 1937.

Kapp, Friedrich. *Immigration and the Commissioners of Emigration of the State of New York.* New York: The Nation Press, 1870.

Stern, Gale F., ed. *Freedom's Doors: Immigrant Ports of Entry to the United States.* Philadelphia: Balch Institute, 1986.

Stolarik, M. Mark, ed. *Forgotten Doors: The Other Ports of Entry to the United States.* Philadelphia: Balch Institute Press, 1988.

LOCAL AND REGIONAL STUDIES

Anbinder, Tyler. *Five Points: The 19th-Century New York City Neighborhood That Invented Tap Dance, Stole Elections, and Became the World's Most Notorious Slum.* New York: Free Press, 2001.

Ashkenazi, Elliott. *The Business of Jews in Louisiana, 1840–1875.* Tuscaloosa: University of Alabama Press, 1988.

Bayor, Ronald H., and Timothy J. Meagher, eds. *The New York Irish.* Baltimore: Johns Hopkins University Press, 1996.

Biesele, Rudolph L. *History of the German Settlements in Texas, 1831–1861.* Austin: Von Boeckmann-Jones Co., 1930.

Binder, Frederick M. and David M. Reimers. *All the Nations under Heaven: An Ethnic and Racial History of New York City.* New York: Columbia University Press, 1995.

Bjork, Kenneth O. *West of the Great Divide: Norwegian Migration to the Pacific Coast, 1847–1893.* Northfield, Minn.: Norwegian-American Historical Association, 1958.

Burchell, Robert A. *The San Francisco Irish, 1848–1880.* Berkeley: University of California Press, 1980.

Chen, Yong. *Chinese San Francisco, 1850–1943: A Trans-Pacific Community.* Stanford, Calif.: Stanford University Press, 2000.

Clark, Dennis. *Hibernia America: The Irish and Regional Cultures.* Westport, Conn.: Greenwood Press, 1986.

———. *The Irish in Philadelphia: Ten Generations of Urban Experience.* Philadelphia: Temple University Press, 1973.

Conzen, Kathleen Neils. *Immigrant Milwaukee, 1836–1860: Accommodation and Community in a Frontier City.* Cambridge, Mass.: Harvard University Press, 1976.

Cunz, Dieter. *The Maryland Germans: A History.* Princeton: Princeton University Press, 1948.

Davis, Allen F. and Mark Haller, eds. *The Peoples of Philadelphia: A History of Ethnic Groups and Lower-Class Life, 1790–1940.* Philadelphia: Temple University Press, 1973.

Ernst, Robert. *Immigrant Life in New York City, 1825–1863.* New York: King's Crown Press, 1949.

Faherty, William B. *The St. Louis Irish: An Unmatched Celtic Community.* St. Louis: Missouri Historical Society Press, 2001.

Gerber, David A. *The Making of an American Pluralism: Buffalo, New York, 1825–60.* Urbana: University of Illinois Press, 1989.

Gleeson, David T. *The Irish in the South, 1815–1877.* Chapel Hill: University of North Carolina Press, 2001.

Handlin, Oscar. *Boston's Immigrants: A Study in Acculturation,* revised and enlarged ed. Cambridge, Mass.: Harvard University Press, 1979.

Hershberg, Theodore, ed. *Philadelphia: Work, Space, Family, and Group Experience in the Nineteenth Century.* New York: Oxford University Press, 1981.

Jordan, Terry. *German Seed in Texas Soil: Immigrant Farmers in Nineteenth-Century Texas.* Austin: University of Texas Press, 1966.

Juliani, Richard. *Building Little Italy: Philadelphia's Italians before Mass Migration.* University Park: Pennsylvania State University Press, 1998.

Kamphoefner, Walter D. *The Westfalians: From Germany to Missouri.* Princeton, N.J.: Princeton University Press, 1987.

Machann, Clinton, and James W. Mendl, eds. and trans. *Czech Voices: Stories from Texas in the Amerikán Národni Kalendár.* College Station: Texas A & M University Press, 1991.

Mitchell, Brian C. *The Paddy Camps: The Irish of Lowell, 1821–1861.* Urbana: University of Illinois Press, 1988.

Mullen, Kevin J. *Dangerous Strangers: Minority Newcomers and Criminal Violence in the Urban West, 1850–2000.* New York: Palgrave Macmillan, 2005.

Nadel, Stanley. *Little Germany: Ethnicity, Religion and Class in New York City, 1845–80.* Urbana: University of Illinois Press, 1990.

Niehaus, Earl F. *The Irish in New Orleans, 1800–1860.* Baton Rouge: Louisiana State University Press, 1965.

O'Connor, Thomas H. *The Boston Irish: A Political History.* Boston: Northeastern University Press, 1995.

Peterson, Richard H. *Manifest Destiny in the Mines: A Cultural Interpretation of Anti-Mexican Nativism in California, 1848–1853.* San Francisco: R and E Research Associates, 1975.

Ryan, Dennis. *Beyond the Ballot Box: A Social History of the Boston Irish, 1845–1917.* Rutherford, N.J.: Fairleigh Dickinson University Press, 1983.

Starr, Kevin, and Richard J. Orsi, eds. *Rooted in Barbarous Soil: People, Culture, and Community in Gold Rush California.* Berkeley: University of California Press, 2000.

Struve, Walter. *Germans and Texans: Commerce, Migration and Culture in the Days of the Lone Star Republic.* Austin: University of Texas Press, 1996.

Swierenga, Robert P. *Dutch Chicago: A History of the Hollanders in the Windy City.* Grand Rapids, Mich.: W.B. Eerdmans Publishing Co., 2002.

Van Vugt, William E. *British Buckeyes: The English, Scots, and Welsh in Ohio, 1700–1900.* Kent, Ohio: Kent State University Press, 2006.

Wust, Klaus. *The Virginia Germans.* Charlottesville: University Press of Virginia, 1969.

Wyman, Mark. *Immigrants in the Valley: Irish, Germans, and Americans in the Upper Mississippi Country, 1830–1860.* Chicago: Nelson-Hall, 1984.

NATIVISM

Beals, Carlton. *Brass-knuckle Crusade: The Great Know-Nothing Conspiracy, 1820–1860.* New York: Hastings House, 1960.

Billington, Ray Allen. *The Protestant Crusade, 1800–1860: A Study of the Origins of American Nativism.* New York: Macmillan, 1938.

Feldberg, Michael. *The Philadelphia Riots of 1844: A Study of Ethnic Conflict.* Westport, Conn.: Greenwood Press, 1975.

Franchot, Jenny. *Roads to Rome: The Antebellum Protestant Encounter with Catholicism.* Berkeley: University of California Press, 1994.

Saxton, Alexander. *The Indispensible Enemy: Labor and the Anti-Chinese Movement in California.* Berkeley: University of California Press, 1971.

See, Scott W. *Riots in New Brunswick: Orange Nativism and Social Violence in the 1840s.* Toronto: University of Toronto Press, 1993.

IMMIGRANT LIFE: ETHNICITIES AND NATIONALISMS

Brown, Thomas N. *Irish-American Nationalism*. Philadelphia: Lippincott, 1966.

Chun, Gloria H. *Of Orphans and Warriors: Inventing Chinese American Culture and Identity*. New Brunswick, N.J.: Rutgers University Press, 2000.

D'Arcy, William. *The Fenian Movement in the United States: 1858–1886*. Washington, D.C.: Catholic University of America Press, 1947.

Gordon, Milton M. *Assimilation in American Life: The Role of Race, Religion and National Origins*. New York: Oxford University Press, 1964.

Ignatiev, Noel. *How the Irish Became White*. New York: Routledge, 1995.

Knobel, Dale T. *Paddy and the Republic*. Middletown, Conn.: Wesleyan University Press, 1986.

Neidhardt, Wilfried S. *Fenianism in North America*. University Park: Pennsylvania State University Press, 1975.

Senior, Hereward. *The Last Invasion of Canada: The Fenian Raids, 1866–1870*. Toronto: Dundurn Press, 1991.

IMMIGRANT LIFE: INSTITUTIONS AND CULTURES

Anderson, Arlow W. *The Immigrant Takes His Stand: The Norwegian-American Press and Public Affairs, 1847–1872*. Northfield, Minn.: Norwegian-American Historical Association, 1953.

Arndt, Karl J. R. and May E. Olson. *German-American Newspapers and Periodicals, 1732–1955: History and Bibliography*, 2nd ed. New York: Johnson Reprint Corp., 1965.

Brancaforte, Charlotte L., ed. *The German Forty-Eighters in the United States*. New York: Peter Lang, 1989.

Buenker, John D. and Lorman Ratner, eds. *Multiculturalism in the United States: A Comparative Guide to Acculturation and Ethnicity*, rev. ed. Westport, Conn.: Greenwood Press, 2005.

Clark, Dennis. *Erin's Heirs: Irish Bonds of Community*. Lexington: University Press of Kentucky, 1991.

Diner, Hasia. *Erin's Daughters in America: Irish Immigrant Women in the Nineteenth Century*. Baltimore: Johns Hopkins University Press, 1983.

———. *Hungering for America: Italian, Irish and Jewish Foodways in the Age of Migration*. Cambridge, Mass.: Harvard University Press, 2001.

Dolan, Jay P. *The American Catholic Parish: A History from 1850 to the Present*, 2 vols. Mahwah, N.J.: Paulist Press, 1987.

———. *The Immigrant Church: New York's Irish and German Catholics, 1815–1865*. Baltimore: Johns Hopkins University Press, 1975.

Dudden, Faye E. *Serving Women: Household Service in Nineteenth-Century America*. Middletown, Conn.: Wesleyan University Press, 1983.

Ehrlich, Richard L., ed. *Immigrants in Industrial America, 1850–1920*. Charlottesville: University of Virginia Press, 1977.

Gabaccia, Donna R. *From the Other Side: Women, Gender, and Immigrant Life in the U.S., 1820–1990*. Bloomington: Indiana University Press, 1994.

———. *We Are What We Eat: Ethnic Food and the Making of Americans*. Cambridge, Mass.: Harvard University Press, 1998.

Geitz, Henry, ed. *The German-American Press*. Madison, Wisc.: Max Kade Institute, 1992.

Gjerde, Jon. *The Minds of the West: Ethnocultural Evolution in the Rural Middle West, 1830–1917*. Chapel Hill: University of North Carolina Press, 1997.

Higham, John, ed. *Ethnic Leadership in America*. Baltimore: Johns Hopkins University Press, 1978.

Lagerquist, L. DeAne. *In America the Men Milk the Cows: Factors of Gender, Ethnicity, and Religion in the Americanization of Norwegian-American Women*. Brooklyn, N.Y.: Carlson Publishing, 1991.

Miller, Sally M., ed. *The Ethnic Press in the United States: A Historical Analysis and Handbook*. Westport, Conn.: Greenwood Press, 1987.

Munch, Peter A., ed. *The Strange American Way: Letters of Caja Munch from Wiota, Wisconsin, 1855–1859*. Carbondale: Southern Illinois University Press, 1970.

Pickle, Linda S. *Contented among Strangers: Rural German-Speaking Women and Their Families in the Nineteenth-Century Midwest*. Urbana: University of Illinois Press, 1996.

Seller, Maxine S. *Immigrant Women*. Philadelphia: Temple University Press, 1981.

Shaugnessy, Gerald. *Has the Immigrant Kept the Faith? A Study of Immigration and Catholic Growth in the United States, 1790–1920*. New York: The Macmillan Company, 1925.

Taylor, George R. *The Transportation Revolution, 1815–1860*. New York: Holt, Rinehart and Winston, 1951.

Trommler, Frank, and Elliott Shore, eds. *The German-American Encounter: Conflict and Cooperation between Two Cultures, 1800–2000*. New York: Berghahn Books, 2001.

Way, Peter. *Common Labour: Workers and the Digging of North American Canals, 1780–1860*. Cambridge, England: Cambridge University Press, 1993.

Wittke, Carl F. *The German-Language Press in America*. Lexington: University of Kentucky Press, 1957.

———. *Refugees of Revolution: The German Forty-Eighters in America*. Philadelphia: University of Pennsylvania Press, 1952.

Zucker, Adolf E., ed. *The Forty-Eighters: Political Refugees of the German Revolution of 1848*. New York: Columbia University Press, 1950.

IMMIGRANT POLITICAL LIFE

Anbinder, Tyler. *Nativism and Slavery: The Northern Know Nothings and the Politics of the 1850s.* New York: Oxford University Press, 1992.

Engs, Robert F., and Randall M. Miller, eds. *The Birth of the Grand Old Party: The Republicans' First Generation.* Philadelphia: University of Pennsylvania Press, 2002.

Gienapp, William E. *The Origins of the Republican Party, 1852–1856.* New York: Oxford University Press, 1987.

Holt, Michael. *The Rise and Fall of the American Whig Party: Jacksonian Politics and the Onset of the Civil War.* New York: Oxford University Press, 1999.

Levine, Bruce. *The Spirit of 1848: German Immigrants, Labor Conflicts, and the Coming of the Civil War.* Urbana: University of Illinois Press, 1992.

Luebke, Frederick C., ed. *Ethnic Voters and the Election of Lincoln.* Lincoln: University of Nebraska Press, 1971.

BIOGRAPHIES

Athearn, Robert G. *Thomas Francis Meagher: An Irish Revolutionary in America.* New York: Arno Press, 1976.

Barkan, Elliott R., ed. *Making It in America: A Sourcebook on Eminent Ethnic Americans.* Santa Barbara, Calif.: ABC-CLIO, 2001.

Easum, Chester V. *The Americanization of Carl Schurz.* Chicago: University of Chicago Press, 1929.

Engle, Stephen D. *Yankee Dutchman: The Life of Franz Sigel.* Fayetteville: University of Arkansas Press, 1993.

Greene, Victor R. *American Immigrant Leaders, 1800–1910: Marginality and Identity.* Baltimore: Johns Hopkins University Press, 1987.

Hearne, John M., and Rory T. Cornish, eds. *Thomas Francis Meagher: The Making of an Irish American.* Dublin: Irish Academic Press, 2006.

Hurtado, Albert. *John Sutter: A Life on the North American Frontier.* Norman: University of Oklahoma Press, 2006.

Koerner, Gustave M. *Memoirs of Gustave Koerner, 1809–1896: Life-sketches Written at the Suggestion of His Children,* 2 vols., ed. Thomas J. McCormack. Cedar Rapids, Iowa: Torch Press, 1909.

Schurz, Carl. *The Reminiscences of Carl Schurz,* 3 vols. New York: McClure, 1907–1908.

Shaw, Richard. *Dagger John: The Unquiet Life and Times of Archbishop John Hughes of New York.* New York: Paulist Press, 1977.

Trefousse, Hans. *Carl Schurz: A Biography.* Knoxville: University of Tennessee Press, 1982.

Wittke, Carl F. *Against the Current: The Life of Carl Heinzen (1809–80).* Chicago: University of Chicago Press, 1945.

————. *The Utopian Communist: A Biography of Wilhelm Weitling, Nineteenth-Century Reformer.* Baton Rouge: Louisiana State University Press, 1950.

Wylie, Paul R. *The Irish General: Thomas Francis Meagher.* Norman, Okla.: University of Oklahoma Press, 2007.

THE MEXICAN WAR

Foos, Paul. *A Short, Offhand, Killing Affair: Soldiers and Social Conflict during the Mexican-American War.* Chapel Hill: University of North Carolina Press, 2002.

Hogan, Michael. *The Irish Soldiers of Mexico.* New Orleans: University Press of the South, 1997.

McCaffrey, James M. *Army of Manifest Destiny: The American Soldier in the Mexican War, 1846–1848.* New York: New York University Press, 1992.

Miller, Robert Ryal. *Shamrock and Sword: The Saint Patrick's Battalion in the U.S.-Mexican War.* Norman: University of Oklahoma Press, 1989.

Stevens, Peter F. *The Rogue's March: John Riley and the St. Patrick's Battalion.* Washington, DC: Brassey's, 1999.

THE CIVIL WAR

Bailey, Anne J. *Invisible Southerners: Ethnicity in the Civil War.* Athens: University of Georgia Press, 2006.

Bruce, Susannah U. *The Harp and the Eagle: Irish-American Volunteers and the Union Army, 1861–1865.* New York: New York University Press, 2006.

Burton, William L. *Melting Pot Soldiers: The Union's Ethnic Regiments.* Ames, Iowa: Iowa State University Press, 1988.

Demeter, Richard. *The Fighting 69th: A History.* Pasadena, Calif.: Cranford Press, 2002.

Gallman, J. Matthew. *Mastering Wartime: A Social History of Philadelphia during the Civil War.* Cambridge, England: Cambridge University Press, 1990.

Geary, James W. *We Need Men: The Union Draft in the Civil War.* DeKalb: Northern Illinois University Press, 1991.

Kamphoefner, Walter D., and Wolfgang Helbich, eds. *Germans in the Civil War: The Letters They Wrote Home,* trans. Susan Carter Vogel. Chapel Hill: University of North Carolina Press, 2006.

Karamanski, Theodore J. *Rally Round the Flag: Chicago and the Civil War.* Chicago: Nelson-Hall Publishers, 1993.

Keller, Christian B. *Chancellorsville and the Germans: Nativism, Ethnicity, and Civil War Memory.* New York: Fordham University Press, 2007.

Lonn, Ella. *Foreigners in the Confederacy.* Chapel Hill: University of North Carolina Press, 1940.

————. *Foreigners in the Union Army and Navy.* Baton Rouge: Louisiana State University Press, 1951.

Mahin, Dean B. *The Blessed Place of Freedom: Europeans in Civil War America.* Washington, DC: Brassey's, Inc., 2002.

O'Grady, Kelly J. *Clear the Confederate Way! The Irish in the Army of Northern Virginia.* Mason City, Iowa: Savas, 2000.

Palladino, Grace. *Another Civil War: Labor, Capital and the State in the Anthracite Regions of Pennsylvania, 1840–68.* Urbana: University of Illinois Press, 1990.

Paludan, Phillip Shaw. *"A People's Contest": The Union and Civil War, 1861–65.* New York: Harper and Row, 1988.

Schechter, Barnet. *The Devil's Own Work: The Civil War Draft Riots and the Fight to Reconstruct America.* New York: Walker and Company, 2005.

Underwood, Rodman L. *Death on the Nueces.* Austin, Tex.: Eakin Press, 2000

Vinovskis, Maris A., ed. *Toward a Social History of the American Civil War: Exploratory Essays.* Cambridge, England: Cambridge University Press, 1990.

VIDEO RESOURCES

Denenberg, Barry. *So Far from Home: The Story of Mary Driscoll, an Irish Mill Girl.* [New York]: Scholastic, 1999.

Ding, Loni, and Pat Morita. *Ancestors in the Americas: Chinese in the Frontier West, an American Story.* Asian American history series, pt. 2. Berkeley, Calif.: Center for Educational Telecommunications, 1998.

Grubin, David, Blair Brown, Stephen Stept, and Chama Gazit. *Destination America [the People and Cultures That Created a Nation].* [United States]: PBS Home Video, 2005.

Guggenheim, Charles, and David G. McCullough. *Journey to America.* Alexandria, Va.: PBS Video, 1989.

Hammond, Roy A., Roman Brygider, and Shinyu Yang. *The Chinese Americans.* New York: WLIW21, 1999.

Hammond, Roy A., Roman Brygider, and Gia Amella. *The German Americans.* New York: WLIW21, 2001

Kilbane, Richard, James McDonough, and Keith Kurlander. *The Irish Brigade in the American Civil War.* Venice, Calif.: TMW Media Group, 1998.

Lennon, Thomas, Bill D. Moyers, Ruby Yee, Brian Keane, George Gao, Michael Chin, Richard Nemeroff, and Allan Palmer. *Becoming American: The Chinese Experience.* Princeton, N.J.: FFH Home Video, 2003.

Lennon Documentary Group. *Irish in America: Long Journey Home.* PBS Video database of America's history and culture, v. 272–275. Alexandria, Va.: PBS Video, 1999.

McGliney, Felice. *A Nation of Immigrants: The Chinese-American Experience.* Princeton, N.J.: Films for the Humanities and Sciences, 1999.

Michael Blackwood Productions. *The German Americans: 300 Years in the New Land.* New York: West Glen Video, 1983.

Moberg, Vilhelm. *The New Land.* Burbank, Calif.: Warner Home Video, 1994.

———. *The Emigrants.* Burbank, Calif.: Warner Home Video, 1994.

Pett, John. *Where Have the Germans Gone? Destination America.* Princeton, N.J.: Films for the Humanities and Sciences, 2005.

Rock, Marcia, and Peter Quinn. *No Irish Need Apply.* New York: Cinema Guild, 1993.

Thomas, Rhys, and Aidan Quinn. *The Irish in America.* [New York]: A & E Home Video, 1997.

Veras, George. *The German Americans.* Silver Spring, Md.: Acorn Media, 2004.

Wagner, Paul. *Out of Ireland.* PBS Video database of America's history and culture, v. 211–212. Alexandria, Va.: PBS Video, 1999.

INTERNET RESOURCES

Connecticut State Department of Education. Teacher Resource Guide. *The Irish—The Great Hunger and Irish Immigration to America.* Available at http://www.sde.ct.gov/sde/cwp/view.asp?a = 2618&q = 320932.

Delaware Saengerbund and Library Association. "German American History." Available at http://www.delawaresaengerbund.org/GermanHistoryV3.shtml.

Fordham University's Internet Modern History Sourcebook. US Immigration. Available at http://www.fordham.edu/halsall/mod/modsbook28.html.

German-American History and Heritage. Available at http://www.germanheritage.com/.

Library of Congress "Learning Page." Chinese Immigration. Available at http://memory.loc.gov/learn/features/immig/chinese.html.

Library of Congress "Learning Page." Immigration. Available at http://memory.loc.gov/learn/community/cc_immigration.php.

Nebraska Department of Education Teaching Guide. The Great Irish Famine. Available at http://www.nde.state.ne.us/ss/irish/irish_pf.html.

Norway-Heritage. Hands across the Sea. Available at http://www.norwayheritage.com/.

Norwegian-American Historical Association. NAHA Online. Available at http://www.naha.stolaf.edu/.

Statue of Liberty-Ellis Island Foundation (resources on all eras of immigration history). Available at http://www.ellisisland.org/.

Swedish-American Historical Society. Available at http://www.swedish
    americanhist.org/.
University of Houston Digital History. Immigration. Available at http://
    www.digitalhistory.uh.edu/do_history/immigration/immigra
    tion.cfm.
Vassar College. Views of the [Irish] Famine. Available at http://admin
    staff.vassar.edu/sttaylor/FAMINE/.

Index

About the Author

JAMES M. BERGQUIST is Professor Emeritus of History, Villanova University. He has published dozens of book chapters, journal articles, and encyclopedia entries dealing with immigration and immigration issues in the United States. He is also editor of the Immigration and Ethnic History Society newsletter.